"*Leadership teams* captures the breathtaking effects of the driving force of a team." – **Vadim Makhov**, *Chairman of the Board of Directors, Severstal, Russia*

"This book is a practical and insightful guide to modern team leadership." – **Peter Steane**, *Emeritus Professor, Macquarie University, Australia*

"As we struggle with unprecedented environmental problems at the same time as economic uncertainty, effective leadership and team work has never been so critically important." – **Juliet Roper**, *Professor of Management Communication, University of Waikato, and Associate Dean, Sustainability, University of Waikato Management, New Zealand*

"A well-written text combining intellectual insight with practical common sense." – **Dr Ian Brooks**, *Dean, Northampton Business School, UK*

Other books by Andrew Kakabadse and Nada Kakabadse

GOVERNANCE, STRATEGY AND POLICY: SEVEN CRITICAL ESSAYS (2006) (eds.)

CORPORATE SOCIAL RESPONSIBILITY: RECONCILING ASPIRATION WITH
APPLICATION (2006)
(Andrew Kakabadse & Mette Morsing (eds.))

CSR IN PRACTICE: DELVING DEEP (2007) (eds.)

SPIRITUAL MOTIVATION: NEW THINKING FOR BUSINESS MANAGEMENT (2007)
(Jeremy Ramsden, Shuhei Aida & Andrew Kakabadse)

LEADING THE BOARD (2008)

LEADING FOR SUCCESS: THE SEVEN SIDES TO GREAT LEADERS (2008)
(Andrew Kakabadse, Nada Kakabadse & Linda Lee-Davies)

THE ELEPHANT HUNTERS: CHRONICLES OF THE MONEYMEN (2008)
(Amielle Lake, Andrew Kakabadse & Nada Kakabadse)

Leadership teams

Developing and
sustaining high performance

Geoff Sheard
Andrew Kakabadse
and
Nada Kakabadse

First published 2009 by
PALGRAVE MACMILLAN

Palgrave Macmillan in the UK is an imprint of Macmillan Publishers Limited, registered in England, company number 785998, of Houndmills, Basingstoke, Hampshire RG21 6XS.

Palgrave Macmillan in the US is a division of St Martin's Press LLC, 175 Fifth Avenue, New York, NY 10010.

Palgrave Macmillan is the global academic imprint of the above companies and has companies and representatives throughout the world.
Palgrave® and Macmillan® are registered trademarks in the United States, the United Kingdom, Europe and other countries

ISBN-13: 978–0–230–20190–3
ISBN-10: 0–230–20190–3

A catalogue record for this book is available from the British Library.

A catalog record for this book is available from the Library of Congress.

10 9 8 7 6 5 4 3 2 1
18 17 16 15 14 13 12 11 10 09

Printed and bound in China

CONTENTS

List of figures   viii

Foreword   ix

Preface   xii

Acknowledgments   xviii

About the authors   xix

Chapter 1   Conceptual framework   **1**

Leadership in the 21st century   3
Group development   5
Want to know more?   10

Chapter 2   Mobilizing   **12**

Group development   14
Practical indicators   15
Forming the group   16
Creativity and innovation   18
Decision making   30
Ways of working   36
Fitting behavior   41
Key learning points   46
Want to know more?   47

Chapter 3   Confrontation   **48**

Group development   50
Practical indicators   52
Understanding conflict   53
Managing conflict   60
Fitting behavior   70
Key learning points   76
Want to know more?   77

Chapter 4   Coming together   **78**

Group development   80
Practical indicators   82
Work-based relationships   84
Working in groups   92
Fitting behavior   97
Key learning points   102
Want to know more?   103

Chapter 5   One step forward, two steps back   **104**

Group development   107
Practical indicators   110
The way things are done around here   112
Competencies and capabilities   128
Fitting behavior   137
Key learning points   142
Want to know more?   143

Chapter 6   Behaving as one   **144**

Team development   149
Practical indicators   151
Teams working with other teams   153
Engaging others   165
Fitting behavior   175
Key learning points   180
Want to know more?   181

Chapter 7   Facing the future   **183**

Team development   186
Practical indicators   188
Managing yourself   190
Developing leaders   198
Fitting behavior   207
Key learning points   214
Want to know more?   215

Chapter 8   Grace under pressure   **217**

Grounded under pressure   223
Resilience under pressure   226

Collaboration under pressure 229
Adaptability under pressure 231
Maturity under pressure 235
The audacity of hope 238
It's only a model 240

References 242
Index 247

Figures

1.1   The integrated group development process   9
2.1   The integrated group development process,
stage one: Mobilizing   12
3.1   The integrated group development process,
stage two: Confrontation   48
4.1   The integrated group development process,
stage three: Coming together   78
4.2   Driving change   85
5.1   The integrated group development process,
stage four: One step forward, two steps back   104
6.1   The integrated group development process,
stage five: Behaving as one   144
7.1   The integrated group development process,
stage six: Facing the future   183
8.1   The integrated group development process   217

I have spent my professional life working in and with teams. I can vouch that poor performance of teams is at the root of those issues friends and colleagues raise with me most frequently. The importance of knowing how to transform a group of individuals into a high-performing team can't be overstated. The need for people, in every walk of life, to work together was never more pressing than it is today. That is why this book is so relevant. *Leadership teams* explains how real people facing real problems can learn to create high-performing teams. It explains what ordinary people need to *do* if they are to get extraordinary results.

The authors of *Leadership teams* use a new development of well-proven theory that is rooted in a pragmatic and practical approach to leadership action and team development. They use an academically sound basis to clearly define what leadership action means in practice. The book focuses on the leadership capabilities you must develop and learn to deploy. Critically, the authors clarify the process of group life that plays out when people work together. In so doing they provide insight into why people behave the way they do when working together and, perhaps most importantly, what you should do about it. By providing insight into what can otherwise appear to be the irrational behaviour of others, *Leadership teams* helps you to better appreciate what leadership action is appropriate in a particular context.

This book—more of a handbook—details a stepwise, practical, and rigorous approach that you can really pick up and apply. As the authors say, "anyone who wants to be a better leader can be." If you have tried the more traditional approaches to team development and failed, this book offers a fresh perspective. The linkage between leadership action and team development is laid out in a clear and concise way that makes it accessible.

Making academically sound theory accessible is not easy. In this regard I believe that the authors of *Leadership teams* have excelled. The serialized case study around which *Leadership teams* has been written results in the book reading more like a novel in places. The issues dealt with in the case study apply to all those who are struggling to get the best out of those they work with. The insight you will get reading the case study is readily applied, transforming what might otherwise be dry, abstract ideas and concepts into compelling pictures in your mind. The blend of theory, case study, and analysis makes the book come to life. As such *Leadership teams* is not a textbook, it is a book you can actually pick up and read.

When the authors originally approached me, I was both sceptical and hopeful. I was sceptical that this book could make the difference and at the same time hopeful that it would. Despite my optimism I had to ask, with so many books on leadership already available, is there really a need for another?

In *Leadership teams* the authors have understood that when people accept responsibility for their own actions, this invariably leads to a heightened sense of self-responsibility. In so doing the authors have captured the essence of the leadership qualities that those who presume to lead others must work at developing. *Leadership teams* does not just clarify what you should *do* when taking leadership action, much more significant is that it defines what you must work towards becoming. Leading others is not easy, and it would be naive to pretend otherwise. Those who presume to lead others put themselves under pressure. *Leadership teams* makes explicitly clear why accepting a leadership role will put you under pressure, and the development demanded of you if you are to learn how to deal with that pressure.

It was Ernest Hemingway who famously wrote "Courage is grace under pressure." I fully agree with the authors when they observe that grace under pressure is what anyone who aspires to lead others must strive towards. *Leadership teams* makes explicitly clear what you must both do in the here and now and strive towards in the future if you are to have grace under pressure. I firmly believe that the approach to leadership action and team development presented in *Leadership teams* can help you develop as a leader. That is why I am sure that not only is there a need for *Leadership teams*, but that it is long overdue. I highly recommend this book.

LORD TOM SAWYER OF DARLINGTON
House of Lords, UK.

Leadership Teams clearly shows how organizations can transform dysfunctional groups into a high-performing team in six stages.

This practical, easy-to-read book is intended for busy managers who face the constant challenge of enhancing team performance. After reading this book, managers should be able to confidently harness the leadership skills needed to progress groups into cohesive teams.

The story behind the book

Teamwork is essential in order to realize high performance. Nowhere has this been more evident than in the way world leaders pulled together to address the global financial crisis during the autumn of 2008. We all witnessed an unprecedented level of teamwork and cohesive leadership on an international scale.

Leadership and teamwork have become intertwined for five reasons. First, scale! To become a successful global business, growth is more guaranteed through buying other companies than simply through improving the quality of services and products. We realize considerable economies of scale through merger and acquisition. What really makes such big institutions work?

Second, complexity! Complexity accompanies scale. Managers of today's enterprises require concerted and coordinated effort and skill to successfully lead. Sales and marketing must work together to create an eye-catching global brand. Human Resources (HR) and Information and Communication Technology (ICT) must partner with all other functions of the enterprise to ensure the success of the board. As such, nurturing talent has become a primary lever of competitive advantage. Hence, we have named this obsession as, "the war for talent." Also, ICT, as much as finance, has become the lifeblood of the organization. No wonder that HR and ICT rarely refer to cooperation and collaboration, but rather identify their corporate colleagues as clients, customers, and partners in the same breath.

Third, cost! In the developed world, we live in mature markets. The economic imperative is to drive down costs! Imagine the damage to the morale of management and workforce alike if there were no teamwork behind growing the business while reducing costs.

Fourth, culture! Standing out against the large shareholder-value organizations are the John Lewis Partnership (UK) and Mondragon (Spain), namely the stakeholder culture organizations. Quality, service, and people-count are some of the bywords for the undetected but growing trend of employee-owned enterprises. The irony is that in order to achieve scale and cost reduction, the essence of shareholder value, organizations need outstanding teamwork and leadership. Exactly the same outstanding teamwork and leadership is necessary in the stakeholder-orientated enterprises, where the organization nurtures a culture of care and concern into the financial fabric of the organization.

Fifth, sustainable performance! Today's managers have to contend with ceaseless demands made on their time. Even equipped with all the intellectual, strategic, and managerial skills, no one individual could cope with singly shouldering the responsibilities of the corporation. Therefore, employees share responsibilities. The outstanding team both supports and challenges its workers so that they can sustain high performance. Therefore, from whatever perspective, leadership and teamwork are fundamental to the effective functioning of today's organizations.

Strengths and unique selling points

From extensive research and experience, the authors have identified six critical stages to develop high-performing teams. The challenges organizations face at each stage and the leadership skills to progress through each of the stages, form the essence of this book. The book highlights the actions of an effective leader at each stage of a group's development into a high-performing team.

Organization of the book

This book is structured around eight chapters. The chapters provide a description and analysis of each group development stage followed by the appropriate leadership behaviors to guide the group through to the next stage.

Chapter one introduces the single concept running through this book, that of the Integrated Group Development Process. We thoroughly examine how each of the stages weave together and how groups transform into teams.

Chapter two, stage 1, *Mobilizing*, describes how we form groups, and through so doing, the creative processes necessary to help managers think and act differently from their established ways. Four separate elements comprise *mobilizing*:

- Forming the group
- Creativity and innovation
- Decision making
- Ways of working.

Chapter three, stage 2, *Confrontation*, captures the conflict that arises between group members as the group begins to form an identity, but simultaneously struggles to reconcile some of the differences between individuals. Two elements comprise *confrontation*:

- Understanding conflict
- Managing conflict.

Chapter four, stage 3, *Coming together*, outlines how we form sustainable work-based relationships as the group matures. Two elements comprise *coming together*:

- Work-based relationships
- Working in groups.

Chapter five, stage 4, *One step forward, two steps back*, explores the reactions of certain group members when we challenge group norms, accepted behaviors, and attitudes. This results in further conflict which could dismember the group. Two elements comprise *one step forward, two steps back*:

- The way things are done around here
- Competencies and capabilities.

Chapter six, stage 5, *Behaving as one*, considers how a group meaningfully transforms into a team, assuming that it has survived stage 4. Now, team members exercise their new-found confidence through engaging with stakeholders, inside and outside of their team. Two elements comprise *behaving as one*:

- Teams working with other teams
- Engaging others.

Chapter seven, stage 6, *Facing the future*, focuses on how a transformed team, drawing on their newly found capabilities, learns to positively face the future. Two elements comprise *Facing the future*:

- Managing yourself
- Developing leaders.

The book ends with chapter eight, *Grace under pressure*. As Lord Tom Sawyer mentioned, Ernest Hemingway famously said, "Courage is grace under pressure." We consider the graces (qualities of leadership) most pertinent to those who presume to step into leadership, particularly the leading of high-performing teams. We examine the wisdom that guides leadership action and which, in turn, promotes outstanding team performance.

The research underlying this book was inspired by the work of the American academic and writer, Professor Bruce Tuckman. We hope we have done justice to this truly outstanding intellect.

Another important component of this book is our experience of leadership and teamwork which we have captured in the form of a serialized case study. Interweaving one case, the Traditional Turbine Company, to illustrate each stage of a group's development means capturing the vivid experiences of how a group becomes a high-performing team. Although a real company, we have changed its name and that of the characters to respect the privacy of those involved.

A new engineering director, Harry, joins The Traditional Turbine Co.'s Board of Directors. Drawing on the seniority of his role, Harry decides to reinvent the Traditional Turbine Co.'s product range. In less than two years Harry revolutionizes the company through his leadership of teams.

Harry did not reinvent the company's product range on his own. He was part of a management board led by the Chief Executive, Chris, who together with other critical board members, Natasha (Sales Director), John (Finance Director), as well as Per (Harry's Chief Designer), realigned the company by reshaping its product portfolio.

The story is all the more remarkable as prior to joining the board, Harry had a reputation as a, "hard drinking, pleasure seeker," who spent most of his time in local bars. His sudden elevation to the Management Board brought about an abrupt change in his behavior. Harry recognized that he needed help and advice. He became acutely aware that he was the senior engineer leading a "revolution" in a company with an impressive history and tradition. He had to learn to use his new power wisely. The case study illustrates how Harry navigated a path though the six stages of the integrated group development process, so that outstanding performance became embedded in the organization.

Comment

In this book, we examine the interplay between group members. We highlight frailties and strengths. We emphasize the immense power that emanates from shared ways of working, leading to a heightened sense of self-responsibility. Ultimately, sense of self-responsibility is critical. Without accepting the responsibility for one's actions, how can a cluster of people meaningfully progress to perform better?

Trite as it may be, we capture just what it takes to achieve the magical formula of $2 + 2 = 5$!!

Acknowledgments

We are deeply grateful to Madeleine Fleure for her warm humor and tremendous patience in processing draft after draft in such a prompt and efficient manner. Thank you for dealing with all the queries and changes of mind from the authors and editor.

We also wish to thank Thomas Sigel for his tremendous contribution in turning around extensive scripts into succinct and easily readable text. Thomas, you have brought this book to life.

Our grateful thanks also go to Alexi Mordashov, Vadim Makhov, Dmitry Afanasyev, and Dmitry Kouptsov and the Severstal Corporation for their generous support in sponsoring the studies in this book through the Cranfield/Severstal research program.

Last, we are indebted to all of the managers and directors of the public and private organizations we surveyed and to the community representatives and politicians that we spoke to, all of whom shaped the thinking and research that make up this book. Your experiences have provided an invaluable source of insight for so many people, for so many years to come.

Geoff Sheard, DPhil, PhD, MBA, BEng, CEng, FIMechE, FRAeS, FASME, FCIBSE is currently Vice President—Fan Technology, with the Flakt Woods Group and a director of Flakt Woods Limited, based in Colchester, England. Geoff is also a Visiting Fellow at the University of Northampton Business School and a director of the Air Movement and Control Association. He has doctorate degrees from Oxford University in turbomachinery aerodynamics and from the University of Northampton in leadership and team development. He also holds a masters degree in business administration from Cranfield University and a bachelor's degree in mechanical engineering from Liverpool University. He is a chartered engineer, a Liveryman of the Worshipful Company of Engineers, a fellow of the Institution of Mechanical Engineers, a fellow of the Royal Aeronautical Society, a fellow of the American Society of Mechanical Engineers, and a fellow of the Chartered Institute of Building Service Engineers. Geoff has published widely in both technical and management areas, with his management research focused on leadership and team development. He has published 1 book, 2 monographs, over 60 articles, and is a member of the Journal of Management Development editorial advisory board.

geoff.sheard@flaktwoods.com

Andrew Kakabadse, Professor of International Management Development, Cranfield School of Management. Andrew was the H. Smith Richardson Fellow at CCL, North Carolina, USA and is Visiting Professor at the University of Ulster; Macquarie Graduate School of Management; Thunderbird, and at Swinburne University. His research covers boards, top teams and the governance of governments. He has published 32 books, over 200 articles, and 18 monographs. Most recent books are entitled *"Leading the Board: The Six Disciplines of World-Class Chairmen," "Leading for Success: The Seven Sides* *to Great* Leaders" and *"The Elephant Hunters: Chronicles of the Moneymen,"* published by Palgrave Macmillan. Andrew is coeditor of the Journal of Management Development and Corporate Governance: International Journal of Business in Society.

a.p.kakabadse@cranfield.ac.uk

Nada Kakabadse BSc. Grad.Dip., MSc. MPA., PhD is currently Professor in Management and Business research at the University of Northampton Business School and the coeditor (with Andrew Kakabadse) of the Journal of Management and Corporate Governance: The International Journal of Business in Society. Nada has published widely in areas of leadership, application of IS/IT in corporations, corporate governance, government, boardroom effectivness, diversity management, and ethics; including 12 books, 52 chapters in international volumes, 3 monographs, and over 150 scholarly and reviewed articles. Most recent books are entitled *"Leading the Board: The Six Disciplines of World-Class Chairmen," "Leading for Success: The Seven Sides to Great* Leaders," and *"The Elephant Hunters: Chronicles of the Moneymen,"* published by Palgrave Macmillan. Nada has acted as a consultant to numerous public and private sector organizations.

nada.kakabadse@northampton.ac.uk

CHAPTER 1

Conceptual framework

The empowerment of one heroic leader to run complex organizations, making lone decisions at the top, is anything but rational. Anyone who steps into a leadership role has to learn to develop groups that in turn can help solve organizational problems that are difficult to solve alone. As stated in the Preface, this book presents a model of group development that provides insight into the stages that all groups must pass through if they are to perform to their full potential. Through so doing, we provide readers with an understanding of the process of group life playing out around them, emphasizing that meaningful leadership action necessitates taking full account of context.

Why link leadership with group development? There are two reasons: first, it is important for a leader to focus on how a group is developing and remain aware of the process of group life in order to transform the group into a credible team. Second, the leader must be aware of the choices available when engaged in task activity with the group. Sensitivity to the changing emotions of group members runs in parallel with clear rational thinking.

Most successful leaders share a somewhat unusual trait: a predisposition and capacity to hold in their heads two contrasting ideas simultaneously.Without settling for one alternative or the other, they are able to creatively resolve the tensions between those two ideas by generating a new one that contains elements of the other two, but is superior to both. The process of consideration and synthesis is a discipline that is a defining characteristic of the most exceptional business leaders.

If the development of the group is profoundly influenced by style of leadership, is it reasonable to think of team leadership as either distributed or networked? Is it not more usual to think of exceptional individuals when thinking about leadership? Despite the multiple ways researchers have conceptualized leadership, we have identified two components as central to the phenomenon:

- Leadership is a process. It is not a linear, one-way event but rather a series of interactive events.
- Leadership occurs in groups. Groups provide the context in which leadership takes place.

We can, therefore, view leadership in terms of functions that are important for the survival of the group and the accomplishment of its goals. If we accept this point of view, it then follows that a single individual, two individuals, a subsection of group members, or the entire group can embrace leadership roles.

One reason why group-based leadership can be more effective than any individual within the group is that important decisions about what to do and how to do it are made through the use of an interactive process that involves many different people who influence each other. Again, as emphasized in the Preface, in a complex environment, such as a multinational organization, no individual will possess all the information he or she needs to make a fully informed decision. Therefore, a group that elects distributed leadership has the potential to make better decisions.

The historic origin of a distributed perspective on leadership emerged in the latter part of the 20th century as a result of the changing patterns of work. The rise of the knowledge worker is both a symptom and cause of changing patterns of organizational structure and leadership. Over the last 50 years, the shift from mostly manual laborers performing repetitive tasks to educated workers applying theoretical and analytical knowledge is the process of putting knowledge to work. This has had a profound impact on philosophies of leadership and the structure of organizations.

A continuing shift toward knowledge-based working will result in more work within organizations becoming flexible and varied. This, in turn, will require people to work together in new ways that are conducive to the expression of creativity and innovation. The leadership of organizations will increasingly have to grapple with two challenges, the need for continuous attention to costs and making the enterprise more efficient (resulting in centralization), as well as encouraging innovation resulting in ever more decentralized, networked, distributed, and shared ways of working. Such contrasting tensions are best handled through the platform of sound teamwork.

Leadership in the 21st century

Despite the prolific literature and detailed studies on leadership, we still have little agreement on the characteristics of the great leader or, for that matter, outstanding leadership. This confusion is, in part, because our image of great leaders tends to be of great historical leaders. However, the modern-day manager has relatively little in common with these historical figures.

Scholars advocate two distinctly different interpretations of leadership: (1) the born-to-lead school and (2) the self-development school. The first school takes an upfront and direct approach, requiring strength, courage, and charisma. The latter advocates thinking and negotiation associated with wisdom. The preeminence of the born-to-lead school of leadership is a consequence of the assumption that only great people are capable of achieving great outcomes. Scholars have used an array of terms, skill, strength, vitality, sharpness of mind, and even good looks, to differentiate the great leader from the rest of humanity. Evident displays of outstanding personal, physical, and mental characteristics lead us to assume that leaders are born and not made.

During the late 19th century, the born-to-lead school was th dominant philosophy. Frederick Nietzsche's (1969) *Ubermens* (superman) is a leader because of his unique ability to transform a result of his exceptional human nature. Through the embodin of these extraordinary qualities, the *Ubermensch* leads by crea ever-new values to replace the old ones by destroying the ous ethical, religious, and political order. Leaders, in Nietzs terms, herald nothing short of an ongoing, radical transformation of society. Their guiding philosophy is to dominate those around them, thus fulfilling the image of the ideal leader.

In contrast, the self-development school began with the ancient Greeks. The Socratic question of "what ought one to do?" deeply influenced the Greeks. This question demands an account from individuals as to why they choose one goal over another. Socratic philosophy requires each person to articulate what he or she considers to be good, or at least justify his or her course of action, on the basis that no one truth exists. Indeed, Aristotle (1986) detailed the Socratic origins of humility and the fact that Socrates proclaimed he had no prerogative on any one or other truth. After visiting and conversing with a wise man, Socrates left thinking, "I am wiser than this man: neither of us knows anything that is really worth knowing, but he thinks that he has knowledge when he has not, while I have no knowledge, nor do I think I have."

The Socratic "ignorance" paradox serves as the basis for understanding the deeper nature of leaders who will not say "cannot" and who use the philosophy of aspiring to achieve wisdom as they strive for leadership success. The Socratic message is a continual intellectual and emotional movement, with the ultimate aim of freeing oneself from the presumption of knowledge. The ader-follower relationship, in the Socratic sense, is one that powers the follower, and where both members of the relationship stretch each other to find meaning, and from that emerge penetrating interpretation of the issues at hand.

the concept of wisdom by steering around obstacles eed for justification of action. To achieve wisdom, ness inspiration and must find and/or create path-hindrances and obstacles. By assessing the ques-do, Socrates combined intellect with humility and both those with mature emotive reaction. ination, Socrates argued, no one could mean-e's challenges. On this basis, Socrates posits life is not worth living. Without this, an uld terrorize the individual and paralyze o address future challenges. As such, but the genetic interpretation of born to lead, as no one remains within a box, unless he or she is bound by his or her own perspective.

Scholars have progressively favored the self-development school of leadership during the 20th century. Over the last 20 years, both academics and practitioners have popularized the "functional" approach to leadership. This is a branch of the self-development school. The functional approach to leadership focuses on the ability of an individual to influence, and be influenced, by a group in the implementation of a common task. It is little wonder that functionality has grown in popularity as organizations are, and have been, placing increasing emphasis on the relevance of the functional approach to leadership as they accelerate toward knowledge-based working.

The functional approach to leadership involves focusing the efforts of a group toward a common goal and enabling group members to work together. In order to meet leadership responsibilities, group members need to perform and share certain functions. We define function as what you *do* as contrasted with what you *are* or what you *know*.

So, let us recap. The born-to-lead and self-development schools of leadership constitute fundamentally contrasting philosophical perspectives on leadership. The will to conquer best represents the born-to-lead school. In contrast, humility and a sense of being within a community represent the self-development school. Leaders today face constraints and complexities that require them to display both strength and sensitivity. When leading, they must guide discussion to resolution and also have the good sense and grace not to unduly burden the process with an overlarge ego. Within the context of the 21st-century complex national and global organization, the self-development school of leadership is relevant and its contemporary embodiment in the functional approach to leadership appropriate.

Group development

Our ability to lead begins with the recognition that although our images of great historical leaders are rooted in the born-to-lead school, it is the self-development school generally, and the functional approach to leadership specifically, that is appropriate today. Let us reiterate, the functional approach involves focusing the efforts of a group toward achieving a common goal. As such, an objective of leadership action is to create and develop groups around organizational problems.

Over the last five decades, scholars studying group behavior have advocated various models of group development, some concerned with how to achieve unity, others with how to realize complementarity in order to achieve goals, and certain others with how to address tension and conflict. However, the most widely accepted cluster of group development models is the linear progressive model that advocates a group development sequence. In particular, Professor Bruce Tuckman (2001) advocated that a group development sequence exists and separates two aspects of group functioning: (1) the task activity a group is undertaking and (2) the process of a group's life. A development sequence focuses on the interactions between individuals and the process of group life, asserting that a common development sequence exists for all groups. Different scholars advocate different stages in a group's development. The most widely accepted stages, referred to in the Preface, are as follows:

- Mobilizing
- Confrontation
- Coming together
- Behaving as one
- Facing the future.

During the *mobilizing* stage, group members get to know each other and establish more personable relationships. During the *confrontation* stage, conflict arises. Conflict could emerge over rival leadership challenges or simply because of interpersonal behavior. The source of conflict could be a group's resistance to group influences or task requirements. The group could split at this stage. Assuming it does not, the group moves into the *coming together* stage and focuses on a single leader. Here, the leader establishes behavioral norms and a sense of group cohesiveness. The leader sets new group standards and determines roles for members. The *behaving as one* stage occurs when members start performing tasks together. The leader has established role clarity and members are now working together in a cooperative and complementary manner. The *facing the future* stage occurs as members realize that the group is about to complete the task for which it was created. As a result of the regrouping, members initially feel a sense of loss, but realize that they would not have achieved the task at hand in their former environment. Now they come to grips with the new order. In order to sustain their new-found high level of performance, facing the future and focusing on continual improvement for the future becomes critical.

The concept of a linear development sequence is important as it establishes the existence of generic stages through which all groups pass. However, over a 20-year period, working with and studying groups of managers, we have observed that the vast majority of groups do not pass smoothly through the stages of a linear group development sequence. In practice, individuals opt out, groups regress, and, in many cases, disband. During the course of our research, we recognized that we could consider a linear group development sequence more usefully in terms of a process, specifically a process with two breakdown points.

The first breakdown point occurs as a group attempts to negotiate the transition out of the mobilizing and into the confrontation stage. The breakdown occurs when members become clearly aware of the non-shared assumptions between themselves. Each individual will ask himself, "Do I agree with what the leader is asking this group to do?" Not everyone will agree and some will opt out at this point, visibly, or just switch off. The passive resistance of those who have switched off is not necessarily apparent to other members. As they argue about who will do what and how (the confrontation stage) and finally start to reach a consensus (the coming together stage), the group might appear to be functional. However, some group members have no intention of accepting any decision that involves their doing anything differently from the way they did in the past.

The second breakdown point occurs as a group attempts to negotiate the transition out of the coming together and into the behaving-as-one stage. Individuals ask themselves, "Do I accept the role I will have to play to work in this group?" The sudden realization of what working in the group will actually mean in practical terms results in some instinctively answering "no." As a consequence, at the point where the group could really start to perform, we clearly notice that some have either been opting out, or have suddenly decided to opt out. Passive resistance is now explicit. The group will slip back into conflict, entering a new stage one step forward, two steps back.

We could argue that the one step forward, two steps back stage is little more than a repeat of the confrontation and coming together stages. From a group development perspective, it is undoubtedly true that the group does slip back into conflict, and that members then attempt to reach a consensus as to a new way forward. From a leadership perspective, however, the one step forward, two steps back stage is unique. Those who have accepted their new role and would have been happy to move on must manage their crushing disappointment as the group descends into conflict at the very moment that it appeared to be on the point of really performing. The emotion felt at the start of the confrontation stage is shock. However, the emotion at the start of the one step forward, two steps back stage is anger. If this anger is allowed to continue, it cools into hard disdain toward those who have frustrated the ambition and capacity of the majority.

By identifying two breakdown points and an additional stage, we have created an "integrated" group development process (Figure 1.1)." It is integrated on the basis that it identifies all stages of, and breakdown points within, a group's development:

- Stage One: Mobilizing.
- Stage Two: Confrontation.
- Stage Three: Coming together.
- Stage Four: One step forward, two steps back.
- Stage Five: Behaving as one.
- Stage Six: Facing the future.

The integrated group development process also identifies a recurring cycle within the process, associated with the second question those involved ask themselves at the one step forward,

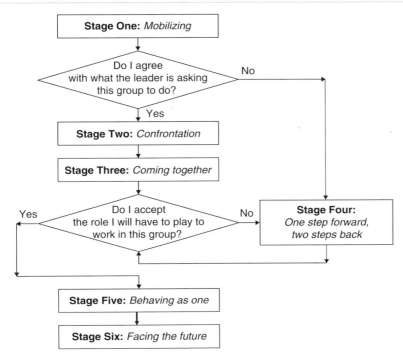

Figure 1.1 The integrated group development process

Source: Compiled by the authors

two steps back stage. The recurring cycle occurs as a consequence of group members never accepting their role, and for this reason the group never progresses beyond the one step forward, two steps back stage. The group members continue to interact similar to the way they interacted on the first day they met. The interaction is minimal but the group is kept together by the obligation the members feel to apply their social interaction skills. They do not generate a positive synergy through coordinated effort. Analysis of the recurring cycle provides reasons as to why many groups perform worse than expected, given the capability of the individuals involved.

It is only as group members accept their new roles that a group transforms into a team. Therefore, the first four stages of the integrated group development process are concerned with group functioning. The fifth and sixth stages, behaving as one and facing the future respectively, are concerned with team interaction and performance. We emphasize that the term "group" and "team" should not be used interchangeably. Groups and teams are not the same phenomenon. For this reason, the integrated group development process defines how a group evolves and the specific point at which it transforms into a team.

The integrated group development process may look complex, and indeed it is! Group development is intricate and we contend it would be naïve to pretend otherwise. Groups in work organizations do not progress smoothly from their initial formation through performance. Anyone who has ever worked with others knows that many groups never go on to realize their full potential. They get stuck, and the members of the group seem to do little more than argue and go round in circles revisiting the same issues and tensions, but without resolution.

Anyone aspiring to lead any part of an organization will have to manage people in groups, and the integrated group development process model shows how they have, do, and will behave in the future. We have observed many managers and boards of directors. The two questions "do I agree ... ." and "do I accept ... ." are generic as is the tendency to get stuck, perpetually attempting to agree and repetitively failing to do so.

So, let us recap. The six stages of the integrated group development process provide a way of explaining how groups develop into teams. Understanding how groups mature and progress enables the leader(s) to adopt appropriate behaviors and actions. Thus, we conceptualize leadership action in terms of a group's development. From now on, we offer the reader insight into how leaders and groups can resolve the tensions between them.

Want to know more?

- For more information on the research behind this book, read Sheard and Kakabadse (2002; 2004; 2007) and Sheard (2007).
- For insights into the characteristics and makeup of leaders, refer to Martin (2007).
- For further understanding of leadership roles see Avolio et al (1996); Manz and Sims (1993), and Pearce and Sims (2000).

- To further understand the dichotomy between the born-to-lead and self-development schools of thought, see Barnard (1926); Fiedler (1967); House and Mitchell (1974); Stogdill (1974); Kakabadse and Kakabadse (1998), and Aristotle (1986).
- To gain further insight into the six-stage integrated group development process, refer to Tuckman (1965); Tuckman and Jensen (1977), and Tuckman (2001). For a broader view on the nature of groups, also read Chidambaram and Bostrom (1996) and Kakabadse (2000).

CHAPTER 2

Mobilizing

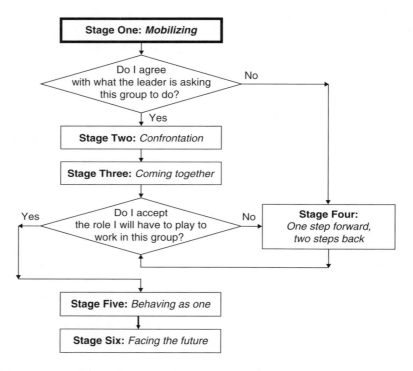

Figure 2.1   The integrated group development process, stage one: Mobilizing

Source: Compiled by the authors

What makes an effective manager? While effective managers differ widely in their personalities, strengths, weaknesses, values, and beliefs, they all have one thing in common: they get the right things done. Effectiveness does not, however, spring only from extraordinary talent. Effectiveness is a discipline, and like every discipline it can be learnt.

The process of accomplishing the right tasks is closely linked to spending time with other people. We can consider a casual conversation with one person as a meeting. In a work environment, effective managers spend most of their day in either formal or informal meetings, working in groups as opposed to alone. We often question what managers are actually accomplishing. They discuss, debate, analyze, and listen. At the end of that process, after considering all the information and the opinions of others, it is a manager's job to make prudent decisions and then make them happen.

Making it happen starts with the mobilization of organizational resources. Four elements comprise the *mobilizing* stage of a group's development:

1. Forming the group.
2. Creativity and innovation.
3. Decision making.
4. Ways of working.

As we previously stated, anyone who presumes to step into a leadership role can learn to form and develop groups that in turn, help him or her solve organizational problems he or she would find difficult to solve alone. As such, the first element of the mobilizing stage is *forming the group*. A key aspect of any group that is to ultimately perform to its full potential is its creativity compared to that of any individual within the group. The creative process allows a group to identify novel connections between the knowledge and perspectives of group members. This leads to the second element: *creativity and innovation*. The third element is *decision making*, the tipping point at which an organization moves from discussing a range of possible ideas to a commitment to the delivery of just one.

If creativity is the original idea, then innovation is the practical implementation of the idea. Innovation is the hard-focused purposeful work we need to convert a creative idea into a new product or service. The work associated with innovative implementation of a creative idea brings us to the fourth element of the mobilizing stage: *ways of working*. A difference between individuals working alone and as members of a group is that they adapt what they do in response to knowledge of the needs of other group members. The way in which group members work can either help or hinder their ability to adapt.

So let us recap. We can break down the mobilizing stage of a group's development into four elements: *forming the group, creativity and innovation, decision making* and *ways of working.* Each is important if we want to successfully mobilize a new group. Before we consider the four elements in detail, we describe the mobilizing stage. We examine the practical indicators that signal a group is first approaching the mobilizing stage. We then explore what occurs as the group evolves.

Group development

The first stage of a group's development, mobilizing, commences as members become aware of other members of the group and begin to interact with them as a consequence of that new knowledge. We characterize the mobilizing stage by group members testing each other to establish how each will respond to various statements coupled with indirect attempts to discover the nature and boundary of his or her task. Essentially, group members attempt to establish what they must accomplish and how much cooperation they demand to do so.

We characterize the mobilizing stage by a sense of "newness" as group members attempt to structure the unknown and find their position in the group. Scholars who have studied group behavior consider that during the initial stage of a group's development, the group works out authority problems by the quick acceptance of, and dependence on, a group structure. The establishment of a hierarchy within the group caters to the dependency needs of members. In essence, group members make an attempt to structure the unknown and find their position in that structure.

In parallel to the group processes playing out associated with establishment of hierarchy and place in that hierarchy, the group also sets forth task activity. Task activity attempts to orient group members to the issues at hand, thus leading to setting goals. In general terms, we can characterize this task-oriented behavior as a search for meaning, an attempt to define the situation and the mutual exchange of information. Often, this task-related behavior occurs in a climate of suspicion and fearfulness toward the situation.

We can best characterize the mobilizing stage of a group's development as a dual form of negotiation. Group members engage in negotiation with each other to establish if each is willing to work with the others. Simultaneously, members negotiate with those leading other groups within the wider organization to establish if their management will accept a particular interpretation of what the goal means in practice if delivered.

Practical indicators

There are three signs indicating that a group has entered the mobilizing stage. First, we see a change in focus from discussing a range of possible ideas and approaches to the discussion of a specific idea, the resources necessary, and how the group will make those resources available given all the other tasks that they must achieve. As debate crystallizes on a specific issue, a nucleus of individuals who have relevant knowledge and experience starts to form. The group may not yet contain a full complement of members, nor have existing members started to formally address pertinent issues. Nonetheless, the mobilizing stage has started.

As a group enters the mobilizing stage, the hardest part is to decide what members will stop doing. It is easier to agree to do something new than it is to agree to stop doing something that has always been done. A common failure among the inexperienced is to either underestimate the time and effort he or she needs to undertake a new project, or if he or she estimates accurately, to fail to recognize that members are already doing something, and that some will have to stop as the group mobilizes.

The second sign is an increasing focus on what skills and expertise the group needs for success. The mobilizing stage is underway, but that does not mean that the group is complete. Core members must decide who to recruit outside the group. They need to identify the key skills and experience that they require and start approaching potential candidates. Once they are recruited, these new members will bring ideas and perspectives to the group that will create new cycles of discussion and debate about the group's goal, what it means in terms of practical activity for members, what necessary skills members lack, and hence who else the group should recruit.

The third sign is an acceptance that group membership is now complete. Discussion progresses to what the goal means in terms of activity for existing members of the group, not activity that prospective new members will undertake. As such, members start to recognize that the more difficult or unpleasant jobs must be tackled by one of them. As they become aware of the reality of the purpose of the group, members begin to realize what membership means. They start to recognize their dependency on others in the group, as the input they will need to deliver becomes clear. The group now focuses debate not only on the detail of what each member will do, but also on what they will need from others in order to do it.

Forming the group

Forming the group comprises the first element of the mobilizing stage. Managers do this when they work together; they spend most of their day in either formal or informal meetings. As the mobilizing stage begins, managers take their first step toward forming not just *a* group, but *the* group that constitutes allocation of organizational resources to achieve a new goal. Therefore, the formation of a very specific type of group begins the mobilizing stage.

With the group's initial formation, members may not have defined the organizational resources they require to achieve a new goal. Indeed, the group will not entirely establish how a new goal translates into tangible deliverables. They will still need to determine the skills and expertise they require. This may lead to recruiting more members. As such, the group has not precisely defined the boundary between the first element of the mobilizing stage, forming the group, and the other elements. Although elements proceed in a generally stepwise fashion, there is a "fuzzy" boundary between elements through all stages of any group's development. At times they overlap, and consequentially we position the elements as sequential steps; however in real life it may not feel like that.

Despite the reservation that elements can at times overlap, a nucleus of individuals forming a group will initiate the mobilizing stage and go on to deliver a new organizational goal. As such, the group processes most relevant are those that play out when people meet for the first time. Specifically, we see the breaking down of barriers and inhibitions between group members. This process between group members is necessary as when people meet for the first time there is a natural tendency to be polite, guarded, and watchful. Members form opinions concerning the strengths and weaknesses of others, and decide whether they think they will be able to work amenably with them.

The group must engage in the process of breaking down barriers and inhibitions between the new group and those leading other key groups around the organization, as other groups that comprise the wider organization must accept the new group's output. Therefore, a new group must establish how its assigned goal translates into deliverables others can accept. The set goal will come with assumptions as to what the organization expects from the group in terms of output. Those groups that must accept the output will have particular constraints on what they are able to accept, in addition to preconceptions as to exactly what they expect.

An organization starts to consider mobilizing a new group as influential individuals begin to realize that the status quo is no longer satisfactory and that the organization needs some change without a specific recognition as to exactly what that change is. The group likely lacks consensus as to the key issues the organization faces. There will be disagreement between the traditionalists who want to continue operating in the same vein, with perhaps some improvement, and the revolutionaries who favor more radical action. This is symptomatic of a lack of vision.

An organization's vision does not just spring into life fully formed; it must start out as an internal vision with a minimum of one individual seeing what life could be like while dealing with life as it is. The trick is to hold this paradox, see the vision and deal with reality without losing sight of either. To be convincing, an individual must have a meaningful vision and must convince those who must support the proposal that it should also be meaningful to them.

So, let us recap. The first element of the mobilizing stage is forming the group. Managers spend most of their day working in formal or informal groups. However, the mobilizing stage begins when people form a group with the specific objective of achieving a new goal. Elements can overlap and therefore there is a fuzzy boundary between the first element, forming the group, and other elements. In order for a group to form, the organizers must have a vision of how this group will help achieve the task or goal at stake, thus justifying the formation. When first forming a group, members will experience the social interaction ritual of breaking down barriers and inhibitions between themselves as they decide whether the existing members are suitable for the group and whether they will be able to establish a positive working rapport.

Creativity and innovation

Creativity and innovation comprise the second element of the mobilizing stage. During the mobilizing stage, creative thinking among members and the process of planning innovative implementation of those ideas enables a group to identify what the goal means in terms of practical activity. We therefore link leadership action during the mobilizing stage closely to fostering creativity. However, as we mentioned earlier, an organization starts to consider mobilizing a new group as influential individuals begin to realize that they need some change. Before we discuss the creative process and how members can plan, it is necessary for you to understand how an organization decides to pursue one goal from the many options available.

As you learned in the Preface, the Traditional Turbine Co. case study tells the story of Harry's journey joining the Traditional Turbine Co.'s Board while in his mid-thirties. However Harry, a capable engineer, lacked Board experience. Adapting to his new role would be difficult for Harry and the challenge was greater because of his personality. Harry took an informal approach to business and was naturally humorous, a combination that enabled his technical competence to come across well to colleagues in small group settings. However, in large group settings, such as Board meetings, where formality was appropriate, Harry's sense of humor was more of a liability than an asset.

Like most engineers, Harry was an introvert, but unlike many, was also assertive. That combination enabled Harry to communicate with other introverted engineers in a way an extrovert simply could not, but simultaneously drove change and accomplished things in a way that the unassertive could not even attempt. At one level, the Traditional Turbine Co. case study is a "coming of age" story about a young man who finds himself unexpectedly in a senior role, and despite his intensely human failings, succeeds. At another level, the case study illustrates the reality of leadership, and in the first instance how Harry settled on developing a new product range as his goal. However, on his first day at work, Harry was focused on the immediate issue at hand: to stay awake while his new boss "droned" on.

Case Study 2.1   The Traditional Turbine Co.—Into the labyrinth

"We have enjoyed a dominant position in our market since the 1950's, but the world has changed around us and we must change too. To be honest, we are still a very traditional company," finished Chris, the Traditional Turbine Co.'s Chief Executive. He sat back and contemplated the view from his fifth-floor corner office window, waiting for a response.

Chris had been talking to Harry, the engineering director he had appointed, and who was starting work that

$\rightarrow$

morning. A capable engineer, Chris selected Harry for this esteemed position because he knew that Harry regarded engineering as a means to an end. The end in question was to produce something the customer actually wanted. This inevitably involved spending significant time with clients, talking to them, and agreeing on timely solutions at a tolerable cost and to an adequate specification. This collaborative approach to new product development was unconventional, but was a formula for success.

Privately, Harry thought he offered a skill set that was more business development than engineering. At his final interview, Harry had pointed this out to Chris who just waved the objection away: "The last thing I need is another engineer on the Board. That's what got us into this mess in the first place."

The mess to which he was referring was an obsolete product range. Although Chris did not explicitly tell Harry to "sort out the mess," Harry recognized this implication in his mandate as engineering director.

However, on his first day, Harry was primarily concerned with fitting in. The last thing he wanted to do was make his life harder than it needed to be by unintentionally making a poor first impression on his fellow Board members. As engineering director, Harry recognized that he had a functional role associated with his job title and the duties it implied. More importantly, he recognized that his presumptions as to exactly what those duties were might be misplaced. No man is an island, and Harry acknowledged that he would need to interact more with other people.

Case Study 2.1 illustrates how Harry was wary of jumping to conclusions about Chris' expectations of him in his new role as engineering director. The recognition that "no man is an island" illustrates Harry's awareness that the Board members who comprised his new peer group were unlikely to speak both openly and fully about what they needed from an engineering director until they got to know him.

While Harry was well aware of his boss's views regarding the company's product range, his caution about assuming anything illustrates that he was both focused on establishing what the company expected him to deliver, and what the implications would be for his peer group. We can understand Harry's caution, but we must acknowledge that his new boss had hired him largely because he hoped that Harry would bring a creative approach to product development. Before Harry could form his own view on the Traditional Turbine Co.'s product range, he needed to turn over a few rocks and discover for himself why the product range was obsolete.

Case Study 2.2   The Traditional Turbine Co.—Truth seeking

When Harry reviewed the company's contracts for the turbines, to his amazement, he was told by Per, his chief designer, that the department had badly compromised the designs, they were more expensive than necessary, and not a very good match to client requirements. Because of both internal and client pressures to deliver the goods in a timely manner, the management did not adequately address such problems. This situation had been endemic for years.

Harry and Per decided to rectify these problems by quietly starting work together on a modular turbine concept. This time nobody was pressurizing them to deliver by a specific contract date. They could tackle more difficult design issues with informal discussion. Per would then speak with key specialists around the company. The feedback would fuel further rounds of debate between Harry and Per that would, in turn, lead to further discussion with other specialists as they identified technical issues and considered options.

$\rightarrow$

This was Harry and Per's first step in data gathering and fact finding for the new turbine concept that would eventually lead to a formal proposal to the Board.

Case Study 2.2 illustrates that Harry did not want to make hasty judgments about faults and weaknesses with the existing product range. He adopted an extended data-gathering approach which enabled him to discover exactly the product range. As Case Study 2.2 shows, contract-to-contract variations required more engineering resources than were available. Engineers rushed the design process with no time to think about how they could embed a new feature into a standard product range. As a result, the firm's opportunity to harness creative ideas and innovatively implement them was effectively zero.

Case Study 2.2 also highlights that Harry was able to establish a working relationship with Per, his chief designer. Harry worked through Per, established their respective roles and responsibilities, and acknowledged that Per had access to an informal network within the Traditional Turbine Co. that he did not have. Thus, Harry was able to focus action around informal communication practices, an appropriate approach, because Harry needed to know the opinions of key personnel throughout the company regarding the product range. Harry used an informal approach via Per's well-established network from his many years of service with the Traditional Turbine Co. Harry recognized that if he had made a formal request for information regarding the product range from other departments around the organization, employees would have responded with the same recycled stock answers they had used for years.

Yes, Harry's first step was to identify the core requirements of a new product range. However, to be successful, he needed to find creative ways of meeting those requirements. Occasionally, a brilliant mind working alone can find creative solutions to problems, but in business we usually associate the creative process with a group. A group can bring different perspectives to a problem, find some novel connections among those perspectives, and in doing so can originate what was not previously an obvious alternative.

So, Harry worked with members of the Board, engaging each in informal and wide-ranging debate in his efforts to define exactly a new product range specification. Yes, each Board member had a different point of view, but Harry linked them together, realizing the one mandatory element of any new product range. This realization did not spring from a flash of genius. For Harry, it was hard-won insight.

**Case Study 2.3   The Traditional Turbine Co.—
Seeing clearly**

While Harry relied on Per, his chief designer, inside the Traditional Turbine Co., he chose to broaden his network, traveling with Natasha, the Traditional Turbine Co.'s sales director.

There was, and had been for over one hundred years, brickworks close to the Traditional Turbine Co. that had historically attracted immigrant workers to the town. Displaced during the Second World War, Natasha's father finally found work at the brickworks in the early 1950's. Determined that his own children should have a better life than him, he encouraged Natasha to work at school, and then take a "proper" job in an office. Over a 20-year career with the Traditional Turbine Co., she had worked her way up from secretary through marketing, into sales and finally onto the Board. To her father, she embodied success. To Harry, he simply could not comprehend how she managed to know so little and still sell a technical product.

Natasha might have lacked the formal technical education that Harry took for granted, but she was not stupid. The first customer visit with Harry went wrong when the client's

$\rightarrow$

technical director decided to show his boss how clever he was. Without being asked, Harry cut in and systematically destroyed him on every point. Natasha was well aware that had she been alone, the sales call would have unfolded very differently. Although she did not admit it to Harry until much later, she had little idea what Harry and the client's technical director were talking about as they argued back and forth. She was well aware that if it had been her rather than Harry who had been answering the technical director's questions, she would have been perceived to be poorly briefed at best.

After the meeting, Natasha pointed out to Harry his effect on the client, how they had sat in stunned silence as he had reduced their own technical director from master to student. Natasha was impressed by the way in which Harry did this without resorting to insult or to personal attack of any kind. In fact, the two men appeared to have actually enjoyed the exchange, and, as the meeting broke up, she found them making arrangements to meet up at a forthcoming technical conference.

As a result, Harry and Natasha became friends. This was not because Natasha enlightened Harry on how to properly engage in a sales meeting, or because Harry instructed Natasha on the correct approach to rotating equipment design. Their friendship sprang from the fact that they both recognized the value of the other's capability.

While travelling with Natasha, Harry discovered why the company had been suffering a decline in sales. They had "missed the cut" ten times over the last two years, and six times in the last nine months, because they did not have an "axial exhaust" turbine. A turbine is a source of power, either electrical or mechanical. Turbines have traditionally discharged redundant gas down toward the ground and hence have a downward exhaust. An axial exhaust turbine has an exhaust that is horizontal discharging redundant

$\rightarrow$

gas along the ground. Discharging redundant gas along the ground requires a complex turbine, but a simple concrete foundation. Discharging redundant gas downwards requires a relatively simple turbine, but a deep and therefore expensive foundation. As such, axial exhaust turbines are more expensive than traditional turbines, but have a lower overall installed cost because of the simple foundation.

During their evenings in the bar, Harry and Natasha debated the various contracts they had both won and lost, looking for common threads. Over time, Harry acquired an encyclopedic knowledge of every design feature that had helped win a contract. Natasha understood the significance of an axial exhaust, but did not believe that the clients who asked for it were willing to pay for it. In her experience, the client budgeted for the turbine itself, and the company rewarded those responsible for the purchasing decision for staying within that budget. That an axial exhaust turbine would reduce the overall installed cost, in her experience, was irrelevant.

With persuasive zeal, Harry convinced Natasha to offer clients an axial exhaust product range by offering a 10% cost reduction program, such that the overall product cost of preparing the new axial turbine for the market remained unchanged. Harry always suspected that Natasha intended to carry on selling traditional turbines at a 10% discount, but despite this reservation, was confident that he had finally understood the needs of the Traditional Turbine Co.'s clients: minimum installed cost, and that meant a range of axial exhaust turbines.

Case Study 2.3 illustrates how Harry established the needs of the Traditional Turbine Co.'s customers: a new product range. You should not underestimate the challenges in adopting this approach. Harry had no authority to compel Natasha, the Traditional Turbine Co.'s sales director, to take him to visit clients, and those clients were not turbine experts. Therefore, they could not say explicitly what technical features they needed in a new product range.

Again, Case Study 2.3 illustrates that Harry chose to clarify the need for an axial exhaust product range. He facilitated this by establishing mutually acceptable roles and responsibilities with Natasha, and Per, Harry's chief designer. This enabled Harry to gather data from both inside and outside the Traditional Turbine Co.

The creative spark for Harry was the realization that whatever else was included or left out of the final product specification, the company needed to offer customers a new product range of axial exhaust turbines. If creativity is the original spark, then innovation is the process by which this is converted into something tangible. This is where a group can help. A group is better able to move on from the generation of more ideas to their systematic evaluation, and thus hit "the innovation sweet spot." This is an innovation far enough from existing products to attract real interest, but close enough to fall within a company's existing positioning strategies and capabilities.

When we refer to a creative group, we allude to a number of attributes, one of which is the group's creativity relative to that of any individual within it. Groups are not intrinsically creative, as they contain individuals who may or may not find the group environment conducive to creativity. Second, creativity is not automatically a good thing in every case. There is a link between creativity, innovation, and leadership. Specifically, we must strike a balance between creativity and conformity.

We design organizations to promote order and routine. We require conformity to varying degrees in the daily functioning of an organization. To understand the potential problem with creativity, we must understand how individuals often wrongly define it. We can define creativity as having great and original ideas. The focus is on the ideas, not how useful they are or how well we implement them. From an organizational standpoint, poor attention to the execution of ideas can become a form of personal irresponsibility as creative idea follows creative idea with no action-oriented follow-through.

This behavior is unacceptable;

- The creative man who tosses out ideas and does nothing to implement them is shirking any responsibility for one of the prime requisites of the business, namely, action.
- By avoiding follow-through, he or she behaves in an organizationally intolerable—or at best, sloppy—fashion.

The nature of the creative process may seem chaotic, one in which management or leadership has little part to play. It is indeed possible for "management" to kill a group's creativity. If we include people from a larger number of functional areas in a group in an overt attempt to improve creativity, it does not necessarily improve. While more ideas may come to the table as diversity increases, group problem solving becomes harder. Information overload can bog down the process, canceling the benefit of having more perspectives and ideas from which to work. Generally, groups should contain no more than six people. Research and experience indicate that with more than six people, working together becomes a strain.

A second reason that high functional diversity does not translate into increased creativity is that group members often hold deep-rooted functional allegiances that can compromise their ability to identify with the new group. It is essential for members to have a strong sense of belonging to the group and a stake in its success, thus encouraging its members to find novel connections among their diverse perspectives. This is the grist of creativity. Strong interpersonal ties between group members however are not automatically a good thing. Critical to the creative process is candid debate, yet high social cohesion among group members can actually suppress the forthright exchange of opinion. Highly cohesive groups tend to focus more on maintaining relationships and thus tend to seek concurrence. However, groups that lack cohesion but enter into unproductive fierce conversation as an integral part of their way of working, all too readily disband because of the tension and possible lack of respect between the members. It is all a question of balance between cohesion and open conversation.

When we consider the creative process, conventional wisdom promotes hands-off management and presumes that groups under the magnifying glass will be inhibited. This need not be the case. Within limits, the signal that management is closely monitoring a group project is important to the group and the rest of the organization. Close monitoring can be a powerful motivator. It enhances the group's creativity and helps make resources available to facilitate the innovative implementation of the original idea.

The regular interest of management can help to motivate a group, and therefore an aspect of a leader's role during the mobilizing stage is to provide the right environment in which creativity can flourish. Providing the right environment can be thought of in terms of "the failure-tolerant leader". There are, of course, failures and failures. Some failures are lethal, contravening health and safety legislation. Others are illegal. There is no suggestion that anyone can be casual about these types of failure. The management of failure, however, is critical when we launch innovative initiatives. When taking risks, something will occasionally not work out as we intend. Things can go "wrong" for one of two basic reasons, either because people do not take due care, or as a consequence of the novelty we are trying.

The failure-tolerant leader identifies excusable mistakes and approaches them as an outcome to be examined, understood, and built upon. Failure-tolerant leaders send clear messages to their organization that constructive mistakes are not only acceptable but also worthwhile. Group members feel that they have been given permission to set out and explore, no longer thinking in terms of success or failure, but in terms of learning and experience—viewing mistakes for the educational tools they are and as signposts on the road to success.

The practical process of generating new ideas raises the question of how much time it takes to do things differently. The pressure of time may drive people to work more and achieve more, and may even make them feel more creative; however it actually causes them to think less creatively. Time pressure affects creativity in different ways depending on whether the environment allows people to focus on their work and conveys a sense of urgency about the task at hand. Creative thinking under low time pressure is more likely when people feel as if they are on an expedition. They

- show creative thinking that is more oriented toward generating or exploring ideas than identifying and addressing problems and
- tend to collaborate with one person rather than with a group.

Creative thinking under extreme time pressure is more likely when people feel as if they are on a mission. They

- can focus on one activity for a significant part of the day because they are undisturbed or protected;
- believe that they are doing important work and report feeling positively challenged by and involved in the work, and;
- show creative thinking that is equally oriented toward identifying problems and generating or exploring ideas.

The mobilizing stage of a group's development is unique in that it is classically associated with low time pressure. That does not imply that managers are not under pressure to decide what action to take. However, we link the other stages of a group's development with delivery of an agreed goal by an agreed date and this specifically puts a group's leader under time pressure. In contrast, at the mobilizing stage, group members are identifying an objective. When the objective is not obvious, it takes time to probe properly in order to discover what the group needs to achieve. For the best results, you should dig beneath the surface when collaborating with others one at a time, rather than in a group situation. You should focus on generating and exploring ideas as opposed to identifying problems.

While management plays a role in providing the environment in which a well-constituted group can be creative, provision of a conducive environment alone is not sufficient. You must convert creative ideas into innovative products and services if an organization is to realize some benefit. While the creative process has a chaotic aspect, innovation requires discipline and attention to work rather than relying solely on genius. Knowledge, ingenuity, and focus are key! There are people who are more talented innovators than others, but the innovative implementation of creative ideas requires hard, focused, purposeful work. If you lack diligence, persistence, and commitment, talent, ingenuity, and knowledge are of limited avail.

So, let us recap. The second element of the mobilizing stage comprises creativity and innovation. Creativity refers to the process of generating novel ideas concerning the nature of the challenge you face. Innovation refers to the process by which a group moves from the creation of more ideas to a debate about how a group will implement them. During the mobilizing stage, the leader's role is to first foster a group environment members find conducive to creative thinking and second, to instill discipline to move from creation of more ideas to the innovative implementation of a few.

Decision making

The innovative implementation of a creative idea begins by considering what implementation means in practical terms. As the reality of the action crystallizes, those involved must decide whether or not to implement this new idea. *Decision making* is the third element of the mobilizing stage. Mobilization of a new group is the practical consequence of a decision to allocate organizational resources to achieve a new goal.

We associate the allocation of organizational resources primarily with groups comprising managers senior enough to have the authority to commit organizational resources to achieve a particular new goal in preference to others. Creating a new group, and its subsequent entry into the mobilizing stage, is therefore a consequence of decision making within groups around the wider organization. Therefore, we can intrinsically link decision making within groups generally, and the mobilizing stage of a new group specifically.

The decision-making process starts when we ask what needs to be done, and then whether it is right for the organization. Answering these two questions provides us with the knowledge we need to make a decision on how we should deploy organizational resources. To be effective, managers must take personal responsibility for a decision and its implementation, irrespective of how many others were involved in the decision-making process. This focuses on an individual's responsibility as a leader. Furthermore, it is important to recognize that the existence of a network of relationships with others within the organization is what facilitates the gathering and synthesizing of data to enable us to identify what we need to accomplish and to ascertain whether it is right for the organization. Therefore, an interactive process that involves many people who influence each other clearly displays that the group is now well into the mobilizing stage. A group's interactive process, rather than individual input, helps make better, informed decisions about how the organization should deploy resources than any individual could do alone.

Distributing leadership responsibilities in a group has the potential to result in better-quality decisions than that of any individual within the group. Individuals take account of others in the group before committing themselves to action. Each, in a positive sense, becomes dependent on the other. Dependency exists within a group when members are capable of action independent of others. As others are capable of action over which any single group member has no control, members must consider the implications of others' responses when contemplating what action to take. Paradoxically, the independence of individuals results in dependency or, better still, interdependency between the group members.

With interdependency between group members, we still have no guarantee a group will emerge with good solutions to address the problems it faces. Certainly, groups that make good decisions, have individuals coordinate their behavior with others, even if they are not consciously aware of doing so. When attempting to make a decision to achieve an organizational objective, managers face three challenges:

- *Cooperation*. The challenge of inducing self-interested, distrustful people to work together, even when narrow self-interest would seem to dictate that no individual should take part.

- *Coordination*. Members of a group must figure out how to coordinate their behavior, knowing that everyone else is trying to do the same thing.
- *Cognition*. Collectively solving problems that have or will have definite solutions to which there may not be a single right answer, and where some answers are certainly better than others.

Managers vividly express the issue of cooperation to be the challenge of gathering together those who can contribute to resolving a specific organizational issue. In turn, attempting to gather members with appropriate skills leads to a problem of coordination—ensuring that a particular group does indeed comprise all who have knowledge and experience relevant to the issue at hand. If we successfully bring together the relevant individuals, the concern becomes one of cognition, as the group gathers and analyzes data, shares it, and participates in providing feedback which hopefully will lead toward making a rational decision.

Decision making is not something that we automatically associate with an established group. It can take place in a group created for no other reason than making a decision on how to respond to a specific organizational issue. No matter how a group makes a decision, the practicality of cooperation, coordination, and cognition is the process by which managers decide to pursue a particular course of action. The decision enables the organization to deploy resources which in turn allows a new group to mobilize around achieving a specific goal. Those involved in the decision-making process will not necessarily be involved in its implementation. If the organization decides to implement a specific course of action, however, at least one of those involved must take personal responsibility for it.

The creation of a new group as a consequence of a decision to deploy organizational resources signals a new group is entering the mobilizing stage. It is the responsibility of the designated individual involved in the decision-making process to implement the decision. This signals that he or she is a leader within the organization, and not merely one of many employees.

Let's now rejoin Harry at the Traditional Turbine Co. Several months have passed and he has managed to build relationships with other Board members. Harry has made the tricky transition from outsider to insider. Without pressure to deliver by any particular date, Harry has been on an expedition, systematically developing a vision of the new product range with the help of his chief designer and fellow Board members.

**Case Study 2.4   The Traditional Turbine Co.—
A leap of faith**

Shortly after Harry joined the Traditional Turbine Co., he persuaded Chris, the Chief Executive, to add "product development" to the weekly Board meeting set agenda. Discussion was initially high level and focused on new enquiries, product attributes the company required, and the order-related engineering cost associated with them. Product development, however, was now on the agenda.

Six months after starting with the Traditional Turbine Co., John, the finance director, presented the new product range business case to the Board, and Natasha, the sales director, presented the sales forecast she expected to deliver which included the new product range. Harry was happy to play a low-profile role at the Board meeting. He recognized that John and Natasha performed better than him at Board meetings, so persuading his friends to pitch the new product range was the low-risk option.

John and Natasha were both the same age as Harry. This was complemented by their extroverted personalities compared to Harry's. For his part, John found Harry unique among engineers in that Harry listened. John's ambition was to move into a CEO role within two years, and to achieve that, he needed to demonstrate that his financial management of the Traditional Turbine Co. was responsible for a sharp increase in both turnover and profitability.

→

Although John had a generally low opinion of engineers, he made an exception in Harry's case. It was obvious to John that Harry was competent to deliver a new product range. Because Harry listened to him, John found it easy to work with Harry. Between them, John and Natasha explained to the Board how the Traditional Turbine Co. would spend the proposed product development budget and the potential return on investment (ROI).

Unfortunately however, the Board meeting did not unfold as Harry had envisioned. The CEO, Chris, asked many negative questions, and at one point Per, Harry's chief designer, was asked to step in to explain a technical point Harry had not handled well. Despite a good start at the Traditional Turbine Co., Chris, who could have been the same age as Harry's father, was not treating Harry like a peer, but like a son. The two also had different attitudes. Chris was most at home in the formal environment of a Board meeting, whereas Harry became quickly bored, did not attentively follow discussion, and consequently was not always ready to handle unexpected questions.

Despite the difficult meeting, the board approved the project. Harry found himself wondering how exactly he would deliver on John and Natasha's promises made on his behalf.

Case Study 2.4 illustrates that Harry recognized the need for Board members to buy into the idea of a new product range. Although he personally found it dull to work through a standard agenda every week, Harry recognized that was how his boss liked to work. The weekly debate, at least, allowed Board members to ask questions and raise concerns. As such, the weekly meetings were the process of cooperation and coordination. Board members provided informal feedback to Harry between meetings. This feedback became the process of cognition that ultimately resulted in the Board's decision to proceed with development of a new product range.

Case Study 2.4 also illustrates that in spite of Harry's poor performance at the critical meeting, Board members approved his proposal. At one level, this constitutes a success as Harry's excellent working relationship with Natasha, John, and Per resulted in a coordinated cross-functional business case Harry could never have developed alone. At another level, Harry also risked sabotaging everything he had worked to achieve with his inability to remain engaged through hours of tedious discussion.

Harry's inability to work well in formal meetings was a negative aspect of his creativity. The personality traits that made him so good at gathering data and finding novel connections made it almost impossible for him to work effectively in formal meetings. Poor performance in formal meetings was the price Harry paid for his creativity. Another unfortunate consequence was his general lack of interest in any kind of formality. This lack of interest extended to formal planning.

So, let us recap. Decision making is the third element of the mobilizing stage. The mobilization of a new group occurs as a practical consequence of one or more managers deciding to allocate organizational resources to achieve a new goal. To be an effective leader, a manager must take personal responsibility for a decision and its implementation, irrespective of how many others are involved in the decision-making process.

When driving an organization toward a major decision to commit organizational resources to one goal in preference to others, a manager must remain aware that other influential managers are capable of independent action, resulting in inter-dependency. As others are capable of action over which any single manager has no control, each individual must consider the implication of others' response when contemplating what action to take.

An objective of leadership action during the mobilizing stage is to gather those who can contribute to the decision-making process. In so doing, a manager helps ensure that the group represents all appropriate skills and expertise that in turn will help ensure that they gather and analyze relevant data. While time

consuming compared to an autocratic decision-making process, if a group works together, they will most likely identify a
better-quality decision that the organization is more likely to
implement.

Ways of working

We associate formal planning with the fourth element of the
mobilizing stage, *ways of working.* At the early stage of a new
project, it is not always possible for us to implement detailed
planning because the necessary details are simply not available.
However, it is possible for us to implement goal-based planning.
The concept of goal-based planning is fundamentally different
from the activity planning that we typically associate with project management. The activity planning process produces a bar
chart that lists the tasks we need to complete a project on the
vertical axis, against the time we require to complete these tasks
on the horizontal axis. The bar chart for a project comprises a
detailed activity plan for the project that identifies every activity
needed, and the order in which those activities must be undertaken. Goal-based planning does not eliminate our need for
activity planning; it complements it by forming a link between
the major milestones through a project and the detailed activity
plans.

The process of goal-based planning breaks each project down
into a set of milestones, each of which we must achieve if we
are to deliver the next. In practice, a network of milestones will
emerge, in which each may impact on more than one other.
Critically, this network includes all key parts of the organization that will be involved in taking a product to market, and is
therefore inherently cross functional. This approach is effective
at overcoming problems when a group may not necessarily comprise of members with all the appropriate skill sets needed to
achieve the goal.

The process works best when we define each milestone in terms
of a tangible deliverable, for example "when the design department issues the last drawing to manufacturing" or "when marketing has printed the product literature." These milestones

each represent very clear end points. A second aspect of good goal-based planning is defining milestones in terms of outcome, not task. By defining milestones in terms of outcome, it becomes more difficult to claim that a participant has reached a milestone simply because he or she has undertaken a task. A milestone is reached when the stated outcomes are evidently achieved.

By identifying milestones within a group, it becomes easier for members to monitor the tasks at hand, and therefore, if certain aspects of the project start running late or are delayed, the issue at stake can be explicitly identified by the members. Essentially, we use goal-based planning to prompt an intervention. By flagging a problem early, members are more likely to resolve the issue quickly enough for a group to still deliver on time. The intervention will, therefore, be relatively positive.

The process of goal-based planning does not influence how a group reaches a particular milestone. The member responsible for a specific milestone is left in control of the tactical approach to delivering it. This freedom allows him or her to be creative and innovative in the approach to delivery, while still providing a high degree of confidence that the "collection of parts" will deliver the overall goal on time, within budget, and to specification.

A practical approach to goal-based planning is the "gated" review process. In a gated review, we specify "gates" that are specifically associated with critical milestones. A group cannot pass through a gate until it completes a formal review. The group decides a date for the next gated review, and the review happens on that date irrespective of the group being ready or not. If the gated review is a success, this stage is approved and the group progresses to the next milestone. If problems arise, then the review focuses on the issues at stake and what the group members can do to resolve them.

Let's rejoin Harry just after the Board meeting, as both his success at gaining Board approval and failure to plan come into sharp focus for the first time.

Case Study 2.5   The Traditional Turbine Co.—
Allocating resources

While Harry might have thought the Board meeting had
not gone well for him personally, it did constitute the formal buy-in of not only his peer group who had helped him,
but also of Chris, the chief executive. In fact, Chris could
not quite identify why, but he had become slightly uneasy
about Harry. Perhaps it was his obvious lack of respect of
formality at Board meetings. Other Board members might
find Harry's comments hilarious, but honestly Chris was
clueless as to what Harry was talking about most of the
time. Nevertheless, he had confidence in the financial director, sales director, and chief designer. That would have
to be enough. If the organization could achieve the sales
forecast, they would revitalize the company.

Harry and Per, his chief designer, found a quiet corner in
which to discuss the Board meeting. Neither had ever had
such a large budget, and both were very aware that however
confident they might have sounded in the Board meeting,
that was not how they actually felt. After some time, they
decided that the best way forward was to form a product
development group comprising the company's best technical specialist in each of the key design areas.

The technical specialists that Harry and Per wanted were in
different departments and had not worked together before.
Over the following week, Harry negotiated with departmental managers, while Per held discussions with the individuals
who would be asked to join. This "two-pronged" approach was
Per's idea, and seemed to communicate the necessary information to both management and staff in a non-threatening way.

Case Study 2.5 illustrates that Harry's inability to engage constructively during Board meetings had undermined his working relationship with his boss. It also highlights both Harry
and Per's lack of experience. At the Board meeting, they had

presented projected man-hours, internal and external costs, that conveyed to the Board they knew what they were doing, but in truth they had not developed a credible project plan to deliver the new product range. The two men made the naïve assumption that tapping into the right people would result in technical problems just melting away.

At the very least, Harry should have developed a basic list of the key milestones that he needed to achieve, and the dependencies between them. Typical milestones through the life of a product's development would be as listed below:

- Feasibility study
- Pre-study
- Preliminary outline
- Detailed design
- Pre and post marketing launch
- Delivery

Best practice is to plan for each of the above milestones, and to hold gated reviews at the end of each. The feasibility study can be informal, and that is essentially what Harry did with Per and Natasha. With their help, Harry was able to identify that a new product range must include an axial exhaust. We classically associate the pre-study with a more formal process, defining the customer needs, gathering market information, developing product costs and attributes, identifying cost targets, and delivery strategies. This is often augmented with an assessment of new technologies and certainly should include a risk assessment and analysis of time to market. This is essentially what Harry presented to the Board, and approval constituted successful passage through the gate.

What Harry and his cohorts were not asked to present at the Board meeting was the project plan that underpinned the budgeted man-hours, costs, and time scales. That was fortunate for Harry, as he didn't have one. The release criteria for preliminary outline should be the review and acceptance of a credible project plan that defines action points plus the budget and resources an organization requires to achieve it.

The Traditional Turbine Co. Board should have approved the preliminary outline only. The Board should have mandated a clear instruction to identify first project goals and a final technical specification. Only then should Harry have returned to the Board with a well-researched and clearly delineated project plan and budget that would have significantly reduced project risk.

Instead, Harry effectively bypassed preliminary outline and moved straight into detailed design. During this phase, the design department produces the product or service design. They also perform prototype testing and appropriate players, such as engineers and financial specialists, calculate delivery costs. In addition, operations addresses supply chain and logistic issues; and design, marketing, and sales produce technical and commercial documentation. The company cannot release the new product or service design until management approves investment in any capital equipment. To bypass preliminary outline and launch into detailed design only invites failure.

A further strength of the gated review process is that in addition to dividing a project into more manageable sections, it also identifies that delivery start-up and marketing launch do not happen by accident. It is astonishing how frequently organizations do not budget or plan for these basic necessities.

Finally, best practice includes a company plan to review new products or services after they first deliver goods. What are the final production costs, and are they anything like the original target costs? What does the market feedback tell us, and are the launch customers good references? What have we learnt that we did not expect, and consequently what will we do differently next time?

In the case study, we see that Harry was able to win Board approval, but with no idea of what he would do next. It is, of course, not realistic for us to expect to plan every detail at the very beginning of a project, but it is realistic for us to expect to follow a planning process. Gated reviews provide any project with a structure and help ensure that the group considers various possibilities. The gated reviews themselves provide a formal, but constructive method for groups to communicate. Members can discuss problems and can collectively debate possible solutions.

So, let us recap. The fourth element of the mobilizing stage is ways of working. Detailed planning may not be possible at the early stage of a project. Goal-based planning is however critical, ensuring that the major milestones through a project are identified. A well-constructed goal plan identifies dependencies between milestones, defining how each impacts the others.

The network of milestones that emerges from the goal planning process should include all key parts of the organization and is therefore inherently cross-functional. As such, a goal-based planning process assists with identifying the key capabilities that group members must possess and which other groups around the organization must provide support. "Gated" reviews provide a mechanism to achieve each major milestone and provide an opportunity for the group to broach problems and raise issues. A manager should make it clear that a group is not permitted to pass through a gate until it completes a formal review. The gated review process therefore provides a relatively positive way in which management can focus on problems and what it can do about them.

Fitting behavior

Despite his lack of planning, Harry remained resolutely optimistic. Realistically, after the initial shock of having the Board approve his product development, he entered a state of denial. Let's rejoin Harry as he conducts a more informal meeting in a far more congenial setting than the Traditional Turbine Co.'s Boardroom.

Case Study 2.6 The Traditional Turbine Co.—Denial

Toward the end of the week Harry and Per, his chief designer, were in their local pub, reviewing the results of

→

---

the week's effort. Overall, they concluded, they had done a first rate job. As lunch slipped effortlessly into late afternoon, they considered the strengths of the various product development group members and discussed how best to break down the technical challenge. That morning they had completed diplomatic negotiations with the last departmental manager, reaching agreement on the terms by which the specialist they wanted could join the product development group.

The two friends congratulated themselves on a job well done. They would hold the first formal product development group meeting next week. Now that all the hard work associated with getting approval to do the project and getting the people to do it was over, Harry was looking forward to the first meeting.

"I am sure it will go really well," he thought to himself, as he wound his way through the now lit streetlights on his way home.

Although they had developed an excellent personal working relationship, at a professional level, Harry and Per tended to seek concurrence and avoided challenging each other. Case Study 2.6 shows that they gave no thought as to how the project would be broken down into pre-study, preliminary outline, and detailed design. While it would have been unrealistic to have expected Harry to plan the marketing launch or delivery in any detail, he should have thought about how the company would manage the design process.

When we consider Harry's behavior during the mobilizing stage of the product development group, he displayed some leadership but there was evidence that he also required development as a leader. Harry was able to align the company around the idea of a new product range and obtain approval to mobilize a group to develop it. While he needed leadership action to gain approval to develop a new product range, his management of the development process itself was not very attractive.

Let us state the obvious: leadership is different from management. Leadership has nothing to do with exotic personality traits. It is not the province of a chosen few. Leadership is not better than management or a replacement for it. The two are distinctive and complementary systems of action. Each has its own function and characteristic activities. Both are necessary for success in an increasingly complex and volatile business environment.

Leadership is about change, making things happen, creating new realities. At the mobilizing stage, leadership is about redesigning the structure and drawing people together from different parts of the organization to form new groups. Leadership action is the part a manager plays in initiating that change. In contrast, management is about systematically working through the complexity change inevitably brings. At the mobilizing stage, management is about bringing order and consistency to the organization by planning and budgeting, establishing detailed steps for achieving those targets, then allocating resources to accomplish those plans. Yes, leadership and management are different, but we need them both.

We can best summarize leadership action through the mobilizing stage as initiating change, making things happen, and creating a vision of how things can be different. What a leader chooses to *do* facilitates the visioning process with action focused on progressively defining the goal the group needs to achieve and establishing the priority of that goal. The process of clearly defining a group's goal must be an inclusive process, seeking input from key stakeholders both inside and outside the organization. In contrast, we associate management action with the formality of identifying costs and establishing benefits associated with pursuing a particular course of action.

It is difficult to be prescriptive as to exactly what a manager should *do* during the mobilizing stage. For example, action appropriate in a traditional manufacturing organization such as The Traditional Turbine Co. will not necessarily be appropriate in a service business. Despite this reservation, we can use the Traditional Turbine Co. case study to identify behavior during the mobilizing stage that can be considered generic and therefore applicable to any group.

The Traditional Turbine Co. case study is a true illustration of how a leader actually mobilized a new group. The case study primarily illustrates the behavior of Harry and the other key characters within the Traditional Turbine Co. We have learned that it is difficult to provide explicit guidance on what leaders should specifically *do* during the mobilizing stage. However, it is possible for us to identify key behaviors that, if adopted, can inform leadership action in any group and any organization.

Prior to Harry joining the Traditional Turbine Co.'s Board, members typically discussed financial reporting, with a focus on prospective new orders and progress on current contracts. After joining the Board, Harry made sure that the members allocate a portion of the meeting to summarize and discuss the current status of the product development initiative. In this way, Harry demonstrated the first leadership behavior at the mobilizing stage:

- Build a consensus between managers across the organization.

The approach Harry adopted, persuading Chris, the Chief Executive, to add the product development initiative to the Board meeting standard agenda was astute for a second reason. Now, Chris, not Harry, would make this a regular agenda item and Natasha, the sales director, and John, the finance director, did much of the talking. As such, the product development initiative became a Board initiative, and not a private crusade on Harry's part. In this way, Harry demonstrated the second leadership behavior at the mobilizing stage:

- Encourage senior management to publicly support a proposal at formal meetings.

Following the meeting at which the Board granted approval to proceed with developing a new product range, Harry's leadership behavior changed. In the case study, we see that he agrees to share leadership with Per, his chief designer, who approached those specialists with whom he had been having informal discussions to now join the product development group. The process of informal discussion followed by a more formal approach centered not only on what a specific individual would do in the product development group, but also identified who else Harry and Per required to join the group. As such, Per facilitated discussion and debate among those who would join the product development group and in so doing demonstrated the third leadership behavior at the mobilizing stage:

- Break down interpersonal barriers within the group.

The case study illustrates how Harry complemented Per's work of negotiating with departmental managers. In this role, Harry was communicating the Board's recommendation to commence with the product development initiative. Harry was both negotiating the release of key technical specialists to enable them to join the product development group and also networking among the Traditional Turbine Co.'s wider management group. Thus, Harry demonstrated the fourth and fifth leadership behaviors at the mobilizing stage:

- Focus on the group's goal and;
- Network with influential managers, reinforcing the need for positive behavior and proactive support for the goal.

So, let us recap. During the mobilizing stage, a manager must initiate change, re-designing the organization to draw people together into a new group. Simultaneously he or she must manage the complexity brought about by that change, planning, budgeting, allocating resources, and then monitoring performance against plan. When taking action, the challenge is to balance leadership and management action. Specifically, it takes time and effort for a group to develop a vision of how the future could be better after the group achieves a new goal, but it also takes time and effort to manage the complexity associated with any change. Above all, a manager must involve group members in dialogue about their roles and responsibilities, and through dialogue, a group achieves a new goal by driving a detailed planning process.

Key learning points

- The mobilizing stage comprises four elements: forming the group, creativity and innovation, decision making, and ways of working.
- The four elements have fuzzy boundaries and therefore we cannot regard them simply as discreet steps through the mobilizing stage. However, those who seek to achieve a new organizational goal will start by forming a group and work through all four elements if they are to be successful.
- As a group first forms, the focus is on breaking down barriers and inhibitions between members as each decides if the others are the sort of people who will be easy or difficult to work with.
- Dialogue within a group is initially characterized by the origination of creative ideas. Fostering an environment group members find conducive to creativity is an aspect of a leader's role during the mobilizing stage.
- The mobilization of a new group occurs as a practical consequence of key organizational stakeholders collectively deciding to allocate resources to achieve a new goal.
- Groups should facilitate innovative implementation of the best creative ideas using a goal-based planning process that includes formal reviews at each key milestone.
- Goal-based planning identifies the major milestones through a project, each of which a group must achieve if the group is to deliver the next.
- A well-constructed goal plan identifies dependencies between milestones, defining how each will impact on the others, with a manager using the goal-based planning process to move on from the creation of more ideas to the innovative implementation of a few.
- Groups facilitate effectiveness during the mobilizing stage by focusing on clearly defining the achievable goal and establishing the priority of that goal.
- The mobilizing stage is above all else the stage at which a group creates a vision which helps in developing the idea and clarifies how the future can be different from the present.
- As a group develops a vision of the future, it must attract members with necessary skills and expertise to expand the vision into a more complete picture of the future.

- However, many people are involved in the process of developing a vision and then deciding to commit organizational resources to achieving it; a manager must take personal responsibility for the decision if he or she is to be a leader within an organization as opposed to merely an employee.
- During the mobilizing stage, leaders initiate change, make things happen, create new realities, and simultaneously manage the complexity that change has created.

Want to know more?

- For more ideas on who is an effective manager, see Drucker (2004).
- For further insights on the nature of the mobilizing stage, read Tuckman (1965).
- For contrasting views on the nature of the vision of the organization, refer to Olivier (2001) and Korac-Kakabadse and Kakabadse (1998).
- For further insights into innovation and creativity, read Goldenberg et al (2003) and Sethi et al (2002).
- To better understand the characteristics of the failure-tolerant leaders, see Farson and Keyes (2002).
- Decision making and taking is a broad subject, but Drucker (2004) and Surowieck (2004) on distributed leadership promise a powerful overview.
- For further information on project management, goal-based planning, and bar charts, see Reiss (1992).

CHAPTER 3

Confrontation

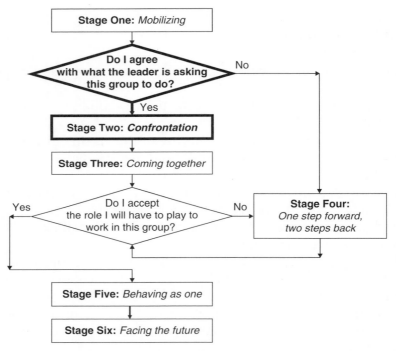

Figure 3.1 The integrated group development process, stage two: Confrontation

Source: Compiled by the authors

How do you get people to work together across internal boundaries within an organization? As competitive pressures continually force organizations to do more with less, few managers have the luxury of relying on their own dedicated staff. Instead, most must work with and through people across the organization, many of whom have different priorities, incentives, and ways of doing things. Attempts at collaboration, however, usually result in confrontation, with most managers focusing on symptoms rather than the root cause of failures. For example, a sales person does not work well with an engineer, because there is a disconnect. The sales person is incentivized on closing a deal to achieve his or her financial goal, thus resulting in a year-end bonus. The engineer may have a monetary incentive at the end of the year as well, but perhaps with an emphasis on research and development. Generally, the mindsets of a sales person and an engineer are on different levels, hence the disconnect that may result in conflict.

It may come as a surprise, but conflict within organizations is inevitable. Scarcity of resources and conflicting priorities are enough in themselves to ensure that conflict occurs when different groups attempt to work together. When you add to the issues of resources and priorities the competition between managers for promotion in today's increasingly flat organizations, then conflict becomes unavoidable.

Even the most senior of managers do not generally appreciate the inevitability of conflict in complex organizations. If they do recognize that conflict is inevitable, they mistakenly assume that management's efforts to increase collaboration will reduce conflict. This is often true even when a manager's attempt at collaboration created the conflict in the first place. Managers underestimate not only the inevitability of conflict, but also its importance to the organization. The disagreements sparked by differences in perspective, competencies, access to information, and strategic focus actually generate much of the value that can come from collaborating across organizational boundaries. Rather than attempting to reduce disagreements, managers need to accept that they are an inevitable part of organizational life and develop methods for managing them.

Conflict is the defining characteristic of the second stage of a group's development. Within this stage, *confrontation*, it is necessary for anyone who aspires to a leadership role to both understand why conflict is occurring and be capable of managing it. The confrontation stage of a group's development comprises two elements:

1. Understanding conflict.
2. Managing conflict.

Any group that is to successfully work through its differences and agree on actionable specifics must contain members who have, at least, a basic understanding of conflict. Without insight into the inevitability of conflict and why it occurs, members' reactions to a deteriorating group situation invariably results in their behavior transforming from a calmer state to a more aggressive level that shows the emotion of conflict. The second element of the confrontation stage is the ability of a person to manage conflict. Managing conflict well requires a skill to intervene positively when group members are in conflict, and in so doing, help all involved to reach some resolution.

So, let us recap. The confrontation stage of a group's development comprises two elements, *understanding conflict* and *managing conflict*. Each is important if a group is to successfully navigate its way through and ultimately out of the confrontation stage. Before considering the two elements in detail, we describe the confrontation stage itself. We examine the practical indicators, such as a group member's change from a calmer state to a more aggressive level, which shows the emotion of conflict and signal that the group has reached and entered the confrontation stage.

Group development

When considering the second stage of a group's development, confrontation, we can separate conflict into task conflict and relationship conflict. We must remain focused on such a difference because it is possible for us to hold strong differences of opinion over what a group should do and why, and it is critical that our disagreement over goals and objectives does not spill over into personal attacks.

It is very easy for an argument about goals and objectives to deteriorate because people tend to make assumptions about what membership of a group will mean to them. The point at which members perceive that conflict is emerging within a group is the point where they begin to realize that their initial assumptions as to what the manager expected of them as an individual, and of the group as a whole, were not right. Differences of view exist between certain group members and the manager, and/or, between group members themselves about what is expected of the group. The transition from the first stage of a group's development, mobilizing, to the second stage, confrontation, therefore results as a consequence of members becoming increasingly aware that they do not fully understand the group environment. Each has a different view of the ultimate goals the group has set out to achieve.

An increasing awareness of the ultimate goals the group has set out to achieve and the expected role each member will play is a move from a false assumption that the group understood its environment to a confused state in which the differences between members' assumptions become clear. Now, the group does not share an understanding of the task they must perform. Members feel irritation, even panic, dread, helplessness, or apathy. The feeling that this group is on the road to failure can overwhelm members. Conflict erupts as anxiety increases. Some members take less care to phrase points in a positive way and others start to overreact. Others blame each other for being responsible for the group's predicament. What started out as a discussion about how to complete a task deteriorates into an argument about what the task is and ultimately, even to the trading of personal insults. Once group members are insulting each other, it is unlikely that the group will ever perform to its full potential.

For groups performing routine tasks, task conflict is detrimental to the group's ability to perform as the members spend time arguing as opposed to performing the task. However, in groups undertaking non-routine tasks conflict is not detrimental, and in some cases can be beneficial. It promotes critical evaluation of problems and options, while simultaneously reducing thoughtless agreement. However, the benefit of task conflict does have its limits. At high levels of task conflict, members become overwhelmed with information and lose sight of the group's goal.

Relationship conflict is detrimental to satisfaction and to members' intent to remain in the group regardless of the task, but it has minimal impact on immediate performance. People simply avoid those with whom they do not get along. It is no surprise that interdependence increases the negative impact of relationship conflict. Some individuals side with others who share their view. Still others become close to those with whom they feel comfortable and who shield them from conflict. Whatever the reason for negative interdependence, the group is seriously distracted from focusing on the task at hand.

The priority for all is to recognize the signs of emerging conflict and take action to curtail it before task conflict deteriorates into full-blown relationship conflict. Fortunately, there are practical indicators that signal a group is approaching the confrontation stage, alerting members that conflict will be emerging soon.

Practical indicators

A group approaches the confrontation stage as its members begin to realize that their initial assumptions about what the group will be doing generally, and what they will be doing specifically, were misplaced or even wrong. There are three signs managers can watch for that indicate a group is approaching the confrontation stage. The first sign is open criticism from members who oppose or disagree with the group's goals and objectives. This overt criticism of goals and objectives goes hand in hand with covert criticism of the group's leader in an attempt to undermine his or her authority and discredit him or her as a leader. It would be too simplistic to suggest that those criticizing openly are also criticizsing privately. In fact, the reverse is more usually true. Those prepared to speak openly do on every subject. However, those who criticize quietly behind closed doors are unlikely to speak up publicly.

The second sign that a group is approaching the confrontation stage is a tendency for debate about issues that will quickly degenerate into interpersonal conflict, sometimes for no "obvious" reason. Initially, one of the more influential group members will step in, change the subject, and brush off the negative exchange as a minor and isolated incident. In reality, however, the increasing frequency of these attacks signals a rapid deterioration of interpersonal relationships within the group.

The third sign that a group is close to open conflict is members' reduced interest in the group's goals and objectives. Polarized opinions create lack of focus among emerging fractions within the group, thus resulting in no apparent opportunity for consensus toward a workable common ground. Members now start to become vocally critical with some openly voicing their blunt disagreement with the group's goals and objectives in spite of more influential group members' efforts to bring calm to the debate. Some adopt a different tactic, simply criticizing any idea, good or bad, while others quietly work in the background to undermine the group's leader in an attempt to get the group disbanded.

The confrontation stage actually starts when the group's leader takes the first "visible" steps. The leader officially ends discussion and now assigns members specific roles and responsibilities. The tasks, in some cases, may be very different from those members originally anticipated, so feelings can run high. Consequently, open conflict emerges as members discuss how they feel about the shift of events. As members express their feelings, talk deteriorates to argument, and the group accomplishes nothing useful.

This unpleasant development feels like a failure of leadership, but is not. Every group passes though the confrontation stage. The challenge is not to avoid it, but to work through it without damaging working relationships to the extent that the group will never be able to perform. For a group's leader, success or failure during the confrontation stage is primarily dependent on his or her working relationship with influential individuals both inside and outside the group. Working together will enable the leader to find a path through the conflict.

Understanding conflict

As the difficulty of what the group needs to accomplish and what it will mean for group members personally becomes clear, members instinctively reject what the leader asks of them. In order to achieve a workable common ground all can accept, it is important for members to understand why conflict has arisen and the specific nature of that conflict.

A psychologist would describe conflict as the behavioral patterns different people adopt when expressing disagreement. But what triggers conflict when people work together? Within a group context, whether the group is formal, informal, or temporary, there are countless social and interpersonal interactions which make members more psychologically aware of themselves and others. These interactions result in group members beginning to influence each other. The interactions lead to an awareness of interdependencies as to the satisfaction or non-satisfaction both of group needs, and of those personal needs and interests each person takes into the group situation.

To understand the personal needs and interests of the key players within the Traditional Turbine Co case study, we must first understand who was asked to join the product development group and why. The first person to join Harry was Per, his chief designer, and it was Per whom Harry relied on when picking other members. Per had advised Harry to approach Doug, the company's chief draftsman. This idea was initially resisted by Harry, as Doug was the supervisor of the company's contract design group and Harry was looking for members who would do the work, not talk about someone else doing it. However, in the end Per had persuaded Harry that Doug's 34-year experience meant that he knew how to get things done.

Once Harry had recruited Per and Doug, the three men had found it easy to identify ideal members for the rest of the group. The men reduced an initial list of over 30 to just 6, each with specific technical competences critical to the development of a new product. There was Jack, a rotor-dynamics specialist; Daniel, a mechanical analyst; Brian, the company's senior blade designer; Mary, a draftswoman; Derek, the company's senior application engineer; and Andrew, a control specialist. They all knew each other, had the technical skills for the task, had worked with one or two others, but had never worked collectively in the same group.

As the first formal meeting of the product development group approached, each member knew with whom he or she would be working, and consequentially there was much informal discussion and debate among the newly formed group members specifically and overall within the company. Harry was largely unaware of the informal debate. The time was rapidly approaching, however, when Harry would have to engage. We rejoin Harry as he prepares for the first formal meeting of the product development group.

Case Study 3.1   The Traditional Turbine Co.—Building credibility

As the first formal meeting of the product development group approached, Harry ran through what he wanted to achieve in his own mind. The purpose of the meeting was to clearly explain why everyone had been asked to join. The objective was to identify key issues associated with design of the new product range. The desired outcome was a set of agreed actions for all, to start the product development process moving forward.

Feeling confident, Harry gathered everyone to present the new product development plan. Harry was at pains to point out that the presentation was the same that he used at the recent meeting when the Board approved the project and its budget.

Harry finished speaking, then Brian spoke up for the first time. In his early fifties, and generally regarded as a world authority on turbine blade design, people listened when Brian spoke. He explained, at some length, that this "preposterous" idea that "those fools" in Sales have foisted on "us" was dependent on the ability of Engineering to design an axial exhaust for the turbine. The competitor information Harry presented was based on much larger turbines. The company had unsuccessfully attempted to scale down before and it would not work now.

$\rightarrow$

Derek, the company's senior application engineer, promptly chipped in, recounting how every time Sales raised the issue of developing an axial exhaust, Engineering shot down the idea. Harry was dismayed as he systematically worked his way round the room, reminding each person, in turn, of the time they had wasted on some long-forgotten proposal that had come to nothing. After ten minutes, he ran out of people to remind, and the group finally fell silent. There appeared to be a collective realization that Harry was still there, as those to whom Derek had been speaking turned to look at him, apparently waiting for a response or comment.

Harry had just "lost the group.". He noticed that Per had become very interested in the ceiling, and that Doug was studying his fingernails intently. Sensing that the others agreed with Brian, Harry thought quickly and abruptly changed his tactics. The objective now was survival, and that meant dashing from the room as quickly as possible. Harry decided to agree with Brian and suggested that Per and Doug review the existing competitor information, while others look through their personal files to come up with any relevant information. The meeting broke up quickly and Harry was pleased to escape.

After the meeting Per apologized to Harry for not thinking to warn him about Brian. Over the years, Brian had developed a reputation as the group cynic. Per noted that, for unknown reasons, Brian's behavior had been much worse the last year or so. Harry was grateful for the moral support, but could not help but think that Brian had actually been right. Harry intended to spend much of the first meeting discussing how to approach the technical problems of designing an axial exhaust. His plan ended in tatters, and Harry was not sure what to do next.

Case Study 3.1 illustrates that at the first formal meeting of the product development group, to Harry's surprise, Brian challenged Harry's leadership. Brian refused to accept that it was possible to achieve the group's goal. Following the challenge, group members effectively rejected their goal. It would have been easy for Harry to react with a personal attack on Brian. Such behavior, however understandable, would have created barriers between Harry and the group. Despite the dysfunctional way in which Brian made his point, Harry recognized that he did have a point, and maintained his respect for Brian's technical competence. He defused the situation by suggesting a review of personal files for additional information. More information would enable them to regroup at a later date and discuss options based on facts. Critically, Harry did not try to resolve the issues in the meeting by forcing consent.

Harry recognized that although the meeting had not gone as he intended, in actuality he did convey important information and members exchanged their thoughts. Preferably, the idea about the axial exhausted design should have been exchanged in a less adversarial way, but it was necessary to communicate this thought with the product development group members. Communication is often adversarial at the confrontation stage because members associate it with feelings of loss at the prospect of leaving a well-established group to join a new one. Anxiety arises about how the new and different group will turn out as an alternative working environment to the "perfectly good one" that will be lost on establishment of a new group.

So conflict is a subjective, personal experience. Although conflict springs from an awareness of interdependencies concerning the satisfaction or non-satisfaction both of group and personal needs and interests, ultimately individuals are the most important factors in understanding, interpreting, and resolving conflict within an organization. Structural explanations for conflict that lay blame with the organization avoid personal responsibility. Individuals come to blame the system, and consequently are disconnected from their actions.

To understand the conflict Harry faced, we must acknowledge that the new product development initiative did represent a divergence of interests between the individuals involved and the organization. Life at the Traditional Turbine Co. was, just as the title suggests, traditional. The business of moving from one contract to another, while complaining about what Sales had sold, was an established routine. Change of any sort represented a threat to the status quo. A new engineering director who threatened to actually do something about the product portfolio was distinctly unwelcome.

The product development group members reacted differently to the divergence of interest. During the mobilizing stage prior to the first formal meeting, both Per and Doug, knew that there would be problems persuading members to cooperate, but they chose to say nothing. When faced with conflict, Per habitually responded by accommodating the other person's point of view. This worked well, at least initially. Although Harry was naturally assertive, he was also cooperative and preferred to work with Per rather then imposing his views. We could characterize Per as unassertive and cooperative, and willing to change his working patterns to accommodate his new boss.

Doug was worse, preferring to avoid conflict at all costs. For Doug, management fads come and go! The path of least resistance was to say as little as possible, do as little as possible, and wait for it all to vanish like all the others had over the years. We could characterize Doug as unassertive and uncooperative. His modus operandi was to employ stealth tactics when dealing with management. He privately believed that all managers were like butterflies and could be guaranteed to "flutter off" to some other more interesting topic before they ever had to actually deliver. That Harry got as far as a formal launch meeting of the product development group came as a most unpleasant shock. In 34 years with the Traditional Turbine Co., Doug could not remember one manager actually following through on anything.

During the first formal meeting, Brian, the company's senior blade designer, behaved dominantly. While Brian spoke about the group's goal, he also attempted to undermine Harry. Assertive and uncooperative in his manner, Brian used his influence over group members to win his own position. At the time, Harry was unaware that management had approached Brian to take the job of engineering director. Declining the offer, Brian explained that he preferred to retain his technical focus. In reality, he feared the next level of responsibility. Despite declining the job, Brian viewed Harry as an inferior appointee. That management had appointed a "mere boy" over him was enough to drive the ferocity of his attack in a way that was simply not rational.

The only other person to play a significant role during the first product development group meeting was Derek, the company's senior application engineer. Derek had little respect for management of any kind, but again could not face conflict, crumbling if somebody openly confronted him on an issue. In truth, he had little leadership potential, preferring to criticize rather than deal with the difficult business of accomplishing tasks. He took action only in the safety of a group where he felt empowered to protest on behalf of others. Perhaps paradoxically, he agreed with the need for a new product range, but disagreed with Harry's approach. If engineers hold any common characteristic, it is that they can become fixated on a particular technical solution. Derek was no different and passionately believed that "epicyclic gearboxes mounted on the generator and not separately," were a mandatory part of any new product development project. It made no difference that the company's clients were conservative and did not want this elegant, but unproven, solution.

During the first product development group meeting, Jack said very little, but was privately against Harry and his motives. The design of a new turbine is "rotor-dynamics limited," and therefore as the Traditional Turbine Co.'s rotor-dynamics specialist, it was critical that Jack should be an active and contributing member of the product development group. Ten years previously, Jack had spent over 80% of his time undertaking tedious manual calculations. Now he spent less then 20% of his time engaged in the same work, having successfully developed one of the best rotor-dynamic programs in the world. In the early years this development effort was at a huge personal cost, working late into the night developing, debugging, and testing his program.

However, at present, he had a life of leisure four days out of five, pursuing his technical interest with little outside intervention.

That changed when Harry arrived. Harry needed help to develop a new product range, and becoming a member of the product development group would require Jack to cease working on his beloved code and start spending time working with other people. Jack did not share his true feelings regarding the situation, but privately started to criticize weaknesses in Harry's product development plan and leadership behind his back. To his shock, it wasn't until over a year later that Harry discovered how his boss had been kept so promptly informed about any error of judgment he might have made, or setback in the development of the new product range.

Unwittingly, Harry put together a product development group that included four members who were either overtly or covertly against him. Brian was an overt critic, preferring to openly criticize rather than actually doing anything. Derek was up front and honest about his disagreements with other ideas. Doug was a covert critic, not wanting much change but preferring to undermine Harry. Jack was the "traitor", wanting Harry and his project to fail to avoid disrupting a status quo that, over time, had shifted from one that required him to work beyond endurance levels to one in which he effectively had a paid hobby.

So, let us recap. The first element of the confrontation stage requires understanding of the conflict at hand. The creation of a new group will invariably involve members leaving other established groups and consequently disrupt the status quo which, while not perfect, is at least predictable. Individuals react differently when in conflict and in expressing their disagreement. However, managers can learn to understand how different people respond in different situations and in so doing, adjust their leadership to meet the challenge of their context.

Managing conflict

Many managers regard conflict as a regrettable experience or set of circumstances that in more favorable times would disappear.

Such a perspective ignores the inevitability of conflict within the workplace, and the fact that we can not simply ignore it. Therefore, *managing conflict* is the second element of the confrontation stage. As a manager rises through the organization, the need for an internalized strategy for managing conflict becomes more important if he or she is to survive and be effective in his or her role. Unfortunately, Harry was too inexperienced to have developed his own conflict management strategy. We rejoin Harry as he struggles to decide what to do next.

Case Study 3.2   The Traditional Turbine Co.—Working through conflict

The following day, Daniel, the product development group's mechanical analyst, came to see Harry. Daniel was a typical engineer, an introverted specialist who could spend hours lost in an internal world, but when it came to people, found it difficult to look anyone in the eye.

Daniel had brought with him a photograph of a Northern Turbine Industries' axial exhaust. It was something he had brought from Northern Turbine Industries when he had transferred to the Traditional Turbine Co. ten years back. The size of the exhaust was probably six times the size Harry needed. This was no help. Brian, the company's senior blade designer, had made it quite clear that large axial exhausts did exist; the challenge was making them smaller. Not wanting to seem ungrateful, however, Harry thanked Daniel who promptly shuffled out of the room without saying goodbye. An hour later, Harry walked past Daniel who was studying intently at his desk. He showed no sign of ever having met Harry.

Later that day, after Harry briefed Chris, his boss, on "progress", he showed the photo to Per. Interestingly, Per had about a dozen similar photos. Harry's thoughts drifted back to the discussion with Chris. There had been no shock

→

or surprise when he had described what had transpired at the first product development group meeting. Certainly, Chris' half-hearted offer of help had been easy enough to turn down. That had not been the case with Natasha, the company's sales director, or John, the company's finance director. Bad news seemed to travel fast in the Traditional Turbine Co. and both his friends had caught Harry in his office, offering useful advice. Their moral support meant a great deal to Harry, but he managed to convince them to grant him more time to work things out before getting involved.

Harry pulled himself back into the present. Per was still "going on" about Northern Turbine Industries, "... but personally, I don't like the approach their fitters take when they work here ... ." Suddenly it dawned on Harry that Northern Turbine Industries was a part of the same group of companies as the Traditional Turbine Co. He could ask them how they would design a small axial exhaust. He could request Chris to make the arrangements with the Group Chairman. Apologizing to Per, he headed back to Chris's office. This time Chris seemed surprised, but agreed to make the call.

Case Study 3.2 illustrates the strategy Harry adopted to manage the conflict facing him: gather new data on axial exhausts. He hoped that if he provided something new, the product development group members would voluntarily collaborate with him to design a smaller version. While it was naive of Harry to hope that an attempt to improve collaboration would somehow reduce conflict, his focus on gathering new data was not. Having established, however dysfunctionally, that it was not possible to agree how to approach the design of an axial exhaust with the information available within the Traditional Turbine Co., Harry accepted he would look outside.

Despite remaining focused on defining the product development group's goal, Case Study 3.2 illustrates that Harry did not have an internalized strategy for conflict management. Although we tend to think of leaders as dominant and unafraid, many have a tendency to avoid conflict. Many managers have a need to be liked and seek approval from others. The need to be loved echoes in every line scripted for their inner theater. Afraid to do anything that might threaten acceptance, all too often, they are unable, or unwilling, to make difficult decisions or exercise authority.

Conflict avoidance is neither a successful nor, in the end, a popular leadership style. The leader who always appeases is like a man who feeds crocodiles, hoping that they will eat him last. There is nothing bad about being nice, but there comes a point where every leader must face up to the reality that there is conflict, and it is part of his or her role to *do* something about it. Even the most widely respected authorities on conflict do not have an exact formula for success. There is, however, a sure formula for failure and that is to try and please everyone.

We rejoin Harry as he arrives at Northern Turbine Industries. Despite Harry's poor management of the product development group so far, what matters now is how he capitalizes on the opportunity the visit represents.

Case Study 3.3   The Traditional Turbine Co.—Through the looking glass

The following week, Harry and Per, arrived for their appointment at Northern Turbine Industries. The engineers seemed genuinely flattered that anyone would travel half way across the country to listen to them talking about their work. They took great pleasure in presenting preliminary designs for the world's biggest axial exhaust, something that, if built, would be 15 times bigger than anything the Traditional Turbine Co. needed. Gradually, Harry could feel himself losing the will to live. He started daydreaming about his student days at Oxford. Perhaps, he should never have left!

→

After three hours of listening to the Northern Turbine Industries engineers, Per finally spoke explaining that the Traditional Turbine Co. made small, high-speed turbines, and they were actually looking for something smaller not bigger. Listening for so long to inputs that did not make sense for Harry's business gives you, the reader, some clue of the non-challenging culture of the Group let alone the Traditional Turbine Company itself.

"Well then, you need to see plans for the Vizag job in India," said the Northern Turbine Industries chief designer.

"You should have said ... ." The engineer disappeared and shortly returned with a new roll of drawings. The axial exhaust for the Vizag turbine was only about twice as big as needed for the new Traditional Turbine Co. product range.

"It's still in development, so we don't know if it works or not," the Northern Turbine Industries chief designer commented, rather unhelpfully. "It is well outside our normal design envelope, but we are seeing many more enquiries for these micro turbines."

The idea that anyone could consider something three meters diameter "micro" struck Harry as most odd, but he thanked the engineers for their time and the drawings, assuring them their meeting had been useful. Privately, he could not help but think that these nerdish engineers desperately needed to develop a life outside the realm of work.

Case Study 3.3 illustrates how groups have different perspectives, competencies, access to information and strategic focus. At Northern Turbine Industries the product development drive was toward larger axial exhausts. While Harry possessed many strengths, patience was not one of them, and, in truth, it was Per who facilitated a successful meeting. Again, the case study illustrates what Harry chose to *do*. Even though the meeting at

Northern Turbine Industries was only marginally productive, Harry recognized that expertise could exist around the wider group of companies within which the Traditional Turbine Co. was a component.

In the case study we see that by remaining focused on defining the product development group's goal, Harry is still trying to please everyone. Despite not yet having a fully developed conflict management strategy, following the first product development group meeting, Harry had hit upon what would become the first and second parts of his trademark conflict management style. First, accept negative feedback and second, do not rise to other people's dysfunctional feedback. We rejoin Harry after he has the chance to recover from the traumatic events of the day. Having reestablished his equilibrium, he has to decide what to do next.

Case Study 3.4   The Traditional Turbine Co.—Poultry in motion

Despite the dubious reputation of British railways, Harry and Per were pleasantly surprised with the tasty chicken Caesar salad and the well-stocked cellar in the first class dining car. With a splendid glass of Chardonnay in his hand and a roll of drawings under his arm, Harry discussed the next step with Per, who was quiet for a moment and then said: "Tomorrow morning would be a good time for another meeting. Very good actually. You see, Brian is off-site all day. No need to take up his valuable time with an exhaust, nothing to do with the blades after all."

Harry did not take much persuading. Clearly, Brian might be a world authority on blade design, but he most certainly did not want to do anything other than design blades the way he had always done. If they could stop him disrupting another meeting, so much the better.

→

The following day Harry gathered the product development group to examine the Northern Turbine Industries axial exhaust. The discussion that broke out immediately took Harry completely by surprise. The group members loudly informed Harry that from an engineering design perspective, the axial exhaust was complete rubbish. Members immediately started arguing how to design it better. Harry groaned inwardly. "This is like herding cats," he thought. "I need to get them out of the room quickly before they blow it." Harry attempted to restore order. "Let's break up now, and reconvene first thing after lunch. Come back with a list of major issues in your area of responsibility and we can work through them together."

To Harry's amazement, it worked. Members dispersed, started making lists, and engaged in animated discussion in smaller groups. Instead of arguing, they were being productive.

Best practice in conflict management suggests that managing disagreement at the point of conflict works best when the parties involved in a disagreement are equipped to manage it themselves. The aim is for people to resolve issues on their own through a process that improves, or at least does not damage, their relationships. Case Study 3.4 illustrates the point at which Harry's attempts to clarify the product development group's goal became a conflict management strategy as opposed to appeasement or conflict avoidance. When Harry accepted that Brian should be excluded from the next product development group meeting, he also accepted that he could not please everyone.

During the second product development group meeting, Harry kept dialogue focused on the task at hand. By ending the meeting quickly, and asking members to list issues in their own area of responsibility, he encouraged them to focus on what the goal meant in terms of issues for them. In so doing, Harry had hit upon what would become the third part of his trademark conflict management style—seek new data and present it in a way that keeps conflict at the level of the task, such that it does not damage, but rather, strengthens working relationships.

Following the second product development group meeting, Harry was in a buoyant mood. He was convinced that the worst was now behind him. His euphoria, however, was short lived. Despite the product development group members now starting to engage with their challenge, the task did not get any easier. We rejoin Harry in the aftermath of the second product development group meeting.

Case Study 3.5   The Traditional Turbine Co.—
Changing role

The next week was a busy one for Harry. The engineers kept getting bogged down in detail, and seemed very reluctant to heed Harry's advice.

"If you don't know, guess. Just do something that looks right, and, then if it doesn't work, we can change it," Harry advised.

Complying, as soon as Harry left, the engineers started to argue about how impossible it was to guess, let alone the unprofessionalism of this nonscientific "technique." A few days later Per had a quiet word with Harry: "I don't think this approach is working."

Harry knew this and deep down realized he had to manage the situation differently. However, he still reacted badly when Per confronted him. After all, these people worked for him, didn't they? Calming himself, Harry started to see Per's logic. The idea of experimenting with different ideas just to see how they would work out was not bad, quite the contrary. Per agreed that this was a good way forward, but had a different way of articulating this notion by casting it to the group with a positive

$\rightarrow$

spin. From his 40 years' experience, Per did not use the word "guess" but suggested revisiting former ideas that might show promise. With his approach, Per was able to put the process of guessing in a positive context and in doing so gain "buy-in" from members in a way that Harry was unable to achieve.

Harry was just getting used to the idea of Per telling product development group members to guess when a second issue of which both he and Per had been unaware became apparent. Group members were confiding in Per that they were afraid to guess. They expressed concern that they were simply unable to implement guesswork because of fear of the unknown. It all boiled down to a matter of time. Feeling conflicted with what Harry had tasked them to accomplish, they felt as though they needed to fulfill their obligations to live contracts first.

Harry had the authority to resolve the conflicting priorities as he was accountable for both the engineering department's live contracts and product development effort. Previously, there had never been a major new product development effort and therefore no conflicting priorities.

The process of resolving conflicting priorities found Harry negotiating with the project managers for a significant part of his day. During his negotiating Harry invariably discovered that parts of a project were delayed. Critical design work could therefore be rescheduled as part of a broader replanning process aimed at bringing the project back on track. After much wrangling and personal guarantees, Harry could usually obtain mutual buy-in from all involved.

Harry's support from Per gave him the confidence to mentally add "diplomat" to his personal skill set. The role of engineering director was not turning out to be anything like Harry had imagined.

$\rightarrow$

His only saving grace during such trying times was the ongoing support of Natasha and John. Both wanted to help, and so Harry suggested that Natasha speak with product development group members on a one-to-one basis, reinforcing the need for an axial exhaust product range using the pretext of asking questions about current enquiries. John agreed to do something that went against all his instincts, he assured the product development group members that the company had unlimited funding for the new product range. This tactic would help dispel the idea that the company would abandon development of the axial exhaust product range. Harry did not really know if these interventions would help.

Case Study 3.5 illustrates that Harry had the good sense and grace to accept that Per could do what he could not. Harry effectively accepted that, for now, Per was leading the product development group. For the time being, Harry saw his role as doing anything he could to support Per. But this was only temporary. Harry needed to resolve issues with group members who were conflicted about how to tackle product development while at the same time fulfill live contracts. Harry needed to negotiate with the Traditional Turbine Co.'s project managers.

Harry was not comfortable negotiating and considered this one of his weak points. In life, however, what we view to be our strengths and how others perceive them are not necessarily the same. Harry was highly intelligent and listened. This combination enabled him to spot opportunities that others simply missed, and, in doing so, identify novel solutions to messy problems. By accepting that it was his responsibility to reconcile the needs of the product development group and those involved with live contracts, Harry accepted that his role had changed. He could no longer direct, but had to facilitate relationships and expose himself to the emotions of others. In accepting his role of managing issues that impacted the group but originated from the outside, Harry developed what was to become the fourth part of his trademark conflict management style. Listen graciously to group members' needs, accept what must be accomplished, and then tackle it.

So, let us recap. The second element of the confrontation stage is *managing conflict*. Although those lower down in the organization may think of leaders as dominant and unafraid, many leaders have a tendency toward conflict avoidance. Many managers have a need for people to like and approve of them, wary of doing anything that might threaten acceptance. However, conflict avoidance is not a recipe for success. Managers need an internalized conflict management strategy, and best practice in conflict management suggests that managing disagreement at the point of conflict works best when the parties involved are equipped to manage it themselves. A manager should facilitate the management of disagreement but first expect conflict. Second, when conflict emerges, do not respond with a personal attack. Third, seek new data to enable those involved to resolve issues through a process that improves, or at least does not damage, working relationships. Fourth, listen and graciously accept the tasks you need to accomplish to resolve that conflict.

Fitting behavior

The change in role for Harry, supporting Per, and working with the project managers enabled the product development group to function. They were accomplishing useful work, but Harry was well aware that failure was a real possibility. We rejoin Harry, as despite his best efforts, the product development group continues to struggle.

Case Study 3.6 The Traditional Turbine Co.—Closer to the edge

Harry had taken to "managing by wandering about." He knew that he could escape from irate and frustrated project managers only for so long by hiding in his office. He would need to face reality. His tactic was such: first present the

$\rightarrow$

project managers with a moving target and second, tell the product development group members they were doing a good job, but not push them on specifically what they were doing. Harry left that to Per. After a week, Harry asked Per's opinion about convening a third product development group meeting. "Ahhh, not just yet, not quite ready for that, I think."

Harry knew he was right. People continuously argued. Everything seemed so difficult to them. They were not making progress. "We need a plan." Harry said to Per. "Do you think another week of arguing will actually change anything?" Per had to agree that they were going round in circles. The two friends mulled over the problem in the pub at lunch. Harry observed that presenting the Northern Turbine Industries drawings to the group had been a good strategy to appease the group, even though the drawings were marginally useful.

"What we need is another drawing," Harry said, rather peevishly. Per looked thoughtful, and then said, "You know, you might be right. We know all we are going to know any time soon. We do need to get it onto paper."

They returned to the office and asked Doug, the company's chief draftsman to join them. Soon, they compiled a list of previous contracts and some sketches which Doug reluctantly agreed to "cobble together" into a single picture (he refused to call it a drawing). In truth, he did not want to do what Harry and Per were asking, but knew that if he said "no," Natasha, and the finance director, John, who both seemed intent on engaging him in discussion, would only return to waste yet more of his time. On balance, the least bad thing to do was to agree to Harry and Per's wishes.

That night, Harry wondered if this approach would work. Doug was hardly enthusiastic. He clearly articulated that he had enough "proper" work to do on live contracts without this additional burden.

$\rightarrow$

Harry found himself wondering whether the product development group were up to the task on hand. Perhaps it was just too difficult! Should he try to find a redeeming way of telling the Board that he had been overambitious, and that it had not been a good idea? But if it were not a good idea, if it could not be done, how was it possible for their competitors to do it? Harry felt his resolve stiffen. He would ensure that something representative of the product development group's achievements would be put in on paper.

Case Study 3.6 illustrates that leadership action during the confrontation stage of a group's development can be likened to selling an idea to people who are not interested in buying. The group's leader must clarify the tasks each group member will need to undertake, while promoting a sense of belonging within the group. At least, initially the selling process starts with listening. Some concerns and criticism will be valid, and listening will help a group's leader to see errors or oversights in his or her original planning. Also, listening is a form of cooperation, which signals a willingness to cooperate. Few cooperate with people who are against them. Therefore, showing willingness to cooperate also signals that despite the conflict, the leader is working with others and not against them.

Harry's behavior during the confrontation stage of the product development group's development indicates that Harry was starting to develop as a leader. He was willing to listen to negative feedback, and critically recognized the reality that he could not keep everyone happy all the time. An acceptance that universal popularity and leadership are mutually exclusive was an important developmental step. Following the realization that his critics would not be happy no matter what his actions were, Harry's management of the conflict within the product development group improved.

Leadership action thorough the confrontation stage can perhaps best be summarized in terms of a paradox: maintaining an internal vision of how life could be, while dealing with life as it is. The trick is to see the vision and deal with reality without losing sight of either. At this point, a manager finds out if he or she really wants to be a leader. Does he or she have the inner drive to lead others? To lead any part of an organization, a manager must want to make a difference and have an idea about how to do it. To be a leader, a manager must accept that conflict management is a part of his or her role, and that it is his or her responsibility to develop, and, when necessary, implement a conflict management strategy. At the most basic level, the conflict management strategy must enable those in conflict to continue to communicate, even while accepting that it is not possible to please everyone all the time.

We associate the two elements that comprise the confrontation stage, understanding conflict and managing conflict, with establishing the roles and responsibilities of those in conflict, and maintenance of communication during a time when it would be easier for all to disengage. The first element, understanding conflict, identifies the need for a manager to recognize the inevitability of conflict and therefore his or her responsibility for developing coping strategies that do not involve blaming others for the conflict. The second element, managing conflict, clarifies what a manager must do if a group is to function during a conflict-resolution process.

Although the two elements provide insight into what is important at the confrontation stage, in practice it is difficult to be prescriptive as to exactly what a manager should *do*. Conflict is a highly subjective and personal experience and as such, what is appropriate in one situation will not necessarily be appropriate in another. Despite this reservation, the Traditional Turbine Co. case study helps identify behavior during the confrontation stage that we can consider generic and therefore applicable to any group.

The Traditional Turbine Co. case study illustrates how Harry's approach during the mobilizing stage did not work during the confrontation stage. The mobilizing stage involved one-to-one discussion with members of the Board, followed by formal Board meetings at which they discussed nothing new, and decisions the members had already taken privately were little more than publicly approved. In contrast, the confrontation stage began with a product development group meeting that was anything but predictable.

Despite the disappointment of the first product development group meeting, Harry's working relationship with Per remained strong and a source of both technical and moral support. In this way, Harry demonstrated the first leadership behavior he needed during the confrontation stage:

- Focus effort on developing relationships with those group members who naturally have the highest sociability within the group to facilitate informal feedback on the actual as opposed to the intended impact of behavior.

After the first product development group meeting, both Natasha and John spoke with Harry to volunteer advice and suggest ways in which they could help. However well-intentioned they were, Harry intuitively knew that his credibility as the product development group's leader depended on him finding a way forward. Harry did not decline offers of help, but neither did he accept them. By asking his friends to give him more time, Harry demonstrated the second leadership behavior he needed at the confrontation stage:

- Discourage senior management from imposing solutions on the group.

Harry used his bought time to gather data that might help product development group members design an axial exhaust. After an initial attempt at data gathering inside the Traditional Turbine Co., Harry recognized the need to take more risk and look outside. The tactic paid off and the Northern Turbine Industries' axial exhaust drawings provided a basis for product development group members to finally engage in the design process. Thus, Harry demonstrated the third leadership behavior he needed at the confrontation stage:

- Help group members to achieve the group goal.

The product development group's progress made after its second group meeting cannot be attributed only to the axial exhaust drawings from Northern Turbine Industries. Both Harry and Per had collaborated to ensure that Brian, the company's senior blade designer, was off-site when they convened the second product development group meeting. Upon Brian's return, it was Per, not Harry, who briefed him on what the group agreed upon. The relational conflict between Harry and Brian, although not resolved, was at least managed. In this way, Harry and Per demonstrated the fourth leadership behavior they needed at the confrontation stage:

- Address the emerging interpersonal issues.

The practicality of managing Brian was not Harry's only challenge. Despite the success of the second product development group meeting, Harry's management of product development group members following the meeting did not work well. At this point, Per approached Harry saying, "Why don't you let me tell them to guess instead?" It would have been easy for Harry to refuse, but he did not. By being approachable and by listening, Harry demonstrated the fifth leadership behavior he needed at the confrontation stage:

- Utilize interpersonal skills to address sensitive issues.

Despite his change in role and Per's support, Harry still had much to achieve. Intuitively, Harry knew that success was close, but it was also frustratingly elusive. At the point where he felt it all starting to slip away, Harry agreed with Per that they should approach Doug to attempt to get the achievements down on paper. At this point, the support of Natasha and John paid off. Harry had asked both to lobby with the product development group members on a one-to-one basis. It is likely that if they had not, Doug would have found some plausible excuse as to why he could not help just now. In so doing, Harry demonstrated the sixth leadership behavior he needed at the confrontation stage:

- Enlist the help of other influential individuals to reinforce organizational commitment to the group's goal.

So, let us recap. During the confrontation stage, a manager must be flexible, dealing with life as it is while maintaining an internal vision of how life could be. Anyone who attempts to lead a group through conflict will need an internalized conflict management strategy. However a strategy that works for one person will not necessarily work for another as a consequence of different individual strengths, weaknesses, and personalities. Every manager must therefore develop an approach to conflict management that works for him or her, using established best practice in conflict management techniques as a starting point.

When taking leadership action, a manager has to be willing to listen to negative feedback and take action based on that feedback. However hard it may be, anyone who wishes to lead a group successfully through conflict must be willing to swallow his or her pride and get on with accomplishing tasks if the group of which they are a part is to progress. At times what we need to do may be radically different from an individual's preconceptions as to what his or her role would entail. If a group is to progress, the leader must have a sense of humility and a willingness to first see and second, accomplish the task at hand.

Key learning points

- The confrontation stage comprises two elements, understanding conflict and managing conflict.
- An understanding of the origins of interpersonal conflict in a group context is essential if behavior is not to escalate emerging conflict.
- The inevitability of conflict in the workplace makes it critical that managers have an internalized strategy for managing conflict.
- As conflict erupts, a manager must manage the conflict such that working relationships are not so badly damaged that a group can never go on to perform.
- Although we tend to think of leaders as dominant and unafraid, many have a tendency toward conflict avoidance with a desperate need for people to like and approve of them.

However, conflict avoidance is neither a successful nor popular leadership style.

- There is no exact formula for success when managing conflict. However there is a sure formula for failure and that is to try to please everyone.
- Best practice in conflict management suggests that managing disagreement at the point of conflict works best when the parties involved are equipped to manage it themselves.
- We can manage conflict through the use of a four-point conflict management strategy:
  - ➤ However well a group's members may appear to be working together, expect conflict.
  - ➤ When conflict emerges, don't respond with a personal attack; conflict is an inevitable group process.
  - ➤ To facilitate working through conflict, seek new data to enable those involved to resolve issues through a process that improves, or at least does not damage, working relationships.
  - ➤ Listen and accept what needs to be accomplished, and then gracefully tackle it.
- What leaders *do* during the confrontation stage is support those who are in conflict in such a way that group members are able to resolve the conflict themselves.

Want to know more?

- For further information on working across organizational boundaries, see Weiss & Hughes (2005).
- For differences between task and relational conflict, refer to Jehn (1995) and Thomas (1976).
- For analysis on conflict avoidance and why each manager needs to find his or her own approach to conflict handling, see DeVries (2001).
- For deeper insight as to why people need the safety of groups and use them as a crutch, see Analoui & Kakabadse (1991).
- For insights on how groups should face up to their internal conflicts and manage that tension themselves, see Weiss & Hughes (2005).

CHAPTER 4

Coming together

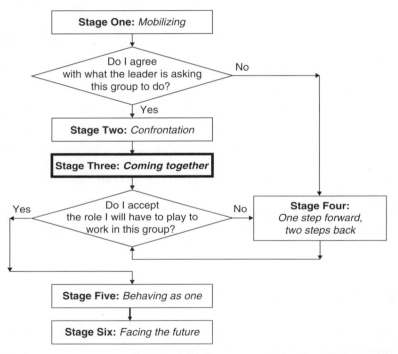

Figure 4.1   The integrated group development process, stage three: Coming together

Source: Compiled by the authors

What does a group need to come together, more leadership or more management? Management is about bringing order to complexity. Good management brings a degree of consistency to key dimensions like quality and profitability of services and products. An organization's formal structure enacts management. Leadership, by contrast, is more about driving through and coping with change. Therefore, management and leadership are two distinctive systems of action. As stated, each has its own function and characteristic activities, and a complex organizational environment requires both to achieve success.

Organizations manage complexity by first planning and budgeting, setting goals for the future, establishing detailed steps for achieving those targets, and then allocating resources to accomplish those plans. By contrast, leading an organization to constructive change begins by setting a direction, developing a vision of the future along with strategies that will produce necessary changes to achieve that vision.

Management develops the capacity to achieve its plan by organizing and staffing, thus creating an organizational structure. Jobs then populate the structure for accomplishing plan requirements. Ideally, suitably qualified individuals fill these roles. Management delegates responsibility for carrying out the plan and creates systems to monitor operations. Ultimately, those in management positions broadly monitor the worker bees in the organization who accomplish the tasks in detail. Management is intrinsically bound with the process of first creating, and then monitoring the performance of the formal organization.

The informal structure of an organization responds more to leadership. It was the academic Knowles (2002:97) who recognized that "within the informal structure people tend to self-organize around the work, forming patterns and networks." The informal structure emerges from the particular competences of, and relationships between, individuals. The concept of the informal organization is one of structure emerging from the relationship between members of the organization, rather than imposing a "theoretical" organization that is populated by specified roles and job descriptions that do not necessarily relate to immediate issues. In business management there is a mantra that structure drives strategy, which in turn drives performance. Within the informal organization, it is people and their relationships that drive structure and that in turn drives performance. Ultimately, the strength of an organization's technology orientation does not matter; organizations are people-driven.

For the informal organization to operate effectively, it must have a free flow of information, in order to develop connections, and create interdependence and trust among people. In short, work-based relationships are important for the success of the organization because they constitute one of two elements that comprise the third stage of a group's development, *coming together*:

1. Work-based relationships.
2. Working in groups.

An effective manager must have insight into the nature of supportive and productive *work-based relationships*, in terms of how we can establish, develop, and maintain them. No one works alone in today's organizations, and the ability to develop and then draw upon a network of work-based relationships is fundamental to the process of aligning people around a common objective. The second element of the coming together stage is *working in groups*. Working in groups is the practical process of putting a work-based relationship to work, the place where individuals moderate their behavior in a collective effort to align around a common goal. An ability to work in a group does not however automatically follow the establishment of good working relationships with other group members. We must strike a balance between maintaining a separate identity as an independent individual, and the emotional well-being we associate with group membership.

So, let us recap. The third stage of a group's development, coming together, comprises two elements, work-based relationships and working in groups. Each is important if a group is to successfully negotiate its way into and then through the coming together stage. However, before considering the two elements in detail, we must describe the coming together stage itself. We present the practical indicators that signal a group is first approaching the coming together stage and then the signs that it has entered it.

Group development

The third stage of a group's development, coming together, commences as a group reaches a consensus as to what is expected of it. Having worked through the frustration of the confrontation stage, group members' expectations regarding what they must deliver are broadly aligned, and members generally agree to what is possible. At this point, the group's development allows the group members to start initiating meaningful and sustainable activities as a group, possibly for the first time.

The initiation of work signals that the group is now functioning as a social system. All group members do not have to accept that they are members of the group, and even if they do, it is not mandatory for them to agree with the approach others are taking. However, we must differentiate the coming together stage from the previous stage, confrontation, because now, a majority of group members do have sound-enough relationships allowing them to work together. As such, the group's social system may not include all individuals, but it does include a sufficient number to enable the group to function.

The second reason why the coming together stage differs from the confrontation stage is the ability of group members to work together underpinned by an acceptance that the group is now a permanent feature of the organizational landscape. Many who originally hoped that the group might abandon the new initiative if ignored long enough have changed their opinion. Some people, of course, will still wish for its disbanding. These critics remain waiting and watching for any opportunity to undermine the group or discredit its leader. They, however, do acknowledge and accept that the group is now something with which they must deal and not ignore.

In terms of the work in which members are engaged, we observe some chaotic elements in the coming together stage. The group may now be functioning with general agreement as to what goal they need to achieve, but that does not mean members exactly know the path to that goal. Members are optimistic, but they have not yet carved out a detailed project plan that articulates how they will achieve their goal.

The lack of an agreed plan of action is why the coming together stage feels chaotic as group members start working, and then, almost immediately, find that their approach may not work as intended. Unlike the chaos of the confrontation stage that we associate with overt conflict, the sentiments concerning chaos during the coming together stage is a consequence of group members trying new ideas. Despite the new ideas typically creating more problems than solutions, group members remain engaged in their effort to identify the meaning of their goal in terms of practical activity.

We can best summarize the coming together stage in terms of vision. In this context, vision refers to a shared view of the future and how it can differ from the present. As a group enters the coming together stage, members buy into the vision. For the first time, a majority of members feel that the group can achieve the set goal. However, progress is more than just a feeling. Group members are proactively initiating work, for the first time, aimed at defining how to achieve the goal.

Within the context of the coming together stage, we can think of progress as a process of defining exactly what we need to realize the goal. While the group is making little substantive progress in delivering the goal, managers will more readily accept this, realizing that the group is still establishing what they need to accomplish. As the name coming together implies, members have, at least, now come together as a group. For the first time, they are more than just a collection of individuals.

Practical indicators

A group approaching the coming together stage of its development is different from a group firmly stuck in the confrontation stage. The difference is that despite the conflict between members, some actions help clarify what the group needs to achieve its goal. Prior to entry into the coming together stage, we clearly observe strong resistance from group members to every proposed approach. Despite the conflict, as group members start putting time into tasks to accomplish the goal, a manager has cause for cautious optimism. The group is on the verge of transitioning into the coming together stage.

Transition into the coming together stage is not necessarily immediately apparent to either those directly involved or those observing a group from outside. We still characterize the coming together stage by conflict even if that conflict is now more positive, associated with disagreement over how the group will deliver a goal. There are, however, four signs that indicate a group has entered the coming together stage. First is the emergence of unforeseen problems that cast doubt on the viability of realization of the group's goal. The emergence of unforeseen problems may not feel like progress, but in actuality is. Group members must be engaged in relevant work in order for them to identify these unexpected challenges. The useful work, not the problems, constitutes progress.

As group members work more effectively together, they may find an endless stream of challenges. The sheer number of emerging concerns can overwhelm a group's leader. On this basis, the second sign that a group has entered the coming together stage is a tendency for the leader to perceive the group in increasingly negative terms. The leader is tempted to blame group members for both the existence of problems and the lack of progress in solving them.

As a group's leader continues to find a way forward, he or she can feel progressively more negative about the group's members. As a result, the leader's motivation starts to falter. The third sign is a lack of motivation from inside the group. While outsiders might perceive the group as functioning better and making progress, this is not the case. The group now identifies the nature and causes of the problems and realize they must address them. This is when the group begins to understand the true magnitude of the task. This can result in an overwhelming feeling that the goal is, in fact, impossible to achieve after all.

Once members lose motivation, the overwhelming feeling leads to a loss of focus on what they need to achieve. This is the fourth sign of the coming together stage. At this stage, certain members of the group recognize the increasing list of problems, but instead of focusing on addressing them, they become disconnected from the original vision.

As we stated earlier, any vision is also a paradox; see the future and deal with the present while not losing sight of either. As some group members lose sight of the vision, task-related conflict tends to reemerge with the associated risk that it will spill over into relationship-based conflict. Despite the reemergence of conflict, there is an important difference between the coming together stage and the confrontation stage that preceded it. Because group members have worked together, they are able to identify problems. They will have discussed, debated, agreed, and disagreed. At this stage, they will have already broken the barrier of not knowing one another. In short, they have established some sense of work-based relationships.

Work-based relationships

Work-based relationships comprise the first element of the coming together stage. It is the existence of relationships between group members that differentiate a group from a collection of individuals. It is as a consequence of the existence of work-based relationships that group members start to moderate their behavior. In essence, the existence of a relationship moderates the way an individual responds because maintaining a relationship is now important. Moderation of behavior is a consequence of the existence of a relationship that signals that a collection of individuals is now becoming a group. They place some value on the relationships with other group members and the social system those relationships collectively constitute.

The Traditional Turbine Co. case study has illustrated how Harry developed good working relationships with Per, his chief designer, Natasha, the company's sales director, and John, the company's finance director. The network of relationships enabled Harry to work with Per who was able to have the product development group members work toward defining the group goal at a detailed technical level. It also enabled Harry to persuade Natasha and John to reinforce the importance of the group's goal, without which it is almost certain that Doug, the company's chief draftsman, would have pursued his own line and then have the product development group back him.

As Harry waited to see what Doug would present, he was not optimistic. Feeling emotionally low, Harry started to focus on the endless problems that the product development group members raised with him. The evening before, Harry let slip to his wife that the product development group was "as much use as a chocolate tea pot on a hot stove." His increasingly negative attitude was starting to show. As the third formal meeting of the product development group approached, Harry mentally prepared for failure. We rejoin Harry as the third meeting starts.

> **Case Study 4.1**   The Traditional Turbine Co.—Driving change
>
> Harry was in shock. Sitting in the conference room, looking at the drawing that Doug had just pinned up, words failed him. It looked "right." Somehow, Doug had pulled the "bag of bits" together into a layout that looked like it would work. It was obvious that everyone else felt that way too. The staid atmosphere in the room transformed into an electric feeling.
>
> →

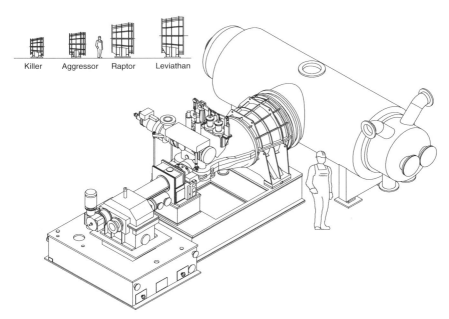

Figure 4.2   Driving change
Source: Compiled by the authors

When Doug finished taking the product development group through the drawing, Harry spontaneously started to clap, quickly followed by Per, and then the rest of the group. Doug was speechless; no one had ever given him as much as a "well done" before. Harry knew that they must now consolidate their gain. Harry asked Doug to list one major problem in each member's area of responsibility. The group immediately attempted to solve the first problem, which Harry cut off after about ten seconds: "Don't solve it now; just tell me who you need to help solve it."

For each product development group member, Harry recorded his or her "problem for the day" and composed a list of members who would help solve it. Harry realized he needed to schedule another meeting soon in order for members not to lose enthusiasm or momentum. "Right, same time Wednesday, and then we can look at Version Two!"

It seemed to do the trick. Everyone knew their task at hand, who was to help them accomplish it, what others had to achieve, and the timeline in which they had to work. This was a very different work style, but the product development group members were warming to it.

Case Study 4.1 illustrates that Harry had timed the third product development group meeting well. His own increasing lack of motivation was mirrored in the product development group members. If a way of pulling what had been achieved together had not been found, it is likely that the good work that had been done would have simply slipped away. Had it not been for Doug's preliminary layout and the enthusiastic response to that layout, the product development group never would have reached the coming together stage. Harry could now rally together the members and assign them various group tasks. The product development group still faced challenges, but Doug's preliminary layout created a positive energy among them. He identified the problems, thus allowing Harry to make the decision to focus the product development group members only on those issues.

The preliminary layout was eye-catching not because of the artistic license Doug used to create it, but because of the extent to which he had consolidated previous work. Every member of the product development group could see some part of his or her own work in the layout, making it easier for them all to accept. Using the preliminary layout, Doug was able to rely on the product development group members' expertise to identify gaps. Case Study 4.1 illustrates that Doug was able to now lead the product development group as a result of his due diligence in researching and consolidating previous development work, and presenting it to the group in a way that demonstrated that a realistic solution was possible. The process of consolidation also clarified the product development group's critical challenges, and in so doing, clearly defined the immediate short-term concerns that group members had to address.

With the group's acceptance of Doug's first layout, this validated his responsibility for fulfilling this task. As the company's chief draftsman, nobody was better qualified to create the first layout, something that both Harry and Per knew. In acknowledging this, Harry and Per validated Doug's role and responsibilities.

Because Doug had been a covert critic of both the idea of an axial exhaust product range generally and Harry specifically, Doug's rise to the challenge both prior to and during the third product development group meeting surprised Harry. Prior to the third product development group meeting, Doug was polite when speaking to Harry, but quietly worked behind his back in an ongoing effort to get the new product range abandoned. Harry was well aware that his working relationship with Doug was not as good as that with Per, Natasha, or John. Harry's approach when dealing with Doug was to leverage his working relationship with all three. While Harry was not aware of how good working relationships with Per, Natasha, and John would help him manage those with whom his working relationship was less good, he at least had the good sense to recognize that he needed the help of others if he were to succeed.

Managers do need good working relationships in order to succeed. But, that comes at a price. The time and effort we need to develop robust work-based relationships are substantial, and the time we take in building relationships is time that we do not spend engaged in task-related work. As such, the downside of relationship building is clearly apparent and we must set it against the uncertain benefit that good relationships may provide in the future. Second, what constitutes relationship building and what constitutes wastage of time is by no means clear as it is difficult for us to define a sound work-based relationship.

Scholars find the study of work-based relationships challenging as there are many variables involved. Identifying the most relevant variables is not easy, resulting in researchers generally adopting a fragmented approach. Despite the inherent difficulty scholars associate with the study of work-based relationships, all relationships depend upon some degree of attraction, and on factors such as proximity and frequency of interaction of participants, similarity, reinforcement, reciprocity, emotional state, and self-disclosure. These are some of the more critical factors that influence the formation, maintenance, development, or demise of relationships.

Of course, our additional challenge is to settle on a definition of a relationship in order to allow for meaningful categorization. A generally accepted definition suggests that relationships refer to regular encounters with certain people over time, emphasizing the importance of explicit "rules" of the relationship. An alternative perspective is that relationships are systems, which include among other things two individuals who interact with each other in characteristic ways. We can link the idea of continuity of association in a relationship or regular encounters with expectations among participants that the relationship will continue for at least some time in the future.

It is important to draw a distinction between social interaction and a relationship. A series of totally independent interactions do not constitute a relationship, and an essential characteristic of a relationship is that other interactions within that relationship influence each interaction. A relationship exists only when the probable course of future interactions between the participants differs from that between strangers. Relationships may have many meanings whereas an interaction will be characterized by one meaning or focus.

The importance of meaning as a context for relationships is because of the extent to which each party in the relationship can understand, shape, and identify with the meaning system of the other person. As two people get to know each other, each tries to explain the behavior of the other and subsequently construct the other person's system of meaning. Each party in a relationship has his or her own personal system of meanings, with a meaning system comprising personality, values, opinions, attitudes, and past knowledge of which the other person is largely unaware. Relationships are based upon the extent to which both parties in the relationship deal with that fact.

We must also consider similarity between individuals in a relationship. Similarity in this context refers not just to how people are similar, or infer similar meanings, but how the use of similarity in a relationship is the process which exerts most influence in shaping the relationship. In effect, a belief in similarity is one way of connecting two realms of meaning. We successfully relate and revise initial commonalities successively over time, until the parties in a relationship interpret events in a similar way. When two people interpret events in a similar way, they have developed "shared meaning."

The concepts of shared meaning and psychological similarity are closely linked. Psychological similarity is based upon the extent to which parties in a relationship construe and interpret a range of events in similar ways and ascribe similar meaning to events. People are persuaded by similarity. It is important for us to consider the identification of both specific and broader general ways in which two people are psychologically similar.

To establish similarity and shared meaning in relationships, those involved must ask themselves if there is any commonality between them and whether they both know that a common element exists in each other's history. Assuming a common element and both individuals involved are aware of it, there is still no guarantee that they will use the same mental framework to evaluate events. To help develop a common mental framework, each person must know how the other interprets events and evaluates performance. An awareness of common elements in each other's history and a shared mental framework enables two people to interpret events in a common way that results in shared meaning between the individuals concerned. Shared meaning, when interpreting events and evaluating performance, characterizes individuals as psychologically similar.

Similarity of meaning is critical in forming and sustaining relationships, having a primary impact on an individual's perception about how well he or she can execute an action. Individual judgments influence the activities people believe themselves capable of managing and also how much effort they will expend. Personal judgments about capability influence thought patterns and emotional reactions during anticipatory and actual exchanges in relationships. Thought patterns and emotional reactions will influence behavior such that individuals may fail to perform successfully even though they have the required skills to know what to do.

We sometimes overlook the fact the way in which individuals describe the development of a relationship is really a story or narrative imposed on a number of events. It is important for us to examine the subtler influences on the way in which we conduct relationships. The contexts within which events take place enact "social norms" or invite judgment about behavior. Others will ultimately judge acceptable behavior; thus in any work-based relationship people are aware that their behavior may be judged by others. Many people allow bad relationships to perpetuate because they do not want others to perceive them as failures.

Also, with humans, talking is fundamental to relationships whether the conversation is starting, getting better, getting worse, or just going on. As such, talk is one obvious vehicle for creating and changing relationships. We talk to share attitudes. We express our personalities through talk. We talk about our goals and, in short, we talk to relate to others whether well or badly. We also talk to handle conflict, resolve disputes, and manage irritations. With these activities, we choose the words we use and the descriptions to employ, and consequently, the preferences and judgments that are implicit. Even casual talk selects such descriptive features or registers a decision to stay silent. Silence and words both record our views. In this subtle way, our talk presents to our audience our own way of looking at the world and it attempts to persuade others to endorse that view.

Talking is fundamental to human relations. However, increasing social isolation within organizations can result in a lack of communication among people. Social isolation is the state where one's level of social contact is lower than one's desired level of contact. Particularly, the trend toward communicating by email is a move toward a high volume of communication, but communication that is impoverished in social interaction and shared experience. While email might be highly effective at enabling one person to keep tabs on many people, it does not help build, develop, or maintain relationships. Building, developing, and maintaining relationships is intrinsically connected with talking to others.

Within the context of a small group exists a second aspect to talking. A measure of leadership in a small group discussion is the amount of speech that a person contributes to discussion. The more often someone "holds the floor," the more observers assume that the person is leading the group's activity. The group perceives the most talkative person as the leader, irrespective of what he or she says, and they see the second, most frequent contributor as the most popular. The management of "floor time" is therefore an important method for a manager to enforce and indicate the measure of control over, and status within, a group.

So, let us recap. The study of relationships is challenging, as there are many variables involved. However, we generally agree that relationships refer to regular encounters with certain people over time, linked to an expectation among participants that the relationship will continue for at least some time into the future. We characterize relationships by many meanings, with an aim of those involved understanding the others' system of meaning. This, then, connects two people's systems of meaning, the objective of which is shared meaning. The outcome of establishing shared meaning enables parties to enter a relationship in which they can interpret a range of events in similar ways. Establishing, developing, and maintaining relationships are fundamentally linked to talking with others. A trend toward electronic communication increases social isolation within organizations. Building robust work-based relationships is therefore intrinsically connected with talking to others.

Working in groups

A manager's ability to build and draw upon a network of relationships is critically important if he or she aspires to lead any part of the organization within which he or she works, and therefore *working in groups* is the second element of the coming together stage. Establishing good working relationships, however, does not automatically lead to an ability to work in a group. The coming together stage may be the point at which a collection of individuals start to regard themselves as a group. It may also be the stage at which, for the first time, there is broad agreement as to what, is the group's goal. However, exactly how the group will achieve that goal is not yet clear. Consequently, the group is fragile, and could fall apart as easily as it could go on to perform to its full potential.

If a group could still fall apart at the coming together stage, it follows that the conflict we associate with the confrontation stage has persisted into the coming together stage. We can understand the continued presence of conflict in terms of the second element of the coming together stage. The second element is working in groups, with focus on the group and the social system it has become. We associate the second element with the residual conflict during the coming together stage as a consequence of the conflicting needs of an individual in group situations.

As individuals, we make a trade-off associated with membership of a group. The trade-off is between an individual's ability to maintain a balance of relative independence thus preserving personal identity and self-esteem, and group membership generating a sense of belonging and affiliation. It is essential for us to establish a separate identity in a group for emotional well-being. Fear of losing one's personal identity is a major factor in the reluctance of individuals to join a new group. As a group progresses through the coming together stage and its members engage with each other and the tasks they need to achieve the group's goal, the balance between individual and group progressively shifts. Initially, individuals are involved on their own terms. However, as the group develops, individuals increasingly have to accept that they are now group members. They have gained a sense of belonging and affiliation, but they have lost some of their personal identities, and consequently their self-esteem may suffer.

As we mentioned earlier, the coming together stage comprises two elements, work-based relationships and working in groups. The first focuses on the individual and the second on the group. The key to success for a group's leader is not to lose sight of either. As individuals, our self-esteem is closely linked to the level of respect we receive from our leaders. Consequently, an experienced leader can moderate the negative aspects we associate with working in groups by continuing to build working relationships with group members on a one-to-one basis even when a group is working well.

The Traditional Turbine Co. case study illustrates the importance of good working relationships, without which Harry would have never mobilized the product development group. Harry may have had many positive attributes and redeeming features, but experience was not one of them. An experienced leader might continue to build working relationships with group members on a one-to-one basis, but Harry was not an experienced leader. We rejoin Harry as he becomes progressively more comfortable leading the product development group.

**Case Study 4.2   The Traditional Turbine Co.—
Reaching a consensus**

Over the next couple months Harry fell into the habit of holding product development group meetings every Monday and Wednesday morning. The process became easier as group members started accepting this routine. Per

→

still chatted unofficially with members and relayed concerns to Harry. Harry continued to negotiate with project managers and reach an agreement that Per could then test and offer Harry feedback on.

Initially, Harry paid attention to certain product development group members who required some extra coddling in order to offer them encouragement. As time passed, however, Harry became more absorbed with project management and sales issues. He spent less time with the product development group members and rationalized that they could always talk at the next group meeting.

The constant dialogue with project and sales managers was not the "leading from the front" Harry had expected, but the technique worked. The key difference now was that each product development group member was organized, and with the help of other group members actually producing substantive work. This collaborative approach resulted in members developing an ability to "guess" in a structured way, enabling them to come up with real solutions in time for the next meeting.

Two meetings a week meant that there was always a sense of urgency. Now this enabled the product development group to confront issues. If they could not solve a problem by the next meeting, they would discuss the work they had completed. This feedback among members enabled them to openly communicate and help solve problems.

As the atmosphere in the product development group meetings improved, Harry and Per found more outlets for their sense of humor. Harry would come out of the reviews with his sides aching from having laughed so much. The group members were not sure how to interpret this, but the enthusiasm seemed infectious. They might have been out of their comfort zone, but at least they were having fun!

$\rightarrow$

> This had a strange effect on how other groups within the company perceived the product development group. Other groups would become bogged down on a project, would not openly discuss problems, and, as a result, they were unable to accomplish anything. Frustratingly, they characterized the product development group as having a surreal disrespect for authority and anarchic humor which amazingly led to producing results.

Case Study 4.2 illustrates that management successfully helped harness and establish relationships between product development group members. The relations were now robust enough for members to both work together and challenge each other. Case Study 4.2 also illustrates a key aspect of leadership action on Harry's part. He held product development group meetings every Monday and Wednesday morning without fail. The meetings only lasted an hour, and there was no formal agenda except that each group member had to present a progress report in his or her area of expertise.

Without exactly discussing it, group members learned to sit around the conference table in a specific order. Harry ran the product development group meetings by asking Per to open with a general progress report that included challenges the group had to face. As Per always sat on Harry's right side, group members learned that if they had an urgent issue they should sit next to Per. After half a dozen meetings, the order in which members sat around the conference table came to reflect the priority with which Harry and Per addressed issues.

By acknowledging placement around the table, Harry and Per could address the most pressing issues, often technical in nature, first. Regular meetings with all key players in attendance enabled everybody to discuss problems openly, thus encouraging group members to volunteer ideas on how to solve issues. As such, the product development group communicated clearly and progressively defined goals in terms of practical activity for the group's members.

While Harry might have moderated the product development group meetings, he did not tell members where to sit. This illustrates leadership action on behalf of the members, deciding among themselves as to whose problems were most pressing. Harry accepted that he would not lead from the front. He would discuss issues that were important for product development group members, and then afterward resolve any resultant clashes through negotiation with the project managers. Further, he proactively engaged sales managers to communicate and clarify emerging aspects of the new product range specification. As such, Harry chose to act as facilitator both during and between product development group meetings. During the product development group meetings he facilitated the internal group debate, and after the meeting he did the same with both the project and sales managers.

Harry's leadership of the product development group improved following the third meeting. Subsequent meetings became progressively more positive. However, Harry's inexperience still showed. For example, Harry took no notes at meetings and he never issued any minutes. Harry's lack of formality and disinterest in the tedious business of project planning was not yet problematic as the product development group still attempted to determine in detail what needed to transpire. However, the time was fast approaching when the product development group required the structure and discipline that the company's project managers imposed on every other project. But, Harry found meetings with the project managers dull.

Harry preferred the product development group meetings to other meetings within the Traditional Turbine Co. because the product development group had developed a very different culture from that of other groups in the company. The Traditional Turbine Co. had, over time, stabilized around a relatively homogeneous culture across the various groups that comprised the company. The culture was highly respectful of authority vested in the formal organizational hierarchy. In contrast, the product development group poked satirical fun at the more ridiculous behavior they witnessed in other groups—a blunt refusal to accept that irrational behavior was in the company's best interest. This facilitated a culture within the product development group that fostered creativity and innovation. In reality, however, the product development group's culture was no different from the culture in any other group. It was an extension of its leader's personality, with Harry as the leader, and that was why he found it such a comfortable working environment.

It never occurred to Harry that everyone else did not feel the same way as him about the product development group. With meetings twice a week, the "managing by wandering about" Harry had practiced on a daily basis became less frequent. Harry's focus on one-to-one discussions and building relationships with product development group members started to slip as he became progressively more distracted by other issues outside the group.

Fitting behavior

That Harry overlooked the need to maintain previously established relationships with product development group members never occurred to him. The biweekly product development group meetings were excellent. Consequently, Harry was once again overwhelmingly optimistic about the future; however, this happy state of affairs was not going to continue indefinitely. We rejoin Harry after a product development group meeting that had not gone well.

Case Study 4.3   The Traditional Turbine Co.—Take nothing for granted

The product development group had evolved into a group as opposed to a collection of individuals; however the members could not take this happy situation for granted. The product development group moved into a phase where they required a detailed definition of blades. They needed help from Brian, the company's senior blade designer.

$\rightarrow$

Harry had dodged the issue with Brian and allowed Per to "package" questions and requests so effectively that the work Brian did for the group had been done as a personal favor for Per. As the product development group moved into a phase where it needed to define the blade designs in detail, involving Brian in product development group meetings became unavoidable.

While Harry and Per knew, the product development group was not aware that Brian had opted out, and did not want to change the way he had been working for the past 30 years. As Brian became involved, however, he started to question the recently established norms and working practices the group had developed, and noted that they were not following any of the company's approved design procedures.

A lack of approved design procedures for small axial exhausts was inevitable, as no one had ever designed one before. This resounding obviousness did not stop a split occurring in the product development group. On one side was Harry, determinedly optimistic that they could sort out such "administrative details" once they had crystallized a design concept. On the other side of the split was Brian, who highlighted that although the group was enthusiastic, it was offering sales on an unfinished design.

The product development group members were all long-standing employees and knew that Sales would generate orders sooner rather than later. When they came to reflect on what they were doing, the product development group realized that they, not Harry, would actually have to design an axial exhaust turbine against a contract specification, with no procedures to guide them.

Morale started to drop quickly as did group performance. Harry was painfully aware that as a consequence of this downturn in the group's fortunes, he was becoming vulnerable to critical judgment from his peers. It also became clear that as a consequence of "ignoring" the approved

→

turbine design process, his lack of turbine experience was something that the product development group members were thinking about for the first time in several months.

Harry's frustration at what he perceived as deliberate sabotage of the product development group was overwhelming. "It's a good thing I don't own a gun," he thought to himself through gritted teeth. As the group's performance faltered, Per, his usually calm chief designer, became increasingly tense and abrupt with product development group members. Harry knew he had to do something, but what?

After his disruption of the first formal product development group meeting, Brian had not been invited to any more. Per had worked with Brian on a one-to-one basis between meetings. This approach enabled the product development group to function, while still obtaining necessary technical input. Clearly, as the product development group progressed, somebody should have documented events. Members of the product development group wanted to formalize action points, but did not want to raise the subject publicly, nor had they been able to do so privately.

With more experience, Harry would have known that the company's quality system had approved procedures in place regarding the design process. However, you could write on the back of a very small postage stamp what Harry knew about the Traditional Turbine Co.'s quality system. He was not even aware that contract designs had to go through a formal compliance procedure. Had he known, Harry could have produced easily an initial draft of an axial exhaust design procedure for others to develop.

Despite that, Harry did have the discipline to run highly flexible and effective meetings twice a week. At the same time, he continuously resolved clashes between the needs of the product development group and live contracts as well as working with the various sales managers. By interacting with the sales managers, Harry obtained feedback for the product development group on how they could improve the new product range.

As such, Harry's initial leadership of the product development group was good. However, the first axial exhaust live contract would require organization, formal systems and the monitoring of those systems. In short, it required complex management. It's not that Harry's management of the product development group had been bad. Worse! It had been nonexistent, and this real-ization was what undermined the product development group members' confidence in Harry.

A downturn in the product development group's fortunes was inevitable as the culture it had developed was so radically dif-ferent from the rest of the Traditional Turbine Co.'s groups. The product development group members found themselves torn between the culture of the wider organization of which they had always been a part, and the product development group. Although the formality of the Traditional Turbine Co. culture was stifling, it did ensure that they would produce contract designs in a safe, low-risk manner. The chaotically creative cul-ture of the product development group was excellent for origin-ating novel ideas, but fundamentally incapable of systematically and repetitively implementing them.

The Traditional Turbine Co. case study illustrates the approach Harry and Per adopted to persuade Doug, the company's chief draftsman, to produce the first axial exhaust layout that in turn facilitated the product development group's entry into the com-ing together stage. Prior to the third product development group meeting where Doug presented the first preliminary layout, the number of problems members were having threatened to over-whelm the group. Harry's excellent working relationship with Per enabled them to take into account the reality of group mem-bers' feelings. This realization prompted the two men to make a mental leap, realizing that it was now or never if they planned to capture what work had been done on paper. In this way, Harry and Per demonstrated the first leadership behavior we require at the coming together stage:

- Draw on the relationships formed with the most sociable group members to access informal feedback on group members' concerns.

During subsequent product development group meetings, Per worked with members and between meetings Harry worked with both project and sales managers to clarify and communicate an action plan. The continual questioning by all involved indicated both a high level of interest in, and also anxiety about what the product development group was doing. The clarity Harry and Per brought to the debate created confidence both in them personally and what the product development group was doing organizationally. In this way, Harry and Per demonstrated the second leadership behavior we require at the coming together stage:

- Accept that group members are anxious and focus on clearly communicating the group's objectives.

Harry's unusual approach while running product development group meetings was effective in allowing members to set the priority with which the group addressed issues during meetings. This allowed members to discuss more complex issues associated with critical aspects of the design meeting after meeting. By holding two meetings a week, and never attempting to plan beyond the next meeting, the product development group was able to solve problems over time rather than resolve them in one go. In this way, Harry and Per demonstrated the third leadership behavior we require at the coming together stage:

- Recognize the need to work through ambiguity that is not easy to address, and avoid the temptation to force consent.

The structure of the product development group meetings provided a way in which each group member could participate to the best of his or her ability. By creating an environment in which product development group members could apply their specialist knowledge to problem solving, Harry demonstrated the fourth leadership behavior we require at the coming together stage:

- Reinforce the strengths of each group member to the group, and make sure they use them.

Harry's approach during product development group meetings was only possible because he continued to keep Brian out of the meetings. Harry relied on Per to work with Brian on a one-to-one basis between meetings. This approach to managing difficult people illustrates how Harry demonstrated the fifth, and Per the sixth leadership behavior we require at the coming together stage:

- Confront sensitive interpersonal issues.
- Focus on the effective utilization of interpersonal skills.

So, let us recap. During the coming together stage, a manager must recognize that leadership will become increasingly distributed among group members as each engages with his or her role. As group members positively engage in a process of identifying problems, they start to proactively initiate work to resolve problems they have encountered. All members of a group, including the leader, must adapt both what they and other group members are doing to facilitate resolution of problems. When taking leadership action, a manager should focus on what help and support each group member needs in order for him or her to achieve success. Above all, a manager must have the good sense and grace not to unduly burden others with an overlarge ego.

Key learning points

- The coming together stage comprises two elements, work-based relationships and working in groups.
- Establishing, developing, and maintaining work-based relationships differentiate a collection of individuals from a group.
- Individuals exchange a part of their personal identity for group membership when they work in a group, a process that can impact negatively on their self-esteem.
- An individual's level of self-esteem is closely linked to the level of respect he or she receives from his or her leader, and therefore a part of any leader's role is to develop and maintain his or her relationship with group members to offset negative aspects we associate with working in groups.

- We facilitate effectiveness during the coming together stage by developing communication practices that are appropriate to their context, assisting group members to progressively clarify how they can achieve a goal.
- The coming together stage is above all else the stage during a group's development where problem solving takes place. The objective of leadership action is therefore not to achieve the goal, but to resolve those problems we associate with defining precisely how the goal will be achieved.
- As group members progressively refine the group goal into specific deliverables, they must communicate those deliverables to the key stakeholders outside the group who will ultimately have to accept them.
- Communication with key stakeholders outside the group must be two-way, with ideas, issues, and concerns relating to the planned deliverable fed back to the group and in so doing helping to ensure that a group actually delivers something acceptable.
- Leaders act as facilitators during the coming together stage. A leader's role is to facilitate meetings to enable group members to apply their skills and expertise to solve problems.

Want to know more?

- For what characterizes social interaction as opposed to relationships, see Hinde (1997) and Jaina (2001).
- For how meaning forms between people and becomes shared, see Duck (1994).
- For analysis of shared meaning and psychological similarity, see Jaina and Tyson (2004).
- For the narratives individuals draw on to describe the development, nature, and level of communication in a relationship, refer to Duck (1994), Caldwell and Taha (1993), and Stang (1973).
- For a better understanding of the trade-off and tension between individuals and team identity, see Diamond (1993).

CHAPTER 5

One step forward, two steps back

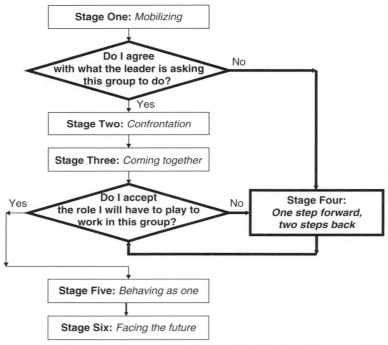

Figure 5.1 The integrated group development process, stage four: One step forward, two steps back

Source: Compiled by the authors

Why do groups go wrong? Within any organization, individuals who comprise groups take for granted the way they work. This is because people tend to assume that "things" will "get done" largely because "things got done in the past." However, this mindset is not appropriate when a group faces a new challenge.

Once a group realizes what it must do collectively, members become aware of how this might impact their individual responsibilities. Quite often, the natural reaction is to reject this new reality.

Group culture consists of the net of accepted norms, values, behavior patterns, rituals, and traditions that collectively constitute "the way we do things around here." Over time, every group develops its own distinctive culture that differentiates between membership and non-membership. How then can an organization have one culture? Within an organization, there are substantial variations between various group cultures. However, if certain assumptions are shared across all groups within an organization, then the organization itself has a culture. Organizations do have common assumptions that come into play during, for example, a crisis. Yet, during normal day-to-day activity, we tend to see the difference between the cultures of various groups within an organization.

When we are faced with a different culture, it is a natural human reaction to perceive it as a threat. This cultural challenge affects people personally. Over time, group members develop specific competencies and skills that they require to achieve their goals. Normally, individuals focus on their competencies, which they apply to the tasks at hand. However, pursuit of competency proficiency is not sufficient as the question that arises is how capably these competencies are applied in order to make that telling difference. Thus, our capabilities are the application of competencies in a way that is contextually relevant. The specific culture which is embedded within a group influences members' capabilities. As such, when somebody challenges a group's culture, individuals involved begin to recognize that the questioning party is undermining capabilities that have previously served the group well. This can result in feelings of inadequacy and insecurity, as individuals do not have the capability to deal with the new demands made on them.

A function of leadership is to manage cultural evolution and change in such a way that a group can survive in a changing environment. However, an established culture defines the criteria for leadership. Acceptable leadership action is rooted in the shared assumption that underpins a group's culture. These shared assumptions are derived from the group's historically successful actions. As such, at the group level, members resist cultural change. Group members invest time and effort to apply their competencies in ways that fit the requirements of the culture within which they are embedded. In so doing, they develop capabilities that complement a group's culture. On this basis, resistance to change at the individual level undermines existing capabilities.

The insight and diagnostic skills leaders need to determine what shared assumptions underpin a group's culture can, in turn, help identify alternative available assumptions and start a process of change towards their acceptance. The identification of shared assumptions underpinning a group's culture is a mechanism for looking below the surface, of asking what is really occurring in a group situation. In effect, we acknowledge that individual and group processes that are not immediately apparent influence decisions. Improved decision making both by individuals and the group will emerge from a clearer understanding of these pressures and allowing for their effects.

The culture that individuals build and maintain by their actions in group situations is the defining characteristic of the fourth stage of a group's development, *one step forward, two steps back*. The one step forward, two steps back stage of a group's development comprises two elements:

1. The way things are done around here.
2. Competencies and capabilities.

The first element, *the way things are done around here*, refers to a group level process whereby certain courses of action prove successful over time, and as these courses of action continue to be successful in solving the group's problems, people take them for granted. A group has an identifiable culture when members share assumptions, nobody questions actions or behavior, and the assumptions increasingly operate out of awareness. "Our" assumptions result as a consequence of members believing their history of success means that their assumptions must be both "good" and "right".

The second element, *competencies and capabilities*, refers to the ability of individuals to deal with changing circumstances we associate with moving into any new situation, for example, a new group. Leaving an established group to join a new one involves change, and even if the consequence of that change is certain to be good (which it almost never is), it is still stressful. The competencies and capabilities that people have always taken for granted and viewed as appropriate may no longer be appropriate. They may need to develop new ones.

The two elements are complementary, each relating to the same cultural issues but from a different perspective. The first element, the way things are done around here, focuses on group processes. The second element, competencies and capabilities, focuses on the individual and the skills and capacity he or she needs to handle the circumstances in which he or she finds himself or herself.

So, let us recap. The one step forward, two steps back stage of a group's development comprises two elements, the way things are done around here and competencies and capabilities. Each is important if a group is to successfully navigate through the one step forward, two steps back stage. However, before considering the two elements in detail, we describe the one step forward, two steps back stage. We then present the practical indicators that signal a group is first approaching the one step forward, two steps back stage, and second, when it has entered it.

Group development

The fourth stage of a group's development, one step forward, two steps back, is intrinsically bound with the two questions individuals ask themselves as a group negotiates its development process. As a group approaches the end of the mobilizing stage, members ask themselves, "Do I agree with what the leader is asking this group to do?" Not everyone will agree, and those who do not will opt out. During the confrontation and coming together stages of a group's development, that some have opted out is not necessarily apparent. If a majority of group members have not opted out, a group can still function.

A group can still function during the confrontation and coming together stages despite some members having opted out because of the task activity within the group. During the confrontation stage, a group argues about the possibility of achieving a goal at all. During the coming together stage, a group establishes exactly how they will achieve a goal. It is only at the end of the coming together stage that it becomes apparent to all members explicitly how they will achieve a goal and consequently, realize their exact roles.

Before a group can leave the coming together stage, members must ask themselves a second question, "Do I accept the role I will have to play to work in this group?" Those who answer "no" to the first question will automatically answer "no" to the second. Some who answered "yes" to the first question may answer "no" to the second. Either way, at the point where what a group needs to truly perform crystallizes into awareness, some will reject it. Scholars studying group development have identified three factors that typically trigger transition from the coming together stage into the one step forward, two steps back stage:

- Individual members, especially new members may challenge certain newly formed practices, procedures, or group norms.
- The group leader may behave in a manner other members find unacceptable, and hence lose their trust.
- The sudden and/or unexpected departure of one or more key members.

Whatever the trigger, at the very moment when we thought that a group would really start to perform, it descends back into conflict. Passive resistance is now overt as the group needs becomes clear and members must now accomplish the task at hand. When it is time to "get off the fence" and commit fully to the group and its goal, those who are not committed, or have just decided to opt out, will simply refuse to cooperate. The group slips back into conflict, entering the fourth stage of its development, one step forward, two steps back.

In theory, it is possible that all group members will want to be a part of what the group is endeavoring to achieve. In theory, it is possible that all group members will welcome the role they need to play if they are to work in a group. Over a 20-year period of studying groups, working with managers and Boards of Directors, the authors have seen this happen once with a group of MBA students. The Cranfield School of Management places MBA students together in groups of between five and seven members. Instructors give students individual assignments and groups group assignments. If group members organize themselves effectively, they can share the work they need to prepare for both individual and group assignments.

As has been said, on one occasion we, the authors, witnessed one group of MBA students that actually did perform, apparently without passing though the one step forward, two steps back stage. That represents about 1% of all groups we observed. The group was so effective its members could spend most of their time socializing with one another while their peers struggled with a mountain of work. Ten years after graduating, that same group still goes skiing together every year, now with wives, husbands, and children in tow. This example remains, regrettably, unique in the authors' experience. In practice, groups do not avoid, bypass, or circumnavigate the one step forward, two steps back stage of their development process. "Naturally" high-performing groups represent a very small minority of all groups. As such, managers must plan for the one step forward, two steps back stage, even if they hope that, perhaps, they will not need to plan this time.

The authors' research demonstrates that if as few as one key individual refuses to let go of the past and accept that he or she needs to move on, then a group will not move on. The group will regress into conflict. However, the conflict is different from that which occurred previously during the confrontation stage. The group has now been through the process of agreeing what they need to accomplish, the coming together stage. As such, during the one step forward, two steps back stage, at least, some group members understand what they must do. We can, therefore, associate the conflict with three specific issues. First, there are members who, based on their own logical criteria, do not accept what the group is doing. Second, members test other members' willingness to moderate their own position in response to an emotional reaction on the part of those who refuse to change.

Third, members struggle with the idea of throwing out of the group the resistant individual or individuals, and then attempting to achieve the group's goal without their contribution.

Practical indicators

A group enters the one step forward, two steps back stage as its members explicitly crystallize their goal into awareness. This is an exciting time for those fully engaged and committed to the group and achieving its goal. With clear understanding of what they must achieve, the group is making real progress. A manager can look for three signs as a group approaches and then enters the one step forward, two steps back stage.

The first sign is members openly criticizing increasingly "visible" activity of a key individual or individuals in the group. Although we primarily associate the coming together stage that precedes the one step forward, two steps back stage with defining exactly how the group will deliver a goal, as opposed to actually delivering it, this does not indicate that the group has not undertaken substantive work. As a group progressively refines its tasks, some work is visible to others and signals the activity a group must undertake in the immediate future. Those who have opted out see that their approach, so far, has failed. The group progresses despite concerns about what the group is accomplishing and how the leader tackles the issues at stake. Thus, certain members of the group now adopt a new tactic— direct and open criticism of the group's visible progress.

The criticism may be a consequence of a legitimate concern regarding the consequences of what the group is doing. However, at this late stage in a group's development, criticism is a challenge to the leadership. Those criticizing may feel they are raising legitimate concerns, but it is too late in the group's development to ask fundamental questions about the prudence of attempting to achieve a goal. The organization made the decision to mobilize organizational resources around achieving a new goal long ago. Yet, we must always question how best to achieve the goal to avoid mindless agreement. The leadership challenge we see is whether or not it makes sense to actually achieve the goal.

The second sign is the emergence of splits and tensions among group members. As a consequence of the open criticism, group members start to focus on the group leader, and begin to question the leader's competence and capability. Factions emerge within a group, with typically one faction firmly uncritical and loyal to the group's leader, a second faction critical and firmly against, and a third, waiting to see how the power struggle plays out. Once separate factions have established themselves, the corresponding leadership battle is now the group's focus.

The third sign that a group is entering the one step forward, two steps back stage is also associated with the visible work a group has accomplished. Despite the group not performing to its full potential—that it has not defined exactly how it will deliver its goal let alone actually deliver it—outsiders perceive the group as performing well. A focus during the coming together stage was to proactively engage others outside the group who have to accept the group's output. An experienced manager communicates a group's interpretation of its goal in terms of actual deliverables and provides feedback to the group as to how key stakeholders outside the group would receive those deliverables. The attitudes of those outside the group become progressively more positive toward those inside as they begin to communicate, listen, and act on feedback. As a consequence, managers outside the group who are under pressure to deliver their own goals are tempted to remove key members of a group for "important" jobs elsewhere.

The one step forward, two steps back stage starts at the point where a group's progress towards achieving its goal stalls. Opposition from those who have opted out has resulted in the group splitting into factions, the group regresses into conflict, and a leadership battle between those factions dominates the group's dynamics.

The group views this unpleasant development as a failure of leadership. Members feel that had the group's leader acted competently, perhaps they could have foreseen and avoided this regrettable circumstance. An experienced leader learns to speak with influential individuals one-to-one, winning them over, or quietly moving them out. However, there will always be those who do not accept either their role or the goal a group endeavors to achieve. Even an experienced manager must sometimes deal with the resistance of some individuals to change before a group can really progress and perform. As such, the one step forward, two steps back stage is not focused on task activity. Working relationships between group members are now good enough to enable concerns to be raised about how they will undertake, raise, and resolve problems associated with task activity. The one step forward, two steps back stage focuses on those who fundamentally disagree with the group's goal and the role they play in achieving that goal.

We associated conflict at the confrontation stage with the rejection of a group's goal. At this stage, some group members refused to accept that it was possible to achieve the goal. The conflict we associate with the one step forward, two steps back stage emerges precisely because group members are now clearly cognizant as to how they can achieve the goal. For the first time, members know how they will achieve this goal exactly. The group realizes the reality that if left to its own devices, it will succeed. At the confrontation stage, conflict would have emerged irrespective of the group's leader. It is only natural for some members to object to the overall group goal. However, at the one step forward, two steps back stage it is not only the goal itself, but the group leader's specific approach that sparks conflict. This time, the confrontation does not result from the leader's suggestions, but from the leader's actions and intended plan. This time, it's personal!

The way things are done around here

The way things are done around here is the first element of the one step forward, two steps back stage. Most managers have worked in and dealt with many organizations, yet find it difficult to understand much of what they observe and experience. We perceive the way organizations accomplish "things" in the most general sense as bureaucratic, political, or just plain irrational. If organizations charge managers with trying to change the behavior of subordinates, the managers often encounter employee resistance to change at a level that seems beyond reason. Anyone who has worked in an organization of any size will have witnessed departments that appear more interested in fighting with each other rather than getting the job done. Even a casual observer witnesses communication problems and misunderstandings between groups that should not occur between "reasonable" people.

Those in leadership roles who strive to bring more effectiveness to their organizations in the face of severe environmental pressure are often amazed at the extent to which groups and individual members will continue to behave in obviously ineffective ways, often threatening the very survival of the organization. Those who have attempted to accomplish "things" that involve other groups quickly discover that they do not communicate with each other, and that the level of conflict between groups in organizations is astonishingly high.

The concept of culture helps explain the above phenomenon, and, further, if a manager understands the dynamics of culture he or she will be less likely to be puzzled, irritated, and anxious when he or she encounters the seemingly irrational behavior of groups and the individuals they comprise. Insight into the dynamics of culture, in turn, helps us understand not only why groups can be so different, but also why it is so hard for us to change them.

Scholars who have studied organizational culture contend that culture and leadership are closely linked, and that neither can be examined nor understood independent of the other. This link enables leaders to create and manage culture. The unique talent of leaders is their ability to understand and work with culture. From the perspective that leadership and culture are two sides of the same coin, we can distinguish leadership from management in that leaders create and change cultures, while managers live within them.

Defining leadership in this manner in no way implies that culture is easy to create or change. Culture is the result of a complex group learning process that leader behavior only partially influences. Despite this reservation, it is ultimately a leadership function to *do* something about the situation when a group's survival is threatened because elements of its culture have become maladapted to a changing environment.

If we accept that leadership and culture are intertwined, there remains the issue that the word *culture* has many meanings and connotations. Most people have a sense of culture, but have difficulty defining it abstractly. When attempting to categorize the phenomena that we associate with culture, scholars have identified as important the observed behavioral regularities when people interact, the language, the customs and traditions that evolve, and that they employ. The implicit standards that evolve in groups comprise group norms, values, behavior patterns, rituals, and traditions and are just some of the many categories scholars have identified.

Group norms, values, behavior patterns, rituals, and traditions are the building blocks of culture in that they deal with things that group members hold in common, but no single one of them is culture. So, why do we need the word culture when we have so many other words? Even a casual observer can see that within an organization of any size there are variations in culture between, for example, senior management and unionized labor groups, so how can an organization have one culture? Undoubtedly true, variations between the cultures of the various groups within an organization can be substantial. If, however, groups within an organization share certain assumptions the organization itself has a culture. It is a normal process of evolution for groups within an organization to produce their own "subculture." Some of these subcultures will be in conflict with each other. In spite of such conflict, organizations do have common assumptions that come into play when a crisis occurs or when they find a common enemy.

Whether at the level of the organization, or one of the groups that comprise the organization, scholars studying culture have recognized that the word culture adds two critical elements to the group norms, values, behavior patterns, rituals, and traditions that comprise the building blocks of culture. The first of these elements is that culture implies some level of structural stability in the group. When we say that something is "cultured," we imply that while it may not be immediately tangible, it is not only shared, but stable. The second element that lends stability is integration of norms, values, behavior patterns, rituals, and traditions into a coherent whole. This integration is the essence of culture. From this perspective, culture is the accumulated, shared learning of a group. For shared learning to occur, there must be a history of shared experience, which in turn implies some stability of membership in the group. Given such stability and shared history, the human need for meaning will cause the various shared elements to form into patterns that we eventually call culture. Therefore, the concept of culture is derivative of our human need for stability, consistency, and meaning.

If we accept that a group's culture is that group's accumulated learning, the question remains: how do we characterize that learning? Scholars studying group behavior have identified two major sets of problems. First, the group members must deal with survival, growth, and adaption to their environment. Second, they must confront internal integration that permits daily functioning and the ability to adapt. Therefore, we may think of culture in terms of the group's accumulated learning that enables the group to survive, grow, adapt to its environment, and at the same time enable members to work together.

The link between culture and leadership in a group starts when one or more members take a leadership role by proposing courses of action. With the success of these courses of action and as the group learns how to solve internal and external problems, members start to take the actions for granted. Members cease to question or debate underlying assumptions. A group develops a culture when it has had enough of a shared history to have formed such a set of shared assumptions. Once members form assumptions and take them for granted, they become a defining property that permits the group to differentiate itself from other groups, and in the process, groups attach value to such assumptions. They are not only "our" assumptions, but by virtue of the group's successful history, unconsciously accept that they must be both "right" and "good."

One main problem in resolving intercultural issues is that we take culture for granted and put value on our own assumptions;

thus we find it awkward and inappropriate to discuss our assumptions or to ask others about their assumptions. We tend not to examine assumptions once we have made them but take them for granted. We normally do not discuss them and if people force us to, we do not examine them but defend them because we have invested in them emotionally.

Ultimately, we may regard culture as an academic term that means the way things are done around here. A helpful, formal, and, perhaps the most widely accepted, definition of a group's culture is that provided by the MIT. (Massachusetts Institute of Technology) Professor, Ed Schein (1992):

> A pattern of shared basic assumptions that the group learned as it solved its problems of external adaption and internal integration that have worked well enough to be considered valid and, therefore, to be taught to new members as the correct way to perceive, think, and feel in relation to those problems.

Any manager who steps into a leadership role should not presume that the culture in which he or she is entering will manage them. What he or she has to be conscious of is that it may! What is critical is to be in tune with the culture. We all desire cultural understanding, but it is essential for leaders if they are to lead.

The case study, the Traditional Turbine Co., illustrates the problems a leader can face if he or she lacks an understanding of the culture within which he or she is embedded. In Case Study 4.3, *Take nothing for granted*, we described Harry's situation at the end of the coming together stage of the product development group's development. The case study illustrated Harry's lack of cultural understanding as the product development group's performance faltered. The company's senior blade designer, Brian, had effectively questioned Harry's competence by drawing the attention of other members that Harry was "ignoring" the company's approved design procedures. Brian chose to overlook that the company lacked procedures for something not yet designed.

In Case Study 4.3, *Take nothing for granted*, we saw that as the product development group's performance faltered, Per, Harry's chief designer, began to panic. For the first time, the arguments he put forth on behalf of Harry failed to persuade the product development group members. We rejoin Harry as he struggles to reconcile the intercultural clash between the product development group and the wider organization within which it is embedded.

Case Study 5.1 The Traditional Turbine Co.—Getting by with a little help from your friends

As Per broke down, not able to win group members to his point of view, for the first time, Harry knew that he had to do something. He intuitively knew that members would block and counter his actions leaving him worse off than if he had done nothing. Harry was acutely aware that when it came to knowing how to get things done in the Traditional Turbine Co., it was Per who always had the answers. With Per floundering, Harry was on his own. It was time to take more risk then he desired, and once again look outside the product development group for help. He needed to call in a favor.

Harry knocked on Natasha's open office door before entering. During his early days with the company, Harry and Natasha had traveled widely together. Becoming progressively more involved in the development of a new product range, Harry's travel diminished, as he was now busy with daily sales meetings with managers who worked for Natasha. After a few introductory pleasantries, Harry got to the point. "The product development group just fell apart and Per, who has always been able to win people round is unable to this time. I'm not sure what to do next."

After some discussion, and no useful new ideas, the two friends decided to regroup with John, the company's finance director, over lunch in the hope of collectively finding a solution.

$\rightarrow$

To Harry's surprise, John found it difficult to believe that the product development group had fallen apart. He continued to emphasize that it was obviously working better than any other group in the Traditional Turbine Co. Harry finally convinced John that the product development group had reacted badly to the lack of approved design procedures. They had to do something.

"Why not just write a design procedure, and then approve it?" John asked rather unhelpfully. Harry explained that while the product development group had almost finished the axial exhaust design, they could not write a detailed procedure until the group actually completed the project. They would not know every detail until they completed every detail of the project.

"Well then, you had better get on and do it ..." Harry wished that they had not invited John, and began to articulate this sentiment when Natasha interrupted:

> You know we could get on and do it if we were pre-pared to break our own rules. We never do any order-related engineering before we actually have an order, but I have an enquiry that I am 99% sure will convert into an order in about three months. The specification is frozen; you could start now.

Working with the sales managers, Harry knew that beyond this enquiry there were at least four others that could convert into orders within the next few months. As a consequence of knowing the details of every enquiry, Harry envisioned a generic design. Because of his good working relationships with the sales managers, Harry could find out what customers truly required. Harry knew this knowledge would make the critical difference between designing a customized turbine for one contract only, and designing a generic turbine that could be reused on other contracts.

$\rightarrow$

John looked thoughtful for a moment before speaking, "There are good reasons why the Traditional Turbine Co. never engages in order-related engineering before actually receiving an order. There are no guarantees in this uncertain world. The Traditional Turbine Co. culture is risk averse, and pre—order-related engineering is just too risky." From the expression on her face, Harry could see that Natasha also regretted inviting John to lunch. John continued:

> In business we must keep in mind that we can reinvent rules, and by combining Harry's encyclopedic knowledge of axial exhaust enquiries with new rules I think we can find a way forward. Harry should not dismiss the need for approved design procedures, but must not stop what the product development group is accomplishing. I see a middle way. We can acknowledge the importance of approved design procedures but must also continue developing a design without them. This compromise should be good enough to enable the product development group members to reengage as long as we do it now, before the first order.

After some discussion about tactics, the three friends agreed that both John and Natasha would attend a "communications brief" the following week at which Per would present the preliminary product range. For her part, Natasha would present the sales department's full list of enquiries, plus the enquiry most likely to turn into an order first. John would act as a referee if things got out of hand. He would also publically approve the budget for order-related engineering without an order.

The briefing was tense and formal as Natasha insisted on inviting all the sales managers. The engineers and sales managers sat on opposite sides of the conference table. It was clear that they did not like each other. Aware of

$\rightarrow$

their poor history of collaboration, Harry felt they were taking an enormous risk bringing these two groups into the same room.

Per had invited Brian, but at the last minute, he was unable to attend. Both Harry and Per suspected Brian would manufacture a plausible excuse not to attend. Harry was not sorry. Without Brian he was able to engage the engineers in debate about how they would undertake the process of first designing a contract turbine and second, documenting the design process in a set of approved procedures.

As he described the ideal design procedure, he started to become aware of the magnitude of the task. Although huge, the engineers could tackle this in small sections. Genuinely relieved that Harry was taking the issue seriously, the engineers did not seem to mind the scale of the task. Although the sales managers could contribute little to this debate, the sheer scale and effort of the task at hand became evident to them. At the end of the meeting, for the first time, the engineers and sales managers engaged in some good-natured banter.

After the briefing, Per and Doug followed Harry back to his office. It would be Doug who would bear the burden and responsibility of writing, and Per the responsibility of checking and approving new design procedures.

"That went well," Per said. Harry looked at him somewhat incredulously. "Well, last week we were stuck and now we know what we are doing next. That's progress, of a sort. All you need to do is figure out what to do about Brian, which neither Doug nor I have been able to do in over 30 years, but I am sure you will think of something...."

Harry could not help laughing. Per was right; they were not stuck anymore so the situation was better than before.

Case Study 5.1 illustrates that previously, Harry could transform the product development group from a collection of individuals into a group, but with no appreciation that the group was still fragile. The fragility sprang from a group culture that its members had not yet fully accepted.

Not every collection of individuals develops a culture. However, we tend to use the word group when there is enough of a shared history so that some degree of cultural formation takes place. The case study illustrates that Harry faced an intercultural clash between the product development group and the wider organization. The Traditional Turbine Co.'s culture was highly averse to risk, with a deeply embedded assumption that each new turbine design must be fully bespoke. In contrast, the product development group formed a creative culture in which they could generally try new ideas, with a basic assumption that every new turbine design could, at least in theory, be semi-standard and based on one of four designs that comprised the new product range.

The case illustrates that together, Natasha and John were able to work with Harry to identify the critical point at which the two cultures clashed: the need for approved design procedures. In effect, the product development group had developed its own subculture within the Traditional Turbine Co., and could maintain this, as long as it did not impact the wider organization in a way that challenged that wider organization's own culture. Cultures, however, started to clash when the company had the prospect of an order, but there were no approved design procedures to move this forward.

Intercultural clash illustrates how culture and leadership are two sides of the same coin in that leaders first create culture when they create groups. Once groups establish a culture, they then determine the criteria for leadership and thus determine who will or will not be a leader. However if culture becomes dysfunctional, the unique function of leadership is to interpret the functional and dysfunctional elements of the existing culture and manage cultural evolution and change in such a way that the group can survive in a changing environment.

Case Study 5.1 illustrates that Harry acknowledged the changing environment within which the Traditional Turbine Co. existed.

Client demands for lower installed cost and shorter delivery time meant the Traditional Turbine Co. had to move away from fully bespoke to more "off-the-peg" designs. However, within the Traditional Turbine Co. employees had the deeply embedded assumption that a new product should be both fully bespoke and designed in accordance with historically proven design procedures.

Within the Traditional Turbine Co., the most assertive engineer after Harry was Brian. The case study in chapters three and four illustrate that during the confrontation and coming together stage of the product development group's development, Harry found a way to move Brian out of the product development group. Between product development group meetings, Per, Harry's chief designer, would speak with Brian such that any work the product development group needed from Brian was effectively done by him as a personal favor for Per. By the end of the coming together stage however the product development group reached a point at which it needed to define blade designs in detail. Consequently in Case Study 4.3, Take nothing for granted, involving Brian became unavoidable. As Brian became aware of what the product development group would do if left to its own devices, he felt empowered to act in defense of the Traditional Turbine Co.'s culture that was not only good and right, but worth protecting and preserving.

Harry did not feel the same way as Brian. Harry had gradually come to the view that the Traditional Turbine Co.'s culture had over the years become increasingly inappropriate to its environment, and that if the culture did not change, the Traditional Turbine Co. would ultimately lose its clients. These two perspectives were so diametrically opposed that they had become irreconcilable.

A more experienced leader might have found a way to manage the product development group's culture such that they could have avoided a "Mexican standoff" between two deeply held but contrasting points of view. Although Harry was able to reengage the product development group members, thanks to assistance from Natasha and John, he was well aware that he only temporarily relieved the symptoms of the intercultural clash. However, when it came to the practical business of finding some acceptable common ground, Harry intuitively knew that confronting Brian directly would only worsen the situation. The time was fast approaching when Harry would need to engage Brian, defender of the Traditional Turbines Co.'s historic culture. If not, Harry would soon face a leadership battle.

Case Study 5.2 The Traditional Turbine Co.— The enemy within

Harry was not having a particularly good day. There were to be four new sizes of axial exhaust turbine in the new product range, and he was attempting to adapt the specification of each so that they could collectively form the basis of a bid for any one of the 42 enquiries he had collected from sales managers over the last few months. Already in a bad mood, he heard his office door open, looked up, and, to his surprise, the product development group marched in.

Without invitation they presumptuously positioned themselves around his conference table. Harry looked around the room and noticed that Per and Doug were on one side of the table, opposite Brian who was flanked by Derek and Jack, the company's senior application engineer and rotor-dynamics specialist, respectively. There was a rather uncomfortable silence.

Harry looked around the room, and for the first time in days found himself relaxing. "So, finally the "old guard" has broken cover. Let's see where this is going," Harry thought to himself. The silence continued and after some time, Brian cleared his throat and spoke. "Are you aware that Daniel is either not here, or when he is does no work?"

Daniel was the product development group's mechanical analyst. Harry had little idea what he did, and certainly was unaware that he was not performing. Harry's relationship with Daniel was positive. He liked him and so did

$\rightarrow$

most other people. Before Harry could answer, Brian spoke again. "His mother is dying of cancer and he is either at the hospital or completely useless when he is in the office. What are you going to do about it?"

Harry saw a look of triumph on Brian's face, as if he had finally found firm evidence of Harry's incompetence. Harry suddenly became calm. He regretted that Daniel' mother was dying. Without thinking, Harry began speaking in a quiet and controlled way.

> The company has a procedure for dealing with employees who cannot perform the duties for which they have been hired. It basically involves firing them. I expect Daniel would be disappointed to learn that those he thought were his friends had asked that he be fired at such a difficult time.

Shocked with this response, Brian realized for the first time he had come up against a hard edge when dealing with Harry.

"So, he is doing no useful work when he is here?" Harry continued. "If I fire him, he will not be here, and will be incapable of doing any useful work. Either way, the result is the same. Per, Doug, speak with the other members of the product development group privately. Ask if they want to cover for Daniel while his mother dies, or have him fired."

Without blinking, Harry looked directly at Brian while he spoke until Brian turned away. He did the same with Jack and then Derek, and when he had finished speaking, buried his head in the notes he had been making before they had entered. Harry could only hear the sound of them leaving.

Case Study 5.2 illustrates that truth can be stranger than fiction. We do not know what transpired behind closed doors that prompted three apparently rational men to use something as horrific as the impending death of a colleague's mother as a weapon in an increasingly bitter leadership battle. Scholars studying culture have long known that an organization's culture is like an individual's character and in part, provides those individuals who comprise an organization with positive direction, self-esteem, and pride. Individuals who do not recognize a need to change will not be able to hear the cultural truths that the organization reveals. They experience a loss of self-esteem because a colleague or a boss, but usually someone new to the organization, destroys some of the myths and ideas about them.

People avoid cultural change when they are not ready for the insight that change will inevitably bring. Insight produces change automatically because we can no longer use certain illusions. If culture is to the organization what character is to the individual, then insight into one's own culture may remove defenses that had been operating and on which the organization generally and some individuals within it specifically had been relying. As such, we can liken an "outsider" coming into an organization and revealing its culture to the "insiders" to an invasion of privacy and therefore, something that some will almost inevitably resist to the last.

Case Study 5.3   The Traditional Turbine Co.—Rock bottom

Per and Doug spoke privately with product development group members, who, in their turn, spoke with those with whom they worked in the wider engineering community within the Traditional Turbine Co. The collective response was one of revulsion.

One would have thought that the product development group would have blamed Harry for what had transpired, but they did not. In truth, the product development group members feared all who occupied a formal role within the organizational hierarchy. Even though they appeared to the casual observer to have a good rapport with Harry, they feared him.

→

In addition to his position in the formal hierarchy, there was a second factor underlying people's feelings towards Harry, a factor that Harry would not realize until much later. With improved relations between Harry and Doug, Doug started asking Harry to participate in design reviews when technical problems arose. Harry complied, looked at the drawings, visualized them in three dimensions, watched the pieces move as he imagined the imposed loads, and asked questions. He would then leave, instructing group members to call him once they were able to answer his questions.

Those watching Harry in action perceived him as unsmiling and uncommunicative. They also found Harry's random questioning strange. The questions were, however, asked for very specific reasons. It was only as group members worked to find the answers to the questions that both the problem and how it could be solved became apparent.

Harry knew what questions to ask as he possessed an incredibly rare gift for three-dimensional thinking. Harry simply thought differently from other people, fitting the classical profile of an iconoclast. It was this gift that made him the one person other engineers wanted around more than any other when they got stuck and didn't know what to do next.

Harry's gift for three-dimensional thinking provides additional insight into why Brian hated Harry with such an irrational passion. Harry could do something he could not, something he very much wanted to be able to do. He was envious.

Within the company, employees unanimously condemned Brian's actions. In contrast, the organization placed Harry on a worryingly high pedestal, with his repeated attempts to climb down simply being characterized as excessive modesty. The leadership battle was over. Harry had won and the wider organization, not just the product development group, ostracized the enemy.

Case Study 5.3 illustrates a way in which a leader developed a new group culture, which the wider organization then accepted. Harry's bitter leadership battle with the "defender" of the old culture led to Harry's acceptance. As has been said, the case study illustrates a way in which we can develop and embed a new culture. Note that we do not intend the case study to imply that a leadership battle is either a desirable or necessary aspect of cultural change.

In mature organizations with a strong culture, that culture defines what people think of as leadership and what they considered "heroic" or "sinful" behavior. Thus, what leadership created now either blindly perpetrates itself or creates new definitions of leadership which may not even include the kinds of entrepreneurial assumptions that initially launched the organization.

The first problem of a mature and possibly declining organization is to find a process to empower a potential leader who may have enough insight to overcome some of the constraining cultural assumptions. The case study illustrates that the Traditional Turbine Co.'s chief executive, Chris, was notable only by his absence during Harry's leadership battle. That a leadership battle transpired was, in part, a direct consequence of a leadership vacuum at the highest level within the Traditional Turbine Co.

What a leader must *do* depends on the degree to which the culture of the organization enables a group to adapt to its environmental realities. If the culture has not facilitated adaptation, ultimately it will not survive. If it is to survive, then it must change its culture, and someone who can break the tyranny of the old culture must lead that change. This requires not only insight and diagnostic skills to determine the old culture, but for the leader to realize the alternative available assumptions and how to implement a change process towards their acceptance. Much of what leaders *do* is to perpetually diagnose the particular assumptions of the culture and determine how to use those assumptions constructively or to change them if they are constraints.

So, let us recap. The learning process for a group starts with one or more members proposing courses of action. As these courses of action successfully continue solving the group's internal and external problems, members take them for granted. A group has an identifiable culture when members cease to question or debate the underpinning assumptions of these courses of action. Shared assumptions increasingly operate outside awareness, and consequently once they form and members take them for granted, they become a defining property of the group. They become not only "our" assumptions, but by virtue of a history of success they become "right" and "good."

A group will develop a culture if there is some level of structural stability in the group. We facilitate stability through the integration of norms, values, behavior patterns, rituals, and traditions into a coherent whole and this integration is the essence of culture. By proposing group members' course of action, individuals occupying a leadership role are instrumental in creating culture. Once the group establishes a culture, it, in turn, determines the criteria for leadership. Despite the difficulty inherent in changing an established culture, a unique function of leadership is to manage cultural evolution and change in such a way that the group can survive in a changing environment.

Competencies and capabilities

The second element of the one step forward, two steps back stage, *competencies and capabilities*, is concerned with the consequences of cultural change for the individuals involved. The first element, the way things are done around here, focuses on the culture a group develops, and why members resist change to that culture when others challenge them. In contrast, the second element, competencies and capabilities focuses on why individuals find dealing with cultural change difficult.

The term competencies refers to specific skills. Competencies are inherently portable and we can take them from one organization to another despite varying culture within different organizations. In contrast, capabilities are far more immediate, far more contextual. How capable are you at using your skills and competencies to make a difference right now? As culture changes, competencies may remain relevant, but we almost certainly undermine current capabilities. As individuals come to realize that the drivers of change will undermine their capabilities, they also realize that this can expose their inadequacies. This realization is a major factor contributing to the resistance we so often encounter when attempting to change organizational culture.

The concept of culture is one of shared assumptions that develop over time as a consequence of the past success of particular courses of action. For members, the group culture largely defines what action they consider appropriate and consequently, as a culture establishes itself, the work behavior it exhibits becomes progressively aligned with the cultural norms of the group.

The convergence of work behavior among members towards that which has proven historically successful is not in itself a bad thing. It would be foolish to deliberately repeat behavior or action that has a known history of failure. However, problems emerge as members take for granted the work behavior that a group establishes as a developed culture. Members cease to question or debate the assumptions governing the way individuals behave. To understand the problems we associate with ceasing to question or debate assumptions about what constitutes good and right work behavior, we must first understand how scholars have studied work behavior.

Scholars have historically believed that it is possible to identify the work behavior of the highest performing individuals. They also believed that identified behaviors could be transmitted through an organization's workforce via well-planned and effectively administered training and coaching. As such, scholars have historically supported the notion that there are both good and right work behaviors.

Some of the earliest research into behavioral variables that successfully predict job performance called these variables "competencies." Following the acceptance of the idea that behavioral variables successfully predicted job performance, scholars further sought to understand what made people in organizations competent. The research enabled the design of training programs where individuals could learn these competencies and consequently become higher performers.

The idea that we can identify and teach competencies is attractive in that it offers the possibility that they can enhance underlying characteristics of an individual that are causally related to superior performance. However, scholars studying competency have been chiefly concerned with providing accreditation of experience. Accreditation of experience refers to an individual having completed a defined activity. The effective demonstration of a managerial skill does not necessarily demonstrate that an individual has the expertise to judge when and if the use of that competency is appropriate in another situation.

Some scholars have argued that the historic focus on competencies fails to define competencies in terms of the organization, its culture, its market place, and business environment. Further, the meaning of competency may depend on the level an individual is operating at within an organization. As such, scholars have focused on the traditional view of competencies, the skills and behaviors organizations require from us to perform a job. However, the ability and willingness to apply competencies within a particular context is also important.

We define capabilities as the ability and willingness to apply competencies within a particular context. We conceptualize context in terms of demands, constraints, and choice. Organizations place demands and, simultaneously, a set of constraints on any individual. Demands might include job requirements, goals, the amount of experience of available personnel, and the amount of necessary personal involvement. Constraints might be available resources, legal and union requirements, technological limitations, and geographic restrictions.

Constraints and demands we associate with any particular situation limit our available choices. Within the constraints imposed upon them, individuals are able to exercise choices when deciding how to comply with the demands organizations place upon them. Choices could include how to actually perform the work, how much to delegate, and how much we need to observe established boundaries. Available choices to an individual fall into one of three following categories:

- What aspect of the job does an individual choose to emphasize in terms of time, effort, and commitment of resources?

- How and what tasks does an individual delegate?
- How does an individual manage boundaries?

As individuals, we first consider awareness in the context of the demands and constraints that competencies place upon us, and second, we become aware of available choices. Individuals willing and able to apply their competencies within the context of the demands others make on them and constraints they impose upon them, are able to make choices and are likely to develop capabilities appropriate to their context.

If we accept that capabilities spring from the ability and willingness to apply competencies in a way appropriate to context, then it follows that the capabilities appropriate in one context may not be in another. Within any organization, culture develops and establishes itself within a particular environmental context. As a culture establishes itself, we cease to question or debate the underpinning assumptions. That the group and/or leader no longer consciously recognizes the underpinning assumptions is not an issue as long as the demands and constraints are handled in such a way that positive outcomes emerge.

Over time, the demands and constraints within an organization do change. Choices that were appropriate, that have a history of success, and have become embedded in an organization's culture will no longer necessarily be the right choices. If no culture existed, members of an organization would assess the demands and constraints actually placed upon them now and make, in some cases, very different choices. However, once an organization establishes a culture, members learn to apply their competencies in specific ways and in so doing develop capabilities that are self-consistent with the culture within which they are embedded.

A change in the demands and constraints facing an organization can result in the possible irrelevancy of capabilities individuals had invested time and energy developing. Whilst competencies may remain relevant, changing context demands individuals develop new capabilities appropriate to that changing context. However, developing new capabilities takes time. If old capabilities no longer apply, and there is no time to develop new ones, then we are able to see an individual's lack of necessary capabilities. Individuals, however competent, will find that as the context within which they applied those competencies changes, their capabilities are no longer necessarily appropriate. They risk exposing their inadequacies. To emphasize a point already made, this, above all else, is why people find dealing with cultural change difficult.

In the case study, The Traditional Turbine Co., the main characters are highly competent; however, the development of a new product range required new capabilities. In the case study, we see that Per and Doug both found that their existing capabilities simply did not apply to the design of an axial exhaust. As highly competent engineers, they did recognize the critical issues in designing an axial exhaust but had not yet developed the new capabilities needed for them to actually do so. Invariably, developing new capabilities "on the job" carries more risk than applying existing capabilities, no matter how competent the individuals. Consequently, both Per and Doug were acutely aware that their inadequacies would likely be exposed in a very public way.

But what about Harry? Serving as engineering director is not turning out to be anything like he expected. As the product development group progressed into and through the mobilizing, confrontation and coming together stages, Harry became aware of the capabilities he lacked, but then mentally set this knowledge aside rather than act on it. However, as the product development group entered the one step forward, two steps back stage, Harry found it increasingly difficult to avoid the reality that he lacked the necessary capabilities to do his job. We rejoin Harry after he has an opportunity to reflect on the events described in Case Study 5.3, *Rock bottom*.

Case Study 5.4   The Traditional Turbine Co.—Senior management

Bad news traveled fast in the Traditional Turbine Co. Harry was unaware that Daniel, the product development group's mechanical analyst, had so many friends.

$\rightarrow$

These coworkers accosted Harry, not with irrational threats, but with offers to cover Daniel's work while he was "ill" rather than see him lose his job. Harry listened and asked for clarification on some points, but otherwise made no comment. He decided to approach Human Resources to find out the procedure for dealing with an employee who was not doing his or her job. Spending several hours behind the Human Resource manager's shut door did nothing to calm the nerves of those who feared the worst.

Shortly after Harry left Human Resources, Per walked into Harry's office, shutting the door behind him. "We don't need much from Daniel at the moment. Until we receive the first axial exhaust order, the other product development group members can cover for him."

Harry looked at Per, and thought about what he had said. It wasn't enough, but before he could think how to phrase his thoughts, Per spoke again. "I mean, the other product development group members want to cover for him. All of them...." Harry looked at Per and raised one eyebrow. "...Brian knows he has gone too far this time. Everyone likes Daniel. No one wants him fired."

Harry looked out the window. The overcast sky and light rain suited his mood:

> Company policy requires that I put him on garden leave if he can't do his job, and then after eight weeks if he does not return to work, we have to stop paying him. If he is not back eight weeks after that, I fire him. Make that clear to everyone, Per. The day anyone mentions this subject again is the day I start implementing company policy.

Per looked at Harry as if he were seeing him for the first time, then looked away and disappeared. He never mentioned the subject again.

Case Study 5.4 illustrates that Harry has finally reconciled his own desire and need to be liked with the need for a capability key to his ability to do his job, the ability to make the darker decision that would likely make him unpopular. The painful reality that Harry had been attempting to avoid was that the capabilities needed to do the job of engineering director were not the competencies needed to get the job in the first place.

Case Study 5.4 illustrates that within the context of the product development group Harry had made a relatively good job of developing new capabilities that complemented rather than competed with those of Per. Within the product development group Per had the best working relationships with members. In contrast, outside the product development group Harry now had the most effective working relationships with other managers. Working together enabled the two men to accomplish what neither could achieve alone.

Despite this positive development, Harry was having a difficult time coming to terms with the capabilities he lacked. In Harry's case, a key weakness was his desire for fellow workers to like him, but specifically, Per. It is normal for us to desire a positive rapport with people, but in Harry's case, he was reluctant to take any action that risked undermining what he perceived to be his most important working relationship. As Case Study 5.4 ends, we see that Harry accepts that he must implement a potentially unpopular decision, and in so doing risk jeopardizing his success as a manager and member of the Traditional Turbine Co. Board.

Case Study 5.4, *Senior management*, highlights that the leadership battle between Harry and Brian, also ends. Despite having won the leadership battle, Harry intuitively knew that it was not enough. If he were to be successful, he knew that he also had to win the peace. As so often before, Per came up with a possible solution. The idea emerged from a conversation in a far less formal setting than the Traditional Turbine Co. boardroom.

Case Study 5.5 The Traditional Turbine Co.—
Grasping the nettle

Comfortably situated in a corner sofa with pints of stout at their local pub, Per looked at Harry and said, "Do you know what the graduate who works for Brian has been doing the last year?" It was a rhetorical question, as Per was well aware that Harry was unaware Brian had a graduate working for him. "He has been using genetic algorithms to create a breeding colony of turbine blades. What he has done is actually very clever and would make a great paper."

The next week Per invited the graduate to present his work at an engineering department meeting. Harry publicly complimented the work and suggested that the graduate transform it into a paper. Harry happened to have with him a call for papers for the next turbomachinery conference, which by good luck was scheduled in Orlando. The prospect of a free holiday in Florida proved highly motivational, so Harry sketched out the structure of a paper on the back of an envelope. Harry and Per had already agreed that Per would broker the deal with Brian, who as the supervisor would act as coauthor.

The writing process went well. Harry was lucky in that Brian was eager to see his work presented at the same conference where his Cambridge University friends published and presented each year. Harry arranged for the three to attend the conference.

The annual turbomachinery conference was the place to be; however, even Harry who knew this was shocked to see the names from the spine of his student textbooks walk into the room to listen to the presentation. After serious and probing questions, it was clear the audience held Brian in the highest regard.

Following the session, Harry invited the graduate to dinner. To his intense relief, some engineers from Northern

$\rightarrow$

Turbine Industries and some PhD students from Cambridge University were hanging around, so Harry decided to be a sport and invited the lot.

To Harry's complete surprise, the evening was rather fun. The young engineers from Northern Turbine Industries and Cambridge University were good company, and most surprising of all, Brian seemed to be in a good mood. Harry recognized that this fortuitous state of affairs was in spite of his presence, not because of it, and so focused on what he perceived to be his four-part role. First, look very interested in what others were saying while himself saying as little as possible. Second, make sure that copious quantities of alcoholic beverages kept arriving at the table while consuming as little as possible personally. Third, pay. Fourth, gently trundle those who were in need of assistance back to the hotel into a taxi without actually burdening anybody with his presence. Harry walked back to the hotel alone. International Drive is actually rather beautiful on a cloudless night at two in the morning, and anyway Harry needed the exercise.

The week passed quickly. Harry and Brian did not discuss personal issues. When they returned to the office however, there was an easing of tension. They had not "cured" the "problem", but as Per pointed out to Harry "we can live with the symptoms." What they had was good enough, so the two friends agreed to live with it, rather than make any further effort to improve it.

Case Study 5.5 illustrates that attending the conference enabled Brian to move on in some ways. We do not know how or why this occurred, as Brian would never speak about the subject. However, if anybody could criticize the Traditional Turbine Co, for anything, it would be that people generally, and Brian specifically, tended to look inwards, focusing only on the company rather than the environment in which it operated. It is possible that Brian focused on events inside the Traditional Turbine Co., and that the conference reminded him that an outside world existed. Most importantly, that world contained people he respected who, in turn, held him in the highest regard.

Again it is speculation, but it is possible that an initial enthusiasm for writing a paper was at some level an indication to Brian that the management respected him and approved of his work. Brian's awareness of the regard in which he was held within the wider community may have made it possible for him to reflect on the level of positive contribution he was making within the Traditional Turbine Co.

So, let us recap. Competencies are skills and behaviors we require to perform a job. Capabilities are how we apply those skills and behaviors. As the individuals who comprise a group's membership begin to realize what the group requires of them, members understand that existing capabilities are not directly applicable in the new culture the group has developed. As individuals, we tend to focus on our competencies which we can apply generally rather than on our capabilities which are contextual. While difficult for us to accept, we must let go of old capabilities and develop new ones. It takes time to develop new capabilities and therefore, during the process, those involved must accept that their inadequacies will be apparent to others.

Fitting behavior

Harry and other key players had accepted their respective roles in the product development group. In doing so, they accepted that the group no longer needed some of their old capabilities and they would have to develop new ones. As all involved moved to accept their roles fully and without reservation, the blocks that had prevented the product development group performing to its full potential fell away.

Despite this positive development, emotionally, Harry was at a low point. This was, in part, because he spent several hours a day working through endless product specifications and procedures. An ability to write product specifications in a way now required by the company was a capability Harry needed, but found desperately dull. However, there was a deeper issue, a sense of childhood's end that resulted in a feeling of despondency. We rejoin Harry as he drags himself through another gray and endless day.

**Case Study 5.6   The Traditional Turbine Co.—
Carrying on**

Daniel opened Harry's office door and shuffled in. Having not seen him in weeks, Harry was surprised.

"I've ... I've just realized what you have been doing. Getting people to cover for me, giving me time ... ." Daniel said, looking at Harry, "I wanted to thank you." Harry didn't know what to say. He had not been expecting such a reaction. "I still need some time to empty the house, deal with the solicitor who is sorting out the will, but I wanted to let you know that I'm back."

The two men looked at each other without saying anything. Harry stood up, and they shook hands. "Take whatever time you need, my friend."

As if orchestrated, a sudden shaft of sunlight lit up Harry's office, and the two men turned to see a glimpse of blue sky and a rainbow where moments before there had been nothing but gray clouds and rain. Daniel looked back at Harry, nodded his head, and shuffled out of the room again. Harry pretended to watch the rainbow and not notice the tears running down his face as he left.

As the clouds scurried across the sky, Harry found himself suddenly staring straight into the shining sun. When he could stand it no longer, he looked away and wiped the tears from his own eyes. He looked around his office, at dust floating in a shaft of sunlight. The faint sound of the world outside his office only emphasized the silence within. He was utterly alone.

Case Study 5.6 illustrates just how difficult Harry found coming to terms with the responsibilities associated with his first senior management role. Was there really a rainbow, and did Harry really find himself staring straight into the sun? Probably not, but that is what it *felt* like. In all probability Harry was drawing on metaphors for hope (the shining sun) and acceptance (the rainbow), but that does not mean he was weak or in some way "lacking moral fiber." Many of those who try to move from middle to senior management roles find it difficult to negotiate the transition. For those that cannot, they are either fired quickly or management quietly moves them out later. That Harry made the transition into his new role is a testament to both his determination and talent.

More than anything else, we associate the one step forward, two steps back stage with the establishment and acceptance of roles and responsibilities and what they really mean in terms of practical day-to-day activity. In practice, it is difficult for a manager to be prescriptive as to exactly what he or she should *do* during the one step forward, two steps back stage. Cultural change and the development of capabilities necessary following change are contextual. As such, what is appropriate in one situation may not be in another. Despite this reservation, we can use the Traditional Turbine Co. case study to help identify aspects of leadership action through the one step forward, two steps back stage that have some generic qualities and therefore are applicable to any group.

The Traditional Turbine Co. case study illustrates above all else that despite his disappointment at the apparent failure of the product development group, at the point when it should have really started performing at its best, Harry did not succumb to the temptation to blame others for the problems he faced. Despite his intense disappointment at the unforeseen downturn in the product development group's fortunes, Harry listened to members, took those concerns seriously, and acted upon them. In so doing, Harry demonstrated the first leadership behavior we need at the one step forward, two steps back stage:

- Listen to the issues and concerns group members raise to help gain insight into the root cause of the breakdown.

The Traditional Turbine Co. case study illustrates the approach Harry adopted as the product development group regressed, approaching his friends on the Board for help. When stuck, asking others for help might seem to be the obvious choice, but many managers will not. Managers often perceive asking for help as an admission that they are not up to the job; however, this perspective is a form of insecurity. As the case study illustrates, by working with others, Harry was able to find a solution he would not have been able to implement alone, even if he had thought of it independently. In so doing, Harry demonstrated the second leadership behavior we need at the one step forward, two steps back stage:

- Enlist the support of key senior managers, making clear the contribution they can make to the group by reinforcing the importance of the group's goal.

Having agreed on a plan of action, Harry did not rush into unilateral implementation. Instead, Harry organized a "communications brief" at which Per and Natasha presented to the group the management's decision and next strategic plan of action. By inviting John, Harry ensured that an independent authority figure was present, should there be a need. Harry kept a low profile, and in so doing demonstrated the third leadership behavior we need at the one step forward, two steps back stage:

- Resist the temptation to "lead from the front" and accept that the deterioration in group performance will take time to address.

Both during and after the communications brief, Harry worked with members of the product development group to identify how they would break down the challenge they faced into manageable sections with which individual members could actually engage. This process of dialogue reinforced both his own commitment to the product development group's work, and second, the importance of each product development team member's individual contribution to achieving the group's goal. In so doing, Harry demonstrated the fourth leadership behavior we need at the one step forward, two steps back stage:

- Focus on reinforcing the importance of the group's goal to individual group members.

Remaining focused on the product development group's goal and reinforcing its importance to members did not mean that Harry was unaware of the leadership battle playing out. Harry and Brian were engaged in an increasingly bitter leadership battle, but Harry did not allow product development group meetings to dwell on it. Harry did discuss the leadership battle with his chief designer and chief draftsman, but did so privately. In public he noted that the Traditional Turbine Co. was fortunate to have such a capable blade designer. In so doing, Harry demonstrated the fifth leadership behavior we need at the one step forward, two steps back stage:

- Maintain a focus on the group's goal; resist efforts by individual members to focus on interpersonal issues.

Last, the way in which Harry managed the underperformance of Daniel, the product development group's mechanical analyst, was important. The path of least resistance would have been to hand a difficult problem over to Human Resources. Instead, Harry found a way to engage product development group members in the issue. He found a way for them to take ownership of both the problem and its solution. In so doing, Harry demonstrated the sixth leadership behavior we need at the one step forward, two steps back stage:

- We need inspirational leadership on the part of the group's leader, a sense that we are all in this together, and no more criticism.

So, let us recap. During the one step forward, two steps back stage, a manager must not overreact to the deterioration of group performance, but listen to the issues and concerns its members raise. In so doing, they can gain insight into the reasons for the deterioration in group performance that can then provide a basis for leadership action. When contemplating what leadership action to take, a manager must enlist the help and support of other senior managers to first, find a way forward and second, reinforce the importance of the group's goal. When taking action, a manager should resist the temptation to lead from the front. The deterioration in group performance is, in part, a consequence of members questioning the group leader's competence, and so a manager must work through others if he or she is to be effective. Whatever action a manager takes, he or she must resist the temptation to be drawn into public discussion about interpersonal issues. Above all, he or she must promote a sense that we are all in this together, there is no "us and them", just people doing the best they can under difficult circumstances.

Key learning points

- The one step forward, two steps back stage comprises two elements, the way things are done around here and competencies and capabilities.
- The learning process for a group starts with one or more members proposing courses of action. As these courses of action continue to successfully solve the group's internal and external problems, members take them for granted. A group has an identifiable culture when members cease to question or debate the underpinning assumptions.
- Shared assumptions increasingly operate outside awareness, and consequently once they form and members take them for granted, become a defining property of a group. They become not only "our" assumptions, but by virtue of a history of success they become "right" and "good."
- A group will develop a culture if there is some level of structural stability in the group. We facilitate stability through the integration of norms, values, behavior patterns, rituals, and traditions into a coherent whole and it is this integration that is the essence of culture.
- By proposing what course of action group members should take, those individuals occupying a leadership role are instrumental in creating culture. Once the group establishes a culture, it in turn determines the criteria for leadership. Despite the difficulty inherent in changing an established culture, it remains a unique function of leadership to manage cultural evolution and change in such a way that a group can survive in a changing environment.
- Competencies are skills that we have developed over time. Capabilities are how we apply those skills.

- As individuals, we tend to focus on our competencies that are generically applicable rather than our capabilities that are contextual.
- It is difficult for us to realize that we must let go of old capabilities as the context changes; developing new ones is difficult to accept. It takes time to develop new capabilities and therefore, during the process those involved must accept that people will notice their inadequacies.
- During the one step forward, two steps back stage, leaders clarify the roles and responsibilities of the individuals who comprise a group's membership. In so doing, a leader helps those involved come to terms with the capabilities required in their new role and thus, help them to accept the role they must play if the group is to perform to its full potential.

Want to know more?

- For further insights into the nature of culture and shared assumptions, see Adair (1986) and for understanding of group development within an established culture, see Kakabadse (1987 a; 1987 b).
- For links between organization culture and leadership, see Schein (1992).
- For attention to language, rituals, values, customs, and traditions, see Jones et al (1988), Trice and Beyer (1985); and Kilmann and Saxton (1983).
- For information on why 'taken for granted' assumptions are resisted at times of cultural change, see Bohm (1990).
- For further insights into the nature of, and distinction between competencies and capabilities, see McClelland (1971); Gladson and Ahiauzu (2008); and Ahiauzu (2006).
- For the training and development of competencies and capabilities, read Stuart and Lindsay (1997), Cheng et al (2003); and Lowe (2003).
- For insightful thought on demands, choices, and constraints, read Stewart (1982).

CHAPTER 6

Behaving as one

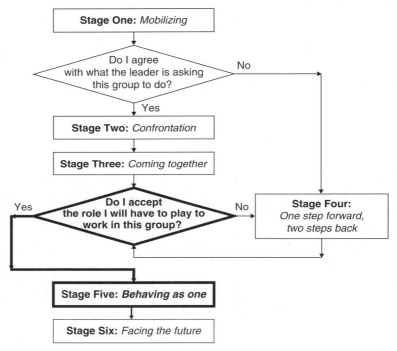

Figure 6.1 The integrated group development process, stage five: Behaving as one

Source: Compiled by the authors

What makes a group of people a team? Groups and teams are not the same thing. We can define a group as two or more individuals, interacting and interdependent, who have come together to achieve a particular objective. The individuals concerned interact primarily to share information and to make decisions to help one another perform within each member's area of responsibility. In this context, the group has no need or opportunity to engage in collective work that requires joint effort. Performance of the group is merely the summation of the group members' individual contributions. There is no positive synergy that would create an overall level of performance that is greater than the sum of the inputs.

In contrast, a team generates positive synergy through coordinated effort. The individual efforts of team members result in a level of performance that is greater than the sum of the individual inputs. A team is a group in which the individuals have a common aim and in which the jobs and skills of each member fit in with those of others. A good working definition of a team is a small number of people with complementary skills who are committed to a common purpose, performance goals, and approach for which they hold themselves mutually accountable.

The above definitions of a group and a team define each, but they do not say explicitly what makes the difference between the former and the latter. Also, the definition of a team could imply that teams are "happy" places to work in which everyone is "nice" to each other. Anyone who has witnessed how the highest performing teams operate will know that this is not the case. When observing high-performing teams, we the authors, have on occasions been shocked at the level of conflict. Exchanges between members can be brutally blunt, resulting in teams being intensely demanding working environments.

Conflict is a consequence of tensions that still exist between members. The existence of tensions results from the difficulty of the issues that we face. However, when we study a team that is dealing with a real challenge, the difference between a group and a team becomes apparent. Within a team, we focus dialogue on the externally imposed challenge, and the choices available to members given the constraints under which they operate. This external reality would be the same for any collection of individuals, whether a group or team. A team fundamentally differs from a group in how it deals with the tensions associated with that external reality.

As we noted earlier, within a team the individual efforts of members result in a level of performance that is greater than the sum of the individual inputs. Increased performance results from reconciliation of personal agendas within a team. The members collectively pursue a cohesive and shared objective. In contrast, individual agendas drive group members' actions.

Individual agendas of group members may be oriented internally within the group, for example, aimed at increasing personal power and influence over other members. They may be oriented externally, for example, providing resources for a "pet" project that the organization is not officially funding. Whatever their orientation, group members choose to focus on how external reality impacts their personal agenda. In contrast, team members, having reconciled individual agendas, choose to focus on how external reality impacts on the team's shared agenda.

Team members do not care whether an idea comes from inside or outside the team, from the most senior or most junior member. Members accept that even if the consequences of recognizing an aspect of the team's external reality is not pleasant, even if the consequences of recognition constitute a realization that it is necessary to follow a course of action all would rather avoid, external reality is what it is. After robust dialogue and debate, members accept the nature of the externally imposed challenges the team must address. Following acceptance, members move on to debate who will do what and how. This ability to move on is why individual efforts of members results in a level of team performance that is greater than the sum of individual inputs.

When working with the highest-performing teams we, the authors, have come to realize that as working environments they are not automatically pleasant places. The difficulty, stress, and conflict we associate with working in a team however are fundamentally different from that we associate with a group. Within a group conflict erupts during the confrontation stage as a consequence of general disagreement between members as to the possibility of achieving a goal. During the one step forward, two steps back stage, conflict erupts again. This time the conflict is as a consequence of some members realizing that the group can and will achieve its goal if left to its own devices. Members who do not agree with the group's mission, or the role they are asked to play, argue with those who do.

The different agendas of group members drive conflict at the confrontation and one step forward, two steps back stages. In contrast, teams that have a cohesive and shared agenda are better able to focus on externally imposed challenges, even when they present members with monumental difficulties. We associate conflict within a team with disagreement over the precise nature of its external reality and how best to respond to the challenge it presents. However, the process of collectively deciding how to achieve the team's goal is an essentially positive process. At the behaving as one stage, conflict is therefore inherently less negative than during the confrontation or one step forward, two steps back stage.

The transition from a group into a team signals transition into the behaving as one stage. The switch from a focus on personal agendas to a focus on how to face the challenges external reality imposes has profound implications for leadership action. Just as a team has become externally focused, so too, must a team's leader if what he or she *does* is to remain relevant. As such, we link facilitating the performance of a team to management of the organizational environment within which it is embedded. Consequently, the behaving as one stage of a team's development comprises two elements:

1. Teams working with other teams.
2. Engaging others.

The first element, *teams working with other teams*, is concerned with taking a broader view, a view that accounts for what is happening outside as well as inside the team. Within any organization there will be individuals who are part of many teams. Therefore, an organization is composed of individuals and the teams to which they belong. The internal life of an organization consists of the relationships between individuals and of the relationships within and between the teams to which they belong. Therefore, we can conceptualize the leadership action we associate with taking a broader view in terms of boundary management. This involves controlling transactions across the boundary between a team and other teams within the organization and the wider environment within which it is embedded. At the heart of leadership action is the debate and dialogue with others outside the team. We may characterize the team as open to exchanges with its environment. The team has now become an "open system" of activity.

An open system's perspective can help managers focus on the environment in which the organization operates and also identify teams within the organization that are potentially reducing overall organizational performance. These are important issues; however, perhaps the most significant is the definition of the manager's role as management of the boundary between the team for which he or she is accountable, and the other teams within the organization with whom he or she is required to interact. The notion that managers are not above those he or she manages, but at the boundary between them and the wider organization redefines a manager's role as that of communicator within the interteam system, that is the organization.

The first element, teams working with other teams, focuses on group level processes. In contrast, the second element, *engaging others,* focuses on the individual. A strong tendency, particularly among young or inexperienced managers, is to blame others for their problems. Often they feel that everyone's behavior is unreasonable except their own. Such a perspective is simply a way for managers to avoid the reality that others, both inside and outside a team, have demands and constraints imposed upon them. The net of these demands and constraints constitutes the team's reality. Insight into that reality automatically requires change as our clear understanding of the demands and constraints on others automatically requires a team's leader and his or her members to make different choices in response to that new knowledge. The ability to engage with reality is fundamentally linked to the ability to engage with others. A process of engaging with key stakeholders helps those involved to see the world from those stakeholders' point of view and then make choices in response to this insight.

The two elements are complementary, each relating to the issues associated with not just working within a team, but the organization and wider environment within which it is embedded. The first element, teams working with other teams, focuses on a team and its relationship with other teams within the organization.

The second element, engaging others, focuses on the individual, his or her perception of events and the choices he or she makes in response to the demands and constraints imposed not only upon him or herself, but also other key stakeholders both inside and outside a team.

So, let us recap. The behaving as one stage comprises two elements, teams working with other teams and engaging others. A willingness on the part of members to work with stakeholders in other teams is a key difference between a group and a team. If members primarily focus on their personal agendas, they are part of a group. If they have a cohesive and shared agenda and consequentially are able to take a broader view, considering the demands and constraints under which others work, they are part of a team.

A group that has transformed into a team is not necessarily an easy working environment for its members. Recognizing the demands and constraints on others requires members to engage with them and constitutes recognition of the nature of the team's external reality. Conflict between members is a consequence of the difficulty we associate with dealing with that external reality. Despite the externally imposed challenges a team faces, leadership action must focus on taking a broad view of the demands and constraints that key stakeholders face outside the team. We cannot ignore the dynamics within a team and between its members, but their management must not prevent members recognizing the nature of the challenges external reality imposes upon them.

The behaving as one stage of a team's development comprises two elements, teams working with other teams and engaging others. Each is important if a team is to first perform and second, continue to perform. However, before we consider the two elements in detail, we describe the behaving as one stage. We then present the practical indicators that signal a team is first approaching the behaving as one stage and second, has entered it.

Team development

We link the transition into the behaving as one stage to a change in members' attitude. Specifically, members now accept their role and undertake the tasks that role implies. The contribution each member must make to the team is now explicit. This change of attitude occurs in spite of successful past working practices no longer being appropriate and new working practices being needed that the team has not yet fully accepted.

When a team is able to recognize the nature of externally imposed reality, they can accept new and unproven working practices. There is a difference between those who resist change generally, and those who resist a specific change to working practices because they feel it is a change for the worse. A common reason for resistance to change is that people have come to benefit from status quo. In their mind, why should they change? Those who resist and those who acknowledge the benefit of change perceive and recognize different external realities. We associate conflict during the behaving as one stage with member's disagreement over the nature of the team's external reality. However, a critical difference between a group and a team is its ability to work with others to gather additional data. If new data supports a member's view that a specific change to working practices would later be bad, then team members accept that the change is inappropriate. If new data does not support a member's view that change is bad, then the team accepts that the change is necessary.

It is disheartening when someone who in the past made critical contributions will not, or cannot see the need for change. In the play, *Inherit the Wind*, about the famous Scopes Monkey Trial, the character who portrays the real-life Williams Jennings Bryan (the defender of creationism), looks at Clarence Darrow (the defender of evolution and change) and says, "Why is it, my friend, you have moved so far away?" Darrow responds, "Perhaps it is you, my friend, who has moved away by standing still."

During the course of our research, we, the authors, have encountered individuals who refuse to see the need for change. At the highest level, Board members and chief executives become too comfortable with the status quo, and they interpret any change as a change for the worse. However, as the world moves on, what once was good becomes good enough, then merely adequate, and finally just plain wrong.

The essence of the behaving as one stage is, as the name suggests, all about behaving as one. Even if individuals have to accept that their role as a team member involves them doing some things that they would rather not, during the behaving as one stage they set aside differences and all members accept their role and what that role implies. Transition into the behaving as one stage occurs as members ask themselves one more time, "Do I accept the role I will have to play to work in this team?" When every member answers "yes" then, finally the behaving as one stage commences.

Transition into the behaving as one stage might involve some members being left behind. Perhaps, if the contribution of one particular member is less important now, the team can continue without his or her contribution. As such, as the behaving as one stage commences, casualties can occur. No one wants to see a friend or colleague fired, demoted, or moved into a " career cul-de-sac." However, the world is a tough place, and we must all either adapt or be left behind. We must evolve and remain relevant or if we refuse to change we risk becoming increasingly marginalized.

Despite the casualties, the sense of lost innocence, and childhood's end, the point at which a team crystallizes into existence is an exciting time. The team understands the goal, the organizational environment is supportive, and members clearly understand what they need for success. Any disconnect between members disappears and productivity surges. All are fully involved and engaged without reservation. Those moving forward quickly forget those who choose not to participate in this brave new world. They slip by as if a distant memory, because it's great to be part of a winning team.

Practical indicators

A team approaches the behaving as one stage despite the setbacks and difficulties of the previous stage, one step forward, two steps back, and a team's leader reconnects with the original vision. Despite the difficulty, participants clearly realize how the future will be better after the team has been successful. The team has now critically established and stabilized both membership and leadership.

Three signs indicate to managers that a team has entered the behaving as one stage. The first sign is agreement, both within a team and around the organization in which it is embedded as to precisely what its goal means in terms of practical deliverables. The key point here is that those both *inside* and *outside* a team *agree* on those deliverables. Do not confuse this agreement with the acceptance of the goal that occurred at the first stage of development, mobilizing. During the fifth stage, behaving as one, agreement is at a much more detailed level and comprises agreement as to specifically what deliverables we can expect.

We associate the second sign that a team has entered the behaving as one stage with leadership style. We characterize the highest-performing teams by little or no observable evidence of leadership. In the most effective teams, each member is the leader in his or her respective area of responsibility with other members flexibly adapting to provide help and support as problems emerge. As such, we can characterize leadership within a team as shared and distributed.

A shared and distributed form of leadership does not imply that the team does not require leadership action. The team now continually identifies and addresses issues. Therefore members know precisely the team needs and they progressively work together, constantly clarifying and refining the deliverables. The team's leader must continually communicate with those providing the necessary support and who must accept its deliverables and then provide feedback to key stakeholders. A team that truly behaves as one encourages feedback to go both ways, from the team to the stakeholder and back. As such, the second practical indicator of the behaving as one stage is a team that appears to be self-managing with a leader who spends more time away from the team, engaged with others, rather than with the team directing its members.

We can interpret the above as implying that a team needs its formally appointed leader less during the behaving as one stage.

However, the leader still needs to remain engaged, his or her role has not diminished. During the behaving as one stage a team identifies and addresses issues far more rapidly than previously. Many issues the team identifies will require skill, expertise, and collaborative working to resolve, with members unilaterally cooperating. In these instances, the leader must communicate the consequences of problem-solving actions the team has implemented without personal involvement in the process of resolution.

However, there will be some issues that require a judgment as to the best choice from multiple alternatives where the best choice is not obvious. The third sign that a team has entered the behaving as one stage is a leader who is both available and able to make the difficult or unpopular judgment calls. Even at this late stage in a team's development, the team might need to make a difficult decision but with no obviously correct answer. The effective leader can draw on his or her links with key stakeholders outside the team. A team can then make a difficult or potentially unpopular decision within the context of what is "least bad" for the organization as a whole.

Teams working with other teams

Teams working with other teams is the first element of the behaving as one stage, and as the name suggests, is concerned with the issues that arise when teams work with other teams. All teams need inputs from others and ultimately require others to accept their output. Consequently, there is interplay between teams that must agree on a coordinated approach to the delivery of organizational goals. Dealing with other teams and the people in them might be difficult, but this is unavoidable. Therefore, we provide you with insight into the processes that play out when teams work together.

Scholars studying team processes have concluded that we can consider a team as an "open system" of activities which is required to perform a task of converting inputs to outputs. The term "open system" describes a team that is "open" to exchanges with its environment. Around it there is a boundary separating what is inside from that outside, across which the team's exchanges with its environment take place. The team needs to regulate these exchanges in such a way that it can achieve its task, and therefore manage the boundary. Multiple teams within an organization have one large boundary around them as well as one around each team. The team must manage each boundary so that all parts function in a coordinated way in relation to the overall primary task of the organization.

Most organizational charts place managers above those they manage. The open system model however locates them at the boundary between those they manage and the organization. It is only from this position that they can carry out their function of relating what is inside to what is outside the team. The flow of information across the boundary requires attention, ensuring that the team has the necessary resources to perform its task and monitor that this task continues to relate to the requirements of the organization and beyond. A manager who loses this boundary position either by being drawn too far into the organization or by being cut off from it can no longer manage effectively.

An open-systems approach defines the organization in terms of interrelated teams. Therefore, the open-system approach places greater emphasis on the environment within which an organization and the teams it comprises exist, an important consideration when making decisions about how the organization will deploy its resources. By taking a broader view that encompasses the demands and constraints the context places on other teams, any one member's choices are more likely to match with the requirements of those teams. When all teams within an organization consider the needs of others before taking action, the overall performance of the organization will improve.

We rejoin Harry in the immediate aftermath of a product development team meeting. The chaotically creative behavior that characterized early meetings has given way to a more restrained approach that at least, in part, mirrors a change in Harry. Although he did not spend much time thinking about it, compared to the young man he had been when he joined the Traditional Turbine Co., he was now less impulsive and more self-assured. That self-assurance, in turn, enabled Harry to think clearly about how to engage others to better manage the unexpected.

**Case Study 6.1   The Traditional Turbine Co.—
Fifth gear**

The conference room was empty, apart from Harry, Per, and Doug, the company's chief draftsman. The other product development team members had left after the meeting. The three men were relieved that the product development team was now performing. The friends agreed they had accomplished more in the last week than the previous month, and had spent much of the meeting complimenting each member on his or her progress. Never one to miss a trick, Harry used the opportunity to publicly recognize not only what the team had achieved, but how it linked to what would be done.

Once Harry was back in his office, Natasha, the company's sales director, dropped by. "I'm not sure if it will be the Toronto Light and Power or the Budapest University bid that converts into a contract first, but I have just committed to final price and delivery on both this morning. It's only the fine detail now. We will have both contracts in weeks not months."

Harry gazed out of his office window for a moment, thinking about everything that had happened to get them to this point. "It would be best if the news came from you. There will be another product development team meeting Wednesday morning. You should present both project specifications then. Try to focus on the differences."

After Natasha departed, Harry visited each product development team member to inform them about the agenda change for the next meeting. There was no shock or drama. Harry assured them that the new product specification covered the requirements of both projects.

The next product development meeting was equally without drama. The engineering community usually greeted news of an impending order in much the same way that the crew of a naval frigate might greet the news that a torpedo

$\rightarrow$

was heading toward them. However, the product development team members asked questions, raised concerns, and behaved generally in a thoroughly professional way.

By focusing on the difference between the two project specifications, Natasha was able to help product development team members work though the problems of getting a single design to accommodate both. All that work on product specifications and design procedures is finally starting to pay off, Harry thought to himself.

Case Study 6.1 illustrates that both the product development team membership and leadership accepted their role fully and without reservation. There is also evidence that both Harry and Natasha managed the flow of information across the boundary between sales and engineering. By asking Natasha to focus on the difference between specifications for the two bids when presenting them to the product development team, Harry was, by implication, asking Natasha to reinforce to the sales managers the need to minimize differences. Minimizing the differences between specifications within the sales department is an example of sales managers setting aside personal agendas in favor of a cohesive and shared agenda. It would always be easier to say "yes" when a client asked for a change in specification. Therefore, minimizing the differences required sales managers to think of others, both in sales and the product development team, before taking action.

Management of the boundary between a team and other teams does not simply concern mediating the flow of information across the boundary. Case Study 6.1 illustrates that for the first time product development team members were fully committed to designing a generic product which could be applied to many contracts. Likewise, those in sales were for the first time making a real effort to minimize contract-to-contract variations. As such, it is not simply management of information across a team's boundary a manager must manage. Far more fundamental is to modify team members' actions in response to that new information.

Case Study 6.1 illustrates that by modifying their actions, the sales and engineering effort became better matched. Essentially Harry had optimized the performance of an inter-team system. To achieve this, the sales community accepted Harry and the engineering community embraced Natasha, as essential to winning a contract for the newly designed axial exhaust turbine.

Acceptance by another team is not an easy matter, and the process by which it occurs has been the subject of extensive scholarly studies. Effectively, an individual has to become a member of more than one team, with each of the teams carrying a greater or lesser degree of sentience or emotional significance to the individual. From this each individual can develop a sense of loyalty and commitment to each team's aims. Invariably, however, individuals belonging to more than one team will sometimes have trouble with conflicting demands from the various teams, and over time the dominant team sentience may shift.

In order to understand the problem with membership of multiple teams, we must recognize that all members of a new team are effectively managing membership of two teams. When a new team first comes together, its members are likely to identify themselves predominantly in terms of the "home" team they have so recently left. This can make it difficult for a new team to work effectively. Different home teams can perceive and understand the same event in radically different ways, with one perceiving an event in highly favorable terms while another sees the same event in an entirely derogatory manner. This phenomenon is referred to as "ethnocentrism" and is so powerful that new team members may be unable to develop a view of reality that is independent of their home team. We may regard ethnocentrism as a team level phenomenon, and associate it with the shared value system that develops within a team. Ethnocentrism is a reason why new teams often fragment into fighting factions.

Over time members gradually invest more in the new team as its tasks take on meaning and importance. The new team builds up a shared value system, as well as relationships between team members. As their sentience shifts, members may become more committed to the aims of the new team than those of their home team. This is likely to happen when members work for the new team outside or away from a home team, or when individuals spend much more time in the new team than their home team. As team members' sentience shifts to the new team, it becomes quasi-autonomous, a closed system whose members have lost touch with the home teams from which they have come and on which their effectiveness depends. Ultimately, the effectiveness of a new team depends largely on its members' ability to manage dual membership. Excessive commitment to either membership at the expense of the other will invariably compromise task performance and lead to problematic inter-team relations.

The process of balancing dual membership is a particular issue for managers. Managers are classically accountable for a team within the organization and therefore, when managers meet they will invariably form a "collaborative" team. Collaborative teams are teams comprised of those who represent other teams. This adds another boundary that the team must manage, as in addition to the boundary between a team and the organization, and the other teams and the organization there is now a boundary around the collaborative team. Managers are therefore not managing dual membership, but multiple memberships of teams and mediating the associated flow of information across each boundary.

A collaborative team forms when representatives of several teams within an organization meet together to establish inter-team relations. The members come together as equals, with no one having authority over anyone else. A problem with collaborative teams can be the absence of any formal management. The question of who is managing what and where authority is located can become critical, with many collaborative teams failing because they do not adequately address this question. The critical questions are (1) who needs to work with whom to carry out this task? (2) What authority will they need? and (3) how and by whom will they be managed?

Case Study 6.1 illustrates that Harry and Natasha had established effective inter-team relationships between the sales managers and engineers within the product development team. While this development was undoubtedly a success, the Traditional Turbine Co. comprised of more than just two teams. The time rapidly approached when this resounding obviousness would become unavoidably apparent. We rejoin Harry as reality makes a most unwelcome intrusion into what up until that point had otherwise been a reasonably relaxing day.

Case Study 6.2 The Traditional Turbine Co.—
Working differently

"Nine months? How can it possibly take nine months to make a turbine casing when we have already designed it?" Harry was speaking to Doug. The look on Doug's face told him that he had expected Harry to receive this news badly. As Harry continued his ranting, it was clear that Doug had been right to expect a window-rattling response. "I told Natasha that she could quote nine months for an entire turbine, not just a casing! What's more she has done, twice...."

There was a rather uncomfortable silence. Natasha had trusted the product development team generally, and Harry specifically, to accomplish what they promised. Per finally broke the silence. "There is three months in that for a new pattern. If we ordered it now we might still be okay. Final assembly takes about a month. As long as we don't get an order for at least four weeks we should get away with it...."

A pattern is a wooden model of a cast component, and when the component is as big as a turbine casing, a pattern has many fine and redeeming attributes, but low cost is not one of them. Per was aware that they had no budget for a new pattern, but Harry knew what Per was thinking. The cost of a new pattern was below Harry's authorization limit. Harry normally approved all contract requisitions for new patterns. If Doug raised the paperwork, Harry could approve it, and no one would be any the wiser until the invoice arrived, by which time they should have both the Toronto

→

Light and Power and Budapest University contracts to book it against. "Doug, raise the paperwork for the pattern for me to approve, but don't advertise what you are doing."

As Doug disappeared, Harry and Per headed for Natasha's office. They explained that they had misjudged delivery time for the first turbine casing, and their plan to resolve it. It was going to be tight. Final negotiations on both Toronto Light and Power and Budapest University were in full swing, but as Harry observed, these things usually took longer than expected. They would probably not sign the first contract for another month.

The conversation with Natasha was slightly strained. That Harry simply admitted that he had erred without any attempt to gloss over or make excuses for his mistake unsettled her. Still, she seemed to pull herself together. "How do you want to manage the minor issue that you have just ordered something without a contract against which to book the cost?"

Harry hoped that this subject would not come up. After Per left, Harry and Natasha headed to John, the company's finance director. After some debate, the three friends decided that it was better to seek forgiveness than permission.

"Why trouble an already troubled mind?" Harry asked, as they speculated on how Chris, the company's chief executive would react if told. They decided that because Chris consistently rejected requests for contract pre-provisioning, this time they would just do it and not tell him.

Case Study 6.2 illustrates how both Harry and Natasha were now working differently. First, they both confronted Harry's error head on, with no attempt to dodge the issue. Second, they both thought in terms of the impact this unwelcome turn of events would have outside the sales and engineering community. The financial implications were significant and they immediately involved John, the company's finance director.

We can consider the team Harry, Natasha, and John formed a classical collaborative team. When they met, they did so as equals with none having formal authority over the others. This was not the first time that Harry, Natasha, and John had worked collaboratively. During the mobilizing stage in Case Study 2.4, *A leap of faith*, Harry, Natasha, and John worked together to prepare the business case for a new product range. Their ability to work together was critical during the one step forward, two steps back stage in Case Study 5.1, *Getting by with a little help from your friends*, and was responsible for remaking rules that allowed the product development team to progress.

The above illustrates that collaborative ways of working may be critical during the behaving as one stage, but are also important at other stages. Boundary management therefore extends beyond simply managing information flow across a boundary between an established team and other teams within an organization. The term boundary management extends to the creation of new boundaries around new collaborative teams. As with any other team, collaborative team members must reconcile their individual agendas and agree to pursue a shared objective. Only by agreeing on a shared objective can collaborative team members direct the teams for which they are individually accountable in a coordinated manor.

When considering a manager's role as that of management of the boundary, in addition to agreeing how other teams will work differently in the future, the manager must understand the consequences for his or her own team. Following understanding, there must be action as a consequence of this new insight. We rejoin Harry as the product development team reacts to the news that they will order a new pattern immediately.

Case Study 6.3   The Traditional Turbine Co.—
The grapevine

Bad news seemed to travel fast in the Traditional Turbine Co. As a result, Harry devoted the next product

→

development team meeting entirely to a plan of action that would ensure that the company could deliver turbine casings in nine months.

Harry listed each task on the conference room white board as product development team members made suggestions. When no one had anything else to add, Harry asked, "Does anyone know of anything else that should be on this list?"

After a long pause, Harry decided to try another approach. "Everyone write down what you do personally, without looking at the white board. When you have finished, we will go around the table and make sure we have captured everything."

Half an hour later, the product development team members finally agreed that the list, now considerably longer, was complete. Harry suddenly realized that neither he nor anyone else had appreciated the complexity of the casing design process. It was a minor miracle that it worked at all. Despite his reservations, Harry spoke again. "Right, we need to work out how to do this faster then we usually do. Let's start with the first task on the list. What are its key deliverables and what other tasks need them as inputs?"

Two hours later, Harry produced a very complex network diagram identifying how all the tasks were interrelated. Following another hour of down-to-earth common sense input from Per, the network diagram became less complex. However, Harry was not worried about the complexity. He was worried about unforeseen changes that might occur as they defined casing final machining requirements.

When the product development team members reflected, they realized that unforeseeable changes in the final machining requirements always result in the pattern design having to be changed. However, they required at least a 1,000 hours to define final machining requirements. It was not enough to have designed the casing. They had to also

$\rightarrow$

define the final machining requirements before the pattern could be made, otherwise they would in all probability make a pattern that was wrong. The atmosphere in the room became suddenly tense as the product development team realized that they had over one 1,000 hours of work to do, and not time to do it.

Harry looked around the room, and for one of the few times in his professional life, he did not know what to say next. In prior situations, he had worked through the problem-solving process successfully, but not this time.

Without Harry asking, product development team members started to discuss among themselves how they would drop their current projects and prioritize in order to accomplish the task at hand. They suggested working weekends and double shifts. They seemed to think that they had no more than two weeks, rather than the usual four months, to finalize casing machining requirements.

"It will be two weeks before the pattern maker starts." Doug, commented to Harry after the meeting, "They will have to process the paperwork and finish what they are doing before they start on our job. As long as we get a revised drawing to them before they actually start, it won't impact delivery."

Time for more shuttlecock diplomacy, Harry thought to himself, as he headed back to John's office to deliver the good news about the overtime that was imminent, and the increase in payroll—more than double—that they had not budgeted for the coming month.

Case Study 6.3 illustrates two key points. First, the product development team members pursued a shared objective, having set aside personal agendas. They were fully engaged, accepting the externally imposed reality of their situation and by implication that they would have to abandon their personal plans for the next two weeks for the good of the team. Second, the product development team was now part of a wider inter-team system, as opposed to working autonomously. The product development team was taking action specifically as a consequence of insight into the demands and constraints that an impending order placed on the Traditional Turbine Co. pattern maker. In so doing, the organization and its wider environment influenced the internal action within the product development team.

It would have been easy for product development team members to evade their responsibility, allowing the manufacture of a pattern that would in all probability have been wrong. They could have done so because Harry did not realize the implications when he ordered the pattern. Per, Doug, and Harry made the decision, but did not realize that a second pass was a necessary and a routine part of the casing design process. A second pass at the casing design would inevitably result in a pattern manufactured to the first design simply being wrong. The product development team was collectively able to recognize the reality of the consequences, and then reorganize to engage with that reality. This illustrates that the product development team was now behaving as a high-performing team.

The Traditional Turbine Co. now operated as an inter-team system, aligning activity within individual teams to optimize overall organizational performance. In actuality, the most radical behavioral changes took place in the team developing the new product range—the product development team. However other teams were also working differently, thus helping facilitate performance of the product development team.

So, let us recap. Despite the difficulty inherent in working with other teams, no team is an island. Teams depend on other teams both for inputs and acceptance of their output. These inter-team transactions require management of the transactions that take place across the boundary that separates a team from the organization and wider environment within which it is embedded.

Scholars studying inter-team processes conceptualize teams as "open systems" in which the team is "open" to exchanges with its environment. For those occupying leadership roles, they too must be open, recognizing the demands and constraints on key stakeholders around the organization and within the wider environment within which it is embedded. By taking a broad view, recognizing the need to coordinate action with others, a team is better able to match what it does with the actual needs of the organization. An appreciation of inter-team processes can help a manager when visiting, communicating, and negotiating with other teams that will, in itself, improve inter-team communication. However, improved communication is not an end in itself. As a consequence of the new knowledge which resulted as a consequence of improved communications, the task activity within a team must change in response.

To facilitate the alignment of the inter-team system that is an organization, managers must form collaborative teams. A collaborative team comprises representatives of other teams who come together to agree how rules will be remade to allow the organization to work differently in the future. Boundary management, therefore, extends beyond simply managing information flow across a boundary between an established team and other teams within an organization. The term boundary management extends to the creation of new boundaries around new collaborative teams, and the reconciliation of collaborative team members' individual agendas.

Engaging others

Engaging others is the second element of the behaving as one stage. The second element identifies that in addition to organizations being inter-team systems, they also comprise of individuals. These individuals rather perversely insist on behaving in highly individual ways. They collectively have a multiplicity of interests, and although they also have shared commonalities, finding those commonalities is not easy. In order to become empowered and take real ownership, individuals within the team must identify with the team's needs.

Identifying individual and team needs does not happen by accident. In addition to a full and clear understanding of the meaning of the team's goal in terms of practical action, members need to fluidly communicate. In addition, team members need to feel a part of the decision-making process, not in a token way, but in a real way which they can see truly impacts events. After all, team members are the frontline experts who know in detail their area of expertise and therefore, can offer needed advice for increased success.

By giving team members both decision-level and practical autonomy, team members and the key stakeholders within the organization and wider environment within which a team is embedded can establish a free dialogue. Only through truly free-flowing information can we create an environment which transparently breaks down "them and us" barriers. As a result, team members are more satisfied and have higher respect for their leader, respect that is earned rather than demanded.

For a manager to effectively engage team members, he or she must be both approachable and ensure that he or she approaches others in the right way. It means allowing room for the diversity of a person's style within the team and cultivating an environment of trust. It means allowing everyone to participate in a healthy debate. A manager must ensure that his or her door is open to others, and that others open their doors to them. It is a balance of encouraging dialogue at multiple levels and a culture of respect for others and their opinions even if they are different. We can summarize this as the need for a positive attitude toward others and a level of maturity that ensures that we always consider others before taking action.

In Case Study 6.3, *The grapevine*, we see that Harry is spending more of his time engaged in what he terms "shuttlecock diplomacy." In effect, Harry encourages dialogue at multiple levels within the Traditional Turbine Co. We also see that Harry had developed a respect for others and their opinions even when they differed from his own. As the Traditional Turbine Co. tries to secure the first axial exhaust contract, we rejoin Harry as the multiple dialogue comes into sharp focus.

Case Study 6.4 The Traditional Turbine Co.—Working with the old enemy

Harry was worried. He had spent the morning with Natasha, working through draft contracts for the Toronto Light and Power and Budapest University projects. He kept finding discrepancies between the two. The discrepancies did not matter in themselves, but the two contract specifications had to fit within the new product specification if they were to have any chance of achieving the promised delivery date. In some instances they were not even self-consistent so compliance with one part resulted in noncompliance with another.

The previous day Harry had approved final machining drawings for a casing designed to the new product specification. It was now simply too late to make changes. Natasha's lack of appreciation for the significance of apparently minor variations between the two project specifications and the new product specification indicated her lack of detailed technical knowledge. Harry knew that she did not have his formal technical education; however the significance of this point was becoming painfully apparent now.

Harry called a crisis meeting with Per and Doug. Back at the local pub, the three friends mulled over the problem: Sales must either sell what the product development team had already designed or only make changes that could be accommodated within the new product specification. After a prolonged pause, Per broke the silence:

> I have a subtle and cunning plan…. Given that no one in Sales knows exactly what we have designed, there is no way they can know what is and is not an acceptable change to the specification. So, why don't I move in with them and finalize the technical aspects of the first two contracts myself?

$\rightarrow$

Both Harry and Doug burst out laughing. The sheer lunacy of the idea! Move in? Do their job? Impossible. But Per was serious. "Why not? Doug can run daily operations in the product development team and anyway, can you think of a better plan?"

The audacity of the suggestion upset Doug's equilibrium, and he excused himself on the pretext of buying the next round of drinks. By the time he returned, Harry and Per were debating tactics.

"Best not to make an issue of it, don't move in, just visit every day, for about eight hours ...."

"She's not in much anyway, probably won't even notice .... At first."

"Best to have a carefully prepared script for when she does work out what we are up to. Diplomacy is what's needed. Flattery often works well, you know ...."

The next week Natasha walked into Harry's office and didn't waste time with introductory pleasantries. "What's Per doing in my department?"

Harry had been expecting this. "Well, as you haven't got a clue what Engineering has actually designed but still have to decide if client requests for changes to the contract specifications are acceptable, we have decided to move in and save you from yourself ...."

As he said it, Harry realized that he could have made his point in a more tactful way. Natasha looked like thunder, but then appeared to melt. "Oh ... I suppose you are right, as usual. So, what *exactly* is he doing?"

Half an hour later dawned a new era in interdepartmental cooperation.

Case Study 6.5 illustrates that both Harry and Natasha had moved beyond "them and us" debates. They were pursuing a cohesive and shared objective, genuinely engaging in dialogue that enabled both to buy into the solutions to the problems they faced. Clear from the case study is that Harry had correctly anticipated Natasha's sentiments and earnestly tried to relate to how she would feel as a consequence of his actions.

Case Study 6.5 also illustrates that Harry was engaged in scenario planning as to the sentiments of Natasha, making educated guesses as to her needs and wants. This anticipation of need may not have been overtly discussed at any length, but undoubtedly impressed Natasha, and despite Harry's rather tactless comments, Natasha more easily forgave him as his intentions were good. This human move uses the science of the head as well as the caring from the heart that was in turn rewarded with a real emotional commitment, securing the good will and willing effort of a peer over whom Harry had no direct authority.

Natasha's goodwill proved vital as the new era in interdepartmental cooperation extended to salesmen and engineers working side by side for the first time. The technical complexity of the task resulted in a level of detail during final contract negotiations with the client that surpassed Natasha's level of expertise. As such, she had to accept the need to delegate part of her role, and effectively empower Harry and Per to negotiate the final contract technical specification.

Overly busy managers classically do not think through the process of delegation and empowerment properly. They become burdened with more responsibilities because they have not developed staff to take over. This may simply be fear about a failed outcome and/or a symptom of a lack of trust in others. However, if managers properly brief and train others, there is no excuse. While a manager may fear not being in control, the mark of a mature leader is good delegation and effective empowerment.

Both Harry and Per were invited to final contract negotiations for the Budapest University contract. Previously, this process had undisputedly fallen into the sole domain of the sales department. Now, Sales trusted Harry and Per to professionally perform in an environment in which Natasha had no control over them. We rejoin Harry six hours after final negotiations had commenced.

Case Study 6.5 The Traditional Turbine Co.—
Celebration day

"Explain to me again exactly why the turbine hall has to look like an upturned Viking longboat?" Harry was speaking to Vlad, the client's architect, who had been somewhat obviously avoiding his questions. The commercial team were arguing about contract terms and conditions, and so it was not the best time or place to attempt to engage Vlad. Finally Harry managed to excuse himself on the pretext of viewing the intended location for the new turbine. Harry, Per, and Vlad were all relived to have escaped the tedium of contract negotiations and consequently were in a good mood. Harry brought up the question of the rather eccentric turbine hall design again.

"Well..." said Vlad. "Off the record?" Harry and Per nodded. "The design will be submitted to the Royal Hungarian Association of Architects. I am hoping to win a gold medal in next year's national awards...."

With a herculean effort Harry managed to keep a straight face, but decided not to risk speaking. Per stepped in to cover for him. "Did you know that our last turbine installation in Denmark won a national award?"

Vlad looked relieved, then said, "Of course! That is why I designed the turbine hall to look like a Viking longboat!"

Harry looked at the plans again, now mentally comparing them to the Danish design. It wasn't as good. "The use of space and glass is impressive, but what about isolating the

→

---

turbine from the surrounding floor to eliminate vibration? Also the inlet pipe-work arrangement doesn't work at all. Can I borrow your pencil?"

As Vlad pressed a pencil into Harry's hand, he started to sketch on the turbine hall layout, redesigning the suspended floor around a cantilevered arrangement that left space around the turbine inlet for a more elegant pipe-work design. An hour later the three men retired to Vlad's office to continue discussion with Vlad's structural engineer. That night Harry briefed Natasha on what they had been up to:

> So, after we modify the turbine inlet, the pipe-work will be symmetrical and balance thermal transient loads better on start-up. It will be much more elegant than the arrangement that took the national award last year in Denmark, so Vlad has a real shot at his gold medal.

Natasha looked mildly irritated. She had spent hours negotiating terms and conditions. You don't get medals for negotiating terms and conditions, you get a headache. While all points had been resolved, it had been tough at times and the client had not invited her to dinner:

> The client will have an internal meeting tomorrow morning. We will then see the vice-chancellor, who has the final decision-making responsibility, after lunch to resolve any final issues. We will either sign the contract or lose it by close of business tomorrow.

The following afternoon Harry, Natasha, and Per found themselves waiting in a large conference room, when the vice-chancellor and his entourage entered. Vlad hurried over to Harry, greeted him like an old friend, and introduced him. It was clear that Vlad had been busy as he presented a heavily revised design for the turbine hall, pointing out the different "world class" features Harry had sketched

→

for him the previous day. Harry and Per chipped in as needed to support the presentation, highlighting the technical elegance and low installed cost of the axial exhaust turbine arrangement.

After about an hour, and with a great flourish, the vice-chancellor produced two enormous fountain pens, passing one copy of the contract and one pen to Natasha who would sign on behalf of the Traditional Turbine Co. After they had signed, Natasha and the vice-chancellor exchanged copies of the contract and signed again to the sound of applause.

"You will be our guest for dinner tonight; my driver will collect you from your hotel," announced the vice-chancellor. That night Harry found himself sitting between Vlad and the vice-chancellor. "...and Harry will arrange for my team to visit Denmark before we finalize the turbine hall design ... ."

As Harry listened to Vlad explain to the vice-chancellor how they would work together, it became obvious that it was not just Vlad who wanted to win a gold medal. The vice-chancellor wanted the university to be associated with award-winning architecture just as much.

As the night wore on, Harry ordered a third bottle of champagne. By the end of the evening both Harry and the vice-chancellor were singing the Hungarian national anthem and had to be helped out of the restaurant. As Natasha and Per assisted Harry to the waiting car, Natasha turned to Per. "How does he do it?" Per looked at her quizzically. "I mean how did he not only convince them to take an axial exhaust turbine, even though we have never actually made one before, but also 'go native.' They treat him as if he is one of them!"

Per was thoughtful for a moment before speaking. "I don't know how he does it. None of us do."

Natasha and Per looked at each other, and then hoisted Harry back into a standing position and dragged him to the waiting car.

Case Study 6.5 illustrates first, that Harry lacked the discipline appropriate in those who presume to lead others and second, that despite this obvious weakness he won the confidence of the client. Successfully closing a major deal involves addressing many commercial and technical challenges. In this instance, the client's architect regarded Harry as he would have regarded a technical expert they had hired themselves. They trusted him, perhaps because Harry seemed to adapt to the local customs and ways of working, or perhaps because he got on particularly well with the key decision makers.

Clear is that as they closed the deal, Harry and Per were working directly with the client's architect. They had established a separate technical communication channel which ran in parallel with the usual commercial communication channel. These parallel communication channels are one example of the multiple dialogues in which Harry engaged both within and outside the Traditional Turbine Co. Scholars who have studied multiple dialogues conclude that they need to exist within an organization. Multiple dialogues make the most effective use of effort and experience. The act of embracing the multidirectional dialogue of many and often conflicting opinions ensures the most informed environment possible.

By undertaking to engage in multidirectional dialogue, a leader stands more chance of providing what the organization actually needs than he or she does alone. A team's competitive advantage effectively increases by using the whole ability of the team. The team incorporates all views into a way forward after appropriate and respectful debate and discussion. We can substitute multiple dialogues with polylogue, from the Greek root poly, suggesting numerous.

The skill of perfecting polylogue lies in the ability to motivate and direct others, value the input they give and pull it upwards in one direction for the good of all. Perhaps this description of polylogue makes things sound easy; however the handling of a range of opinions and personalities requires an ability to communicate, with an open approach to the collection of varied inputs and also their appropriate use. As well as being approachable and ensuring transparent communication, a leader must be confident enough to allow others to shine and not let new talent and different opinions threaten him or her. This is an altruistic stance where the leader thinks less of him- or herself and more about the overall good of the organization.

Polylogue provides a platform for healthy debate that results in a more considered approach and real meaning at the operational levels that really matter. With such multilevel representation of the organization, the resulting decisions are more likely to be the "right ones" as the company reaches them through collaborative conversation which seeks opinions from both junior and senior members of the organization, and from key stakeholders outside. The result is very different from the two-dimensional discussion companies achieve through a more traditional linear approach. Also because organizations arrive at decisions through a voluntary approach, team members really do participate willingly rather than because it is obligatory. As a result, when reflecting on Case Study 6.5, *Celebration day*, perhaps on this one occasion we can forgive both Harry and the vice-chancellor for wanting to open one bottle more of champagne than was necessary.

So, let us recap. In order to engage team members, they need to know more than what to do, why, and where effort fits into the bigger picture. They need to feel a part of the decision-making process, not in a token way but in a real way that they can see has a real impact. In order to feel a part of the decision-making process, team members must have real responsibility and accountability. Delegation of responsibility and accountability on the part of team members occurs as a consequence of decision making and practical autonomy that, in turn, leads to an environment conducive to dialogue and the free flow of information.

The effective management of a team requires everyone to take part in a healthy debate. Nothing else can move individuals from a focus on their personal agenda to a focus on agreeing on a cohesive and shared agenda. Effective management requires balancing dialogue at multiple levels with respect for others and their opinions even if different. The act of embracing dialogue with many others, and the often conflicting opinions that result, ensures the most informed environment possible. The multiple dialogues we associate with simultaneous conversations extends beyond dialogue to polylogue, from the Greek root poly, suggesting numerous. The skill of perfecting polylogue lies in the ability to moderate and direct others, value their input, and, in so doing, give real meaning at the operational levels that really matter.

Fitting behavior

Winning the first contract for an axial exhaust turbine was a major milestone in the development of a new product range. This new contract impacted everyone inside the Traditional Turbine Co. As others started implementing the well-established contract management controls and processes, Harry was able to relax and reflect on his achievement. We rejoin Harry two weeks after winning the Budapest University contract.

Case Study 6.6   The Traditional Turbine Co.—
Cruise control

Harry looked around the conference table as product development team members discussed the critical path for the Budapest University axial exhaust turbine. Compared to the nervous and insecure bunch of misfits who had turned up for the first product development team meeting, they were unrecognizable. They had now each transformed into a leader in their own right, responsible for one aspect of the turbine design.

After winning the Budapest University contract, Harry and Per worked one-on-one with product development team members. They agreed who needed to help each other to deliver his or her part of the design. As a result, the product development team meetings now took on some characteristics of management meetings. Those present spoke in terms of what his or her team achieved, not what he or she accomplished alone.

$\rightarrow$

As Harry listened to the ebb and flow of conversation, he was immensely proud of the product development team's accomplishments. Sometimes it is easy to take the good times for granted, only to recognize them for what they were after they have gone. This was different. Everyone involved knew that this was a golden age. The sound of the conference room door opening aroused Harry from his contemplative state. Natasha, walked in and said, "It just came through, the letter of intent for the Toronto Light and Power contract. They accept the specification as written, if we guarantee delivery within nine months...."

The Traditional Turbine Co. had never delivered a turbine in less than 14 months, but no one was concerned. Per had ensured that the contract contained no nasty surprises. The specification was within the scope of the new product specification they were developing for Budapest University.

Without Harry uttering a word, Per took the lead, working his way round each of the product development team members, agreeing on what additional resources they now required. Nobody complained that they had nine months to deliver and no one doubted that they would deliver the best turbines in the company's history.

Natasha quietly sat in on the meeting, listening to the discussion. Harry watched the way in which product development team members simply accepted her. Difficulties had faded away like mist in the morning sunshine.

Case Study 6.6 illustrates that although the responsibilities of leadership are diffused among members of an organization, the responsibilities come only as a result of individual choice. For most of us, as we look back over our life, we can see that certain choices played a pivotal role in its development. So, too, will the choices we make in the future. Only through choice does an individual become the steward of a larger vision. It is not talent that defines what we really are, but the choices we make.

When we consider Harry's behavior through the behaving as one stage, there is clear evidence that his choices show that he has developed into an effective leader. Harry delegated day-to-day management of the product development team, and focused on the inter-team aspects of his leadership role. More than anything else, we associate the behaving as one stage with team and organizational structures. The case study illustrates how Harry's alignment of different teams became a priority, both around the Traditional Turbine Co. and the wider environment within which it was embedded. In so doing, Harry was able to optimize performance of the inter-team system that was the Traditional Turbine Co.

In practice it is difficult to be prescriptive as to exactly what a manager should *do* during the behaving as one stage. The management of a team within an inter-team context requires both boundary management and inter-team communication that we can characterize as polylogue. Despite this reservation, we can use the Traditional Turbine Co. case study to identify aspects of leadership action through the behaving as one stage that have some generic qualities and therefore, we can consider applicable to any team.

The Traditional Turbine Co. case study illustrates that despite Harry's difficulty and distractions during product development team meetings, he never forgot to recognize the contribution of others. Recognition of achievement is critically important as achievement itself and the recognition of that achievement are the first and second most motivational factors affecting an individual's attitude toward his or her job. By publicly recognizing achievement, Harry highly motivated team members. In so doing, Harry demonstrated the first leadership behavior we need at the behaving as one stage:

- Publicly recognize outstanding individual performance by team members to the organization.

The Traditional Turbine Co. case study illustrates how Harry accepted his role as communicator between teams, but also how he did not overlook the need to communicate within the product development team. Harry knew that he could rely on Per and

Doug to communicate on his behalf within the product development team. As such, he focused his time and effort primarily on communicating with his two most trusted lieutenants. In so doing, Harry demonstrated the second leadership behavior we need at the behaving as one stage:

- Encourage the most sociable team members to network among other team members to improve communication.

While Harry accepted his role as that of communicator within an inter-team system, he did not fall into the trap of the desire to restrict communication flows. Harry positively encouraged Natasha to both be present at, and contribute to product development team meetings. In so doing, Harry ensured that a key manager outside the product development team received information directly and unfiltered. In so doing, Harry demonstrated the third leadership behavior we need at the behaving as one stage:

- Arrange reviews with managers outside the team at which team members present completed work to date plus the plan to deliver the team goal.

We should not underestimate the challenge we associate with inter-team cooperation. Within the Traditional Turbine Co., those in sales and engineering had settled into a comfortable routine that involved blaming each other for their problems and avoiding each other as much as possible. Once the company clinched a new contract, those in sales would "throw it over the wall" into engineering where they received it with the enthusiasm that might greet the arrival of a hand grenade that would soon explode. Finding a way to motivate the engineers was challenging, and the only person who had any chance of pulling it off was Per, given the universal and high regard in which he was held. By finding a way to transfer Per effectively into the sales department, Harry demonstrated the fourth leadership behavior we need at the behaving as one stage:

- Intervene as necessary to defuse interpersonal tensions.

A focus on inter-team processes on a leader's part does not mean that the team can neglect activity. Within the Traditional Turbine Co. case study, a major issue was motivating the product development team to deliver according to approved design procedures. Harry adapted his behavior and became personally involved in the development of approved design procedures, but did not disengage simply because the engineers completed a working draft. Harry realized that the sales department was undermining the achievements of the product development team and he knew he had to change this situation. As a result, Harry dispatched Per to the sales department to change working practices. In an unprecedented move, Harry accompanied Natasha to final contract negotiations to bolster the confidence of the potential customer with the satisfaction that the Traditional Turbine Co. had the technical expertise to deliver the goods. Natasha's lack of technical knowledge could have jeopardized clinching the contract. In so doing, Harry shifted his focus on working practices from those inside the product development team to those outside. Harry demonstrated the fifth leadership behavior we need at the behaving as one stage:

- Be prepared to tackle tasks that the team requires formalizing into new team working practices within the organizational infrastructure, to ensure they become embedded.

So, let us recap. During the behaving as one stage, managers need to recognize that it is no longer necessary to focus on motivating a team to perform. The team is now performing as a consequence of the way in which members are now working together. The focus for leadership action must therefore change from inside to outside the team. The focus is now on aligning other teams around the organization and within the wider environment, and adapting both what the team and other teams are doing to optimize overall organizational performance.

Whatever action a manager takes, he or she must publically recognize outstanding personal contribution and involve key stakeholders. Although the behaving as one stage is not dominated by conflict or interpersonal tensions, a manager must remain aware that he or she is asking all involved to move on and embrace new working practices. Although the best method for a manager to handle the application of interpersonal skills and the defusing of interpersonal tensions is in a low key manner, he or she must, nevertheless, be prepared to take action. A manager must ensure that team members do continue to perform as a team as their team aligns with the organization and wider environment. The goal is to bring all to a point where they can agree on a cohesive and shared objective in order to collectively achieve optimized organizational performance.

Key learning points

- The behaving as one stage comprises two elements, teams working with other teams and engaging others.
- Teams depend on other teams both for inputs and to accept their output. These inter-team transactions take place across the boundary that separates a team from the organization and wider environment within which it is embedded.
- Inter-team transactions require management of those transactions that take place across the boundary that separates what is inside from what is outside a team.
- We can conceptualize a team as an "open system" which is "open" to exchanges with its environment.
- Most organizational charts place managers above those they manage. In contrast, the open system model locates them at the boundary between the team they manage and the organization within which it is embedded.
- The open-system approach's strength is that it defines the organization in terms of interrelated teams with a focus on matching task activity to optimize overall organizational performance.
- Managers must focus on forming collaborative teams. A collaborative team comprises representatives of other teams who come together to agree how rules will be remade to allow the organization to work differently in the future.
- Boundary management extends beyond simply managing information flow across the boundary between what is inside and what is outside a team. The term boundary management extends to the creation of new boundaries around new

collaborative teams and agreement on cohesive and shared objectives.

- An appreciation of inter-team processes can help a manager to manage membership of multiple teams, as his or her role invariably involves visiting, communicating, negotiating, and generally interacting with other teams.
- In order to engage team members, they need to know more than what to do, why, and where effort fits into the bigger picture. They need to feel part of the decision-making process, not in a token way but in a real way which they can see has a real impact on events.
- Responsibility and accountability on the part of team members follows decision level and practical autonomy that in turn, leads to an environment conducive to dialogue and the free flow of information.
- The effective management of a team requires everyone to participate in a healthy debate, without discord or resentment. It is a balance of encouraging dialogue at multiple levels, with respect for others and their opinions even if they are different.
- The act of embracing dialogue with many others, and the often conflicting opinions that result ensures the most informed environment possible. Multiple dialogues of simultaneous conversations go beyond dialogue to polylogue, from the Greek root poly, suggesting numerous.
- The skill of perfecting polylogue lies in the ability to moderate and direct others, value their input, and, in so doing, give real meaning at the operational levels that really matter.
- During the behaving as one stage, leaders clarify team and organizational structures, with the objective of aligning the team, organization, and wider environment. In so doing, a leader embeds new working practices appropriate as a consequence of how a team works, and in so doing, optimizes organizational performance.

Want to know more?

- For further insights on the nature of groups vs. teams, see Robbins (1984) and Katzenbach and Smith (1993).

- For greater insights on open systems thinking, refer to Roberts (1994a) and Miller and Rice (1967).
- For understanding the power of recognizing achievement, go to an old favorite, Herzberg (1987).
- For insights on intergroup relations, refer to Roberts (1994b) and Senge (1997).
- For more in-depth accounts of polylogue, see Kakabadse and Kakabadse (2005) and Kakabadse, Kakabadse, and Lee-Davies (2008).

CHAPTER 7

Facing the future

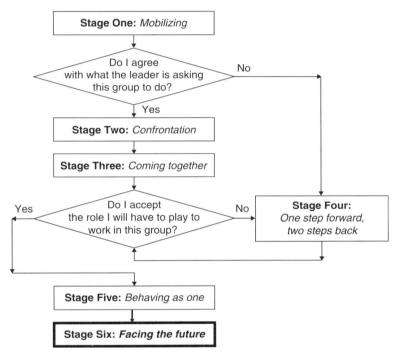

Figure 7.1 The integrated group development process, stage six: Facing the future

Source: Compiled by the authors

How do you let go and face the future? Many leaders arrive where they are because of their ability to fight and win. Sometimes, however, winning is not enough. The ability for us to let go and face the future is intrinsically bound to our ability to manage ourselves, to know when not to fight or when to pick a different battle. Self-insight enables a manager to manage him- or herself, choosing one course of action in preference to others. We underpin the process of managing oneself by reflecting on what it means to be a leader, and consequently what we must do to become a better leader.

The ability to manage oneself is a core characteristic for anyone who presumes to lead others. It is not, however, the only important characteristic. Once a manager actually occupies a specific leadership role, it is no longer enough for him or her to reflect on what it means to be a better leader in general terms. A manager will always associate a specific leadership role with a specific context and the issues associated with that context. A successful manager must understand the demands and constraints under which both he or she and those he or she must lead operate. A manager must make choices that recognize the reality of a situation and allows others to take action appropriate to that reality. In so doing, the manager should be sensitive and diplomatic to all involved in order to gain their trust. However, at the same time, the decisions the manager makes should challenge and motivate those others to develop their own style and philosophy of leadership. In so doing, a manager can help develop not only his or her own leadership capability, but also that of those he or she leads.

The self-insight needed to manage oneself and the choices we associate with developing the leadership potential of team members are the defining characteristics of the sixth stage of a team's development, *facing the future*. The facing the future stage comprises two elements:

1. Managing yourself.
2. Developing leaders.

Managing yourself is the first element of the facing the future stage, and as the name suggests, is associated with making sometimes difficult choices between what is right and what is easy. There are six aspects to managing yourself. The first is listening and reflecting on what people say. Many managers are poor listeners, with little predisposition toward reflection on any part of their lives. However if a manager is to appreciate the second aspect of managing yourself, seeing the bigger picture and how to contribute to it, he or she must both hear what people say and consider the implications for his or her leadership action.

As the reality of a specific situation comes into awareness, a manager must be prepared for the third aspect of managing yourself, taking the initiative, reaching out to others, and engaging, even when it easier for all involved to disengage. We can underpin reaching out to others, particularly those we would rather avoid, with the fourth aspect of managing yourself, 'an ability to control anxiety and "not take it personally."' As a manager, the ability to control anxiety is a critical prerequisite of the fifth aspect of managing yourself, building trust and creating an environment within which others can trust you. A trusting environment underpins your credibility in the eyes of those with whom you work and those who work for you. Credibility in the eyes of others is the sixth aspect of managing yourself and enables a manager to gain support for the pursuit of one course of action in preference to others.

The first element, managing yourself, focuses on the choices a manager makes and the personal consequences of those choices. In contrast, the second element, *developing leaders*, focuses on the choices a manager makes and the consequences of those choices for those with whom they work. There are six aspects to developing leaders. The first is an understanding of context. To be effective in a specific context, a manager must understand his or her context and respond to it, doing things differently as a consequence of the unique aspects of a particular situation. Flexibility is key in understanding context and enables the manager to impact positively on a given situation.

Positioning potentially unpopular messages and timing them with care is the second aspect of developing leaders. Positioning and timing messages underpin the third aspect of developing leaders—picking your moment to give and ask for feedback. Communicating with others and delineating roles comprise the fourth aspect of developing leaders and are both essential if you are to get the best out of others. Getting the best out of others is the fifth aspect of developing leaders. A combination of communications, delineation of roles, and reflection underpins the sixth aspect of developing leaders—a vision about how the future will be different as a consequence of the leadership action all are undertaking in the present. A vision serves as a framework that helps a manager choose one course of action over another, and in so doing, helps ensure that the manager directs others' actions in a coordinated way.

So, let us recap. The facing the future stage of a team's development comprises two elements, managing yourself and developing leaders, each of which comprises six separate and identifiable aspects. Managing yourself requires a manager to both listen to and reflect on what people say. Irrespective of the difficulty of the challenge a manager faces, the manager must control his or her own anxiety, reaching out in an effort to engage, and build trust and credibility with others. Only by engaging, building trust and credibility can a manager gain the agreement of others to take action in ways that enhance the leadership capabilities of those involved as they address the challenges that they face. When others stretch themselves as a result of the choices they make, then those choices help develop the latent leadership potential of all involved. Developing the leadership potential of others constitutes a key aspect of a leader's role. Only by stretching oneself and others can all those involved learn to let go of the past and face the future.

The facing the future stage of a team's development comprises two elements—managing yourself and developing leaders. Each is important if a team is to perform to its full potential. However, before considering the two elements in detail we describe the facing the future stage. We then present the practical indicators that signal a team is first, approaching the facing the future stage and second, has entered it.

Team development

The sixth stage of a team's development, facing the future, commences as members become aware that the task they have been striving to complete is finally within their grasp. We can characterize the facing the future stage by a rising awareness that the team norms and working practices that have become the essence of organizational life are to become obsolete or redundant. They become redundant at the point we clearly recognize that the team will complete the original task, achieve its goal, and will be praised for its achievement. In its natural evolution, the team will soon disperse and its members will move on to other tasks.

We associate the facing the future stage with the loss members feel at the imminent destruction of their team's social system. These negative feelings result in team members naturally focusing on past success, and consequently having difficulty facing the future. The destruction of an established team's social system is something that members will naturally resist, and in practice it is difficult to get them to start the process of disengagement. Therefore, leadership action through the facing the future stage no longer needs to focus on either getting a team to perform or preventing others from stopping it performing.

During the facing the future stage, leadership action must focus on finding new ways to think about the future. Team members' concern with past success must be replaced by debate about current ways of working and how they have resulted in the success all are now enjoying. Refocusing around reasons for success in the present can facilitate dialogue about how new ways of working will influence the way all involved could work in the future. Managers should encourage team members to find new ways of thinking centered in the present and focused on the future to help the individuals involved face the future. Managers help team members identify new opportunities that fulfill both an organizational need as well as individual aspirations. Leadership action must offer hope to members that the conclusion of a team project does not signify a permanent end. Moving on to a new team represents a temporary period of transition as that new team progresses through its own development process.

We closely link the impact of the facing the future stage to the effectiveness with which a team has negotiated its development process. We cannot mourn groups that failed to transform into a team and remained stuck in the one step forward, two steps back stage of their development. Such groups simply drift apart as members complete their task at hand and quickly move on, feeling more a sense of relief than loss. For those groups that successfully transitioned into the behaving as one stage and in so doing transformed into a team, they cannot avoid the facing the future stage. Importantly, we must first recognize the sadness members feel at the prospect of disbanding the team and second, that in the future things will be different. Over enthusiastic attempts for us to raise people's spirits will not help alleviate the emotion they are experiencing.

Those occupying a leadership role should occasionally say something to act as a voice for the team. Such circumstances are never easy and a prescriptive approach is unlikely to work. However, acting as spokesperson comes with leadership territory and effective leaders should not avoid acknowledging the sadness of the moment, but should also remind members of the good times. Instead of focusing on the future when none can envisage a way forward, better to look back at the present from some imagined future. To speak about how all will look back on these times and say to others "I was there" does not explicitly speak about the immediate future. It does, however, remind all that life goes on, and that to have been a part of this was a privilege.

Practical indicators

A team approaches the facing the future stage as its members first realize that they will soon complete the task their team was originally formed to undertake. The work that remains will typically be either fully defined by that which they have already accomplished or associated with formalization and documentation of work they have already completed. During the previous stage, behaving as one, a defining characteristic of the team was its rapid identification and solution of problems in quick succession. In contrast, we do not associate the facing the future stage with problem solving, as essentially, the team has solved all major problems that could prevent it from completing its task. Consequently, team members' attention shifts from problem solving within the team to a more reflective focus on what will happen next.

There are three signs managers can watch for that indicate a team has entered the facing the future stage. The first sign is tangible evidence that the team is completing the task it was originally formed to undertake. Both those inside and outside the team can see clearly that the group is achieving the task-related goals. There may still be some important incomplete parts, but, even here, there is hard evidence of substantial progress. Consequently, the group realizes the purpose and vision for which the team was originally mobilized.

We associate the second sign that a team has entered the facing the future stage with the fact that the team no longer needs to grapple with an endless series of problems. A team enters the facing the future stage as it solves major problems and consequently, the team's leader no longer needs to be a warrior. Therefore, the second sign that a team has entered the facing the future stage is a leader who is him- or herself attempting to imagine new roles and new futures that do not yet exist. The leader has changed from warrior to peacekeeper.

Some organizations are so obsessed with the ongoing battle that the people in them are driven to a point where they do not want to work there anymore. When those leading are only warriors and never peacekeepers they may achieve results, but the people start to look for another place that will actually welcome human beings. To retain good people, a leader must create a welcoming atmosphere that attracts and retains people. A leader must visibly spend time caring about those he or she leads. A leader must take an interest in their welfare, hopes and aspirations and then do whatever possible to help people realize them.

The third sign that a team has entered the facing the future stage is the choices both those inside and outside the team make to publicly recognize the outstanding personal contributions of the highest-performing team members. This is true even if a team's leader is inexperienced or insecure and just plain incapable of recognizing what the group has achieved. Other stakeholders recognize the contribution of key individuals. Team members themselves recognize each others' achievements as they complete particularly challenging pieces of work.

Managing yourself

Managing yourself is the first element of the facing the future stage. There are six aspects to managing yourself, the first is listening to what others have to say and reflecting on what they say. Let us state the obvious; people are as much individuals as you. They perversely insist on behaving like human beings. The only way to discover their strengths, know what they accomplish, and understand their view of the world is to listen to what they say. Scholars who have studied management effectiveness go further, advocating that listening to and reflecting on what people say is not only important in a general sense, but beyond. Failure to listen and reflect is directly responsible for most personality conflicts, as personality conflicts arise when people do not know what other people are doing and how they do their work. They do not know because they have not asked and therefore have not been told.

Throughout the case study, the Traditional Turbine Co., there is evidence that whatever errors of judgment he might have made, Harry did recognize the need to listen to what others had to say. Case Study 2.1, *Into the labyrinth*, illustrates that Harry is primarily focused on listening as he does not want to make a poor first impression as he starts his new job. Harry recognized that his own presumptions as to what people expected of him might be misplaced and that it would take time to find out what his peer group felt was really important.

Although his new boss did not explicitly tell Harry to develop a new product range, Case Study 2.2, *Truth seeking*, illustrates how Harry engaged in what was effectively an extended data-gathering exercise to dig below the surface and find out the real reasons the existing product range was obsolete. Although not immediately apparent, the work Harry initiated to identify technical problems with the existing product range was a form of reflection. Following discussion and debate with his new peer group, Harry then studied relevant aspects of the product range. Harry was able to then continue the dialogue with his peer group on the basis of the new data. In this way, Harry showed respect for others; he listened to what was said, reflected on it, and then sought out factual information to advance the debate.

Over time, the process of listening and reflecting enabled Harry to build a picture of what the Traditional Turbine Co. really needed from a new product range. Case Study 2.3, *Seeing clearly*, illustrates the second aspect of managing yourself, as Harry finally puts the pieces together and sees the bigger picture for the first time. The Traditional Turbine Co. must move away from offering fully bespoke turbines and develop a new range of semi-standard axial exhaust turbines. The way in which Harry could best contribute was to lead the product development team as it developed a new family of axial exhaust turbines, each one smaller than anything available, and, within the industry, widely believed to represent an impossible technical challenge. As such, the case study illustrates how listening and reflecting enabled Harry to first see the bigger picture and second, how best to contribute to it.

Case Study 2.3 may have illustrated how listening and reflecting helped Harry to define his goal, but it did not change the reality that those with whom Harry had to work if he were to be successful worked in different ways. We rejoin Harry as the reality that different people work in different ways comes into focus. The independence that the product development team had enjoyed for so long, with meetings often being more given over to poking fun at "the establishment" rather than actually doing any product development was gone. It was time for the product development team to engage with the wider organization, but in a way that did not destroy what had previously made it successful.

Case Study 7.1 The Traditional Turbine Co.—Personal choice

Project managers! Harry could not escape from them. Company policy required a project manager to oversee a contract, and as there were now two contracts for axial exhaust turbines, it was only a matter of time before a pair of project managers would show their smiling faces around his door.

$\rightarrow$

Harry was aware of the contract-specific submittals and documentation that were both extensive and largely non-technical. It had been hard enough for him to ensure that the technical parts of each contract were consistent with his new product specification. He had made no effort to harmonize the commercial and quality aspects of the contracts. It made sense to have two different project managers, each clearly focused on the needs of one contract only. After all, someone had to take care of the paperwork.

Despite his relaxed approach to a perceived need to split the product development team into two contract teams, Harry was aware of a potential problem. The project managers interpreted the "manager" part of their job title rather more literally than was strictly necessary. They tended to tell others what to do, criticizing them for their lack of action when problems arose rather than getting involved in solving them.

In contrast, Harry perceived himself to be a part of a community, and that his role within that community was to listen, understand, and then ensure his action fit with actual need. Although Harry did not think about it often, he had gradually come to realize that he worked best in a medium-size organization. It was too easy to get lost in a large organization, and too easy to become distracted in a small one. As the Traditional Turbine Co. was a medium-size organization, Harry believed that the way he worked was more appropriate to the needs of the organization, but that did not change the reality that the project managers worked differently.

To worsen matters, the product development team was still working to draft design procedures. They could not finish the design procedures until they completed and finalized the first axial exhaust design. New project managers questioning the product development team's recently established working practices could disrupt its performance. →

Suddenly Harry thought, "Why work it out alone? Why not just ask the product development team members how they wanted to manage the project managers?" Harry knew this was the right approach. The product development team members had a track record of working with the project managers on many other contracts. That track record could help.

Case Study 7.1 illustrates that Harry had understood the third aspect of managing yourself—the need to reach out to others and engage with them, even though it would have been easier for him to disengage. The case study also illustrates that Harry genuinely valued the contribution of product development team members, recognizing that they had knowledge that he did not and further, that that knowledge was valuable. Far too many, and especially people with high knowledge in one area, are contemptuous of knowledge in other areas or believe that being "bright" is a substitute for knowing. Such thinking is intellectual arrogance, a form of personal irresponsibility, and a sign that no matter how gifted an individual, he or she can't reach out and engage others.

Bright people, and especially bright young people, can find engaging with others difficult because they underestimate the importance of good manners. When people work together, there is always the potential for conflict. Good manners are the "lubricating oil" that enables people to work together. Simple things like actually remembering someone's name and saying "please" and "thank you" mean a great deal, facilitating engagement in what could be termed "marginal" situations where it would be easier for those you approach to avoid engagement if given even the smallest of excuses.

Case Study 7.1 illustrates that Harry recognized an obstacle that effectively prevented him from reaching out and engaging with the project managers. Harry was also bright enough to realize that in this instance, approaching the project managers politely would not be enough. If he were to be successful in his efforts to engage the project managers, he needed to work with and through others. Although he was not entirely sure what the obstacle to engaging with the project manager was, Harry hoped that it was an issue over which he could reach a shared view with the product development team members. At least this way, Harry would not face unified resistance. We rejoin Harry as the product development team debates how it should manage the project managers now that they had won the Toronto Light and Power and Budapest University contracts.

**Case Study 7.2   The Traditional Turbine Co.—
One little victory**

In the next product development team meeting, Harry led the discussion on how the two contracts could be run without losing sight of the objective, they were developing one new generic turbine design with each project being no more than a project-specific implementation of that generic design. Despite delivering two turbines, it was critical that they produce one design with the flexibility to accommodate both.

As dialogue continued, clearly Harry could feel that the product development team members were still stuck in their old mind-set, knowing that they needed to apply a generic design to each contract but somehow, they still felt compelled to design two bespoke turbines. After some debate, Doug, the company's chief draftsman spoke up:

> We seem to be missing the point here. I know that we keep falling into the trap of designing bespoke turbines, but it doesn't matter because we keep catching ourselves doing it. We continue to make mistakes but are good enough to catch and correct them before we do any real damage. There is no need to change anything we are doing; we just need to do something about the project managers to ensure that they do not impose unwanted change.

→

Harry was about to point out to Doug that what he had just said was essentially no different from what he himself had said an hour ago when he opened the meeting, but before he could utter a word, Doug continued:

> All we need to do is what we are doing now, but add formal contract reviews between Harry, Per, our chief designer, and me with a project manager. Throw the dog a bone, let them run different meetings the way they want, but don't invite them to any product development team meetings. If any good points emerge from the contract reviews, we just feed them into the next product development team meeting.

Harry thought the idea was almost too simple. He opened his mouth to speak but realized that he had no idea what he was about to say, so shut it again. What would they do? The room had fallen silent, and everyone cast their eyes on Harry as they awaited his decision on how they would oversee the project managers.

"Well," Harry thought to himself, "I asked them for their opinion and they have given me their opinion. I don't like it much but can't think of a better idea. What is the point of asking people what they think if you then ignore what they say?" The silence resonated as a result of the group agreeing with Doug's proposal.

"Let's give the idea a try, Doug," In order to mitigate the tense silence that was overshadowing the meeting room, Harry said,

> Write to all the project managers explaining how we will be working and ask them to confirm which project manager will oversee the Toronto Light and Power contract, which one will handle the Budapest University contract, and when they would like to hold the first contract reviews.

Later, Harry had to admit that he had been wrong to think the approach would not work. Contract reviews were set

$\rightarrow$

up on a biweekly schedule, such that they reviewed one of the two contracts every week. In contrast, the product development team met twice a week, and so remained the main forum for debate.

After the first couple of contract reviews, the project managers each commented that the axial exhaust projects were "self managing" and asked why this was not possible on other projects. Harry avoided telling them that other projects were beset with problems, in no small part, due to their control management style. If this style ever had been appropriate, it most certainly was not now, as the Traditional Turbine Co. reinvented its product range.

Case Study 7.2 illustrates that Harry had, perhaps for the first time when making an important decision, successfully controlled his own anxiety and did not take the product development team's preference as a personal criticism. In so doing, Harry finally understood the importance of the fourth aspect of managing yourself—controlling anxiety and not taking matters personally. Harry's choice to accept Doug's suggestion was a personal choice to put what was best for the team before what was best for him. Harry would have preferred to delegate contact with the project managers to others, thus enabling him to avoid them completely. As we learned earlier, Harry did not like working with the project managers.

Case Study 7.1, *Personal choice,* and Case Study 7.2, *One little victory,* illustrate the latent tension between the product development team that had learned different ways of working and the project managers who had not. Doug's proposed approach for dealing with the situation was insightful. It separated those who were still learning how the new ways of working translated into daily activity from those who had not yet recognized the need to let go of old ways of working.

Specifically, the product development team members were still writing in-depth new design procedures. However, the project managers had no reason not to want to do what they had always done. By holding separate contract and product development team meetings, Harry enabled the product development team to continue formalizing a strategy and implementing what it had so recently learned to do. Simultaneously, the project managers had time to see that the product development team was now working more effectively. Therefore, separate meetings gave the project managers the time they needed to manage their own anxiety while dealing with the prospect of a new way of working.

Case Study 7.2, *One little victory,* also illustrates that Harry was finally developing the trust in others to not reject Doug's idea simply because he did not like it. Harry's newly found trust in others was a consequence of others trusting him. The product development team members' trust in Harry was in part a consequence of Harry's rising awareness of his place within the Traditional Turbine Co. Case Study 7.1, *Personal choice,* illustrates that as Harry matured into his role as the Traditional Turbine Co.'s engineering director, he progressively realized that he "fitted" into a medium-size organization like the Traditional Turbine Co. in a way that he did not fit into either small or large organizations. In this respect he was prepared for the opportunities that came his way because he knew what he should contribute and in turn, what he should expect from others.

A key aspect of Harry's performance was not simply the scale of his contribution to the Traditional Turbine Co. but that he did not think in terms of what he wanted to contribute or what people told him to contribute. The time and effort Harry put into ensuring that the project managers were managed appropriately and effectively illustrates that Harry thought in terms of what he should contribute. Deciding on what he should contribute started with listening to others, reflecting on what they said, and, through a process of dialogue and debate, seeing the bigger picture and how he could contribute to it. As Harry engaged with others he learned to control his own anxiety and not to take proposals from others personally. Harry's increasing ability to "rise above" the issue was a consequence of learning to trust others who in their turn learned to trust Harry.

Harry's leadership action gave him credibility in the eyes of both those with whom he worked and those who worked for him.

Managing yourself such that you have credibility is the sixth, and possibly the most important aspect of managing yourself. It is also the aspect Harry came to appreciate last, and perhaps more than anything else was responsible for the problems he faced.

So, let us recap. We associate managing yourself with making sometimes difficult choices between what is right and what is easy. There are six separate identifiable aspects to managing yourself that underpin any manager's ability to become a better leader:

1. Listening and reflecting on what people say.
2. Seeing the bigger picture and how to contribute to it.
3. Reaching out to others and engaging, even when it would be easier for all involved to disengage.
4. Controlling anxiety and not taking it all personally.
5. Having trust in others and having them trust you.
6. Credibility and others seeing you to have credibility.

Together, the above will enable a manager to first identify what he or she should contribute, and second, gain support for the pursuit of a specific course of action that a manager needs to realize a chosen goal. In so doing, the ability to manage yourself is intertwined with the ability to take leadership action, with the latter facilitated by focusing on the former.

Developing leaders

Developing leaders is the second element of the facing the future stage. Many organizations view leadership as a source of competitive advantage and invest in the development of the individuals occupying leadership roles accordingly. We define leadership development as expanding the collective capacity of organizational members to engage effectively in leadership roles and processes. Leadership roles refer to those that come with and without formal authority. Leadership processes are those that enable teams of people to work together in meaningful ways.

Leadership development involves building the capacity of teams of people to learn their way out of problems that they could not have predicted or arise from the disintegration of traditional organizational structures. Within the context of leadership development, we may consider increased capacity to provide better individual and collective adaptability across a wide range of situations and in so doing, helping those involved when they face unforeseen challenges. Leadership development can help people to break with the past. In practice, leadership development comprises the redesigning of roles to fit actual, as opposed to past, needs, networking and encouraging coordination, and commitment between members of an organization. As people develop as leaders, they are then better able to mould a new future.

Throughout the case study, the Traditional Turbine Co., there is evidence that Harry regarded networking as important and encouraged coordination and commitment between members of the product development team and wider organization. Case Study 3.5, *Changing roles*, illustrates how Harry worked with others and was willing to work differently in response to what he perceived as the needs of others if they were to work effectively. In so doing, Harry demonstrated an appreciation of the first aspect of developing leaders, an understanding of the context within which he found himself and a willingness to do things differently as a consequence of his insight. Working differently enabled the product development team members to engage more fully, and in so doing, start to lead work in their own areas of speciality for the first time.

We traditionally think of leadership as something individuals do, with a sharp distinction between leaders and followers. Within this tradition, consultants and trainers purport that development occurs primarily through training to develop individuals' interpersonal skills and attributes. However, these training approaches ignore the complex interaction between an individual holding a designated leadership role and the social and organizational environment within which they are embedded. In addition to building individual leaders by developing their interpersonal skills and attributes, a complementary perspective approaches leadership as a social process that engages everyone within an organizational community.

Conceptualizing leadership as a social process results in us considering each individual within an organization as a leader. Leadership is then an effect of the way in which individuals work together rather than a cause. From the perspective that leadership is a social process, leadership is an emergent property of effective organizational design. Leadership development from this social perspective consists of using the relational ties between individuals to help build commitment among members of a community.

Throughout the case study, the Traditional Turbine Co., there is evidence that despite his task-oriented personality, Harry recognized the importance of relationships with key stakeholders. Case Study 3.6, *Closer to the edge*, illustrates the way in which Harry focused on developing relationships with key stakeholders inside and outside the product development team. Significantly, the case study illustrates how Harry demonstrated an appreciation of the second aspect of developing leaders—focusing on timing the message to Doug that it was time for him to "get off the fence" and create the first axial exhaust preliminary layout. The case study clearly indicates that Doug did not want to cooperate. Only as a consequence of Harry developing his relationship with key stakeholders inside and outside the product development team did people hear his message.

Timing and positioning the message is the second aspect of developing leaders and is critical to success when attempting to influence others. Case Study 3.6, *Closer to the edge*, illustrates how Harry convinced Doug that as the company's chief draftsman it was his job to create the first axial exhaust preliminary layout. There was no one better qualified for the job and in speaking to Doug, Harry was now focused on the third aspect of developing leaders—giving feedback in a difficult situation. However, not all feedback is either verbal or difficult. Case Study 4.1, *Driving change*, illustrates how a spontaneous round of applause after Doug presented the first axial exhaust preliminary layout did more to communicate how managers regarded Doug than words could have done.

This feedback more than anything else secured Doug's emotional commitment to the aims and objectives of the product development team and was the real tipping point in his development as a leader. Fully committed to the product development team, Doug was able to give team members technical feedback at a level of detail beyond anything Harry could have provided. With over 30 years of experience, Doug simply knew more than Harry about detailed aspects of turbine design. Thus, the giving and receiving of feedback became the mechanism by which Harry facilitated Doug's transformation from reluctant follower to proactive leader.

No doubt, Doug's transformation was a major factor in the eventual success of the product development team. However, in Case Study 7.2, *One little victory*, it is Harry's change that results in Doug really beginning to lead the product development team. Harry accepted Doug's proposal as best for the team, despite personally feeling it was not best for him.

As Case Study 7.2, *One little victory* ends, we see Harry accept that his role as leader of the product development team is now effectively redundant. As product development team members have developed as leaders, they are now capable of achieving independently what Harry had assisted them with previously. We rejoin Harry as he starts to become aware of the reality that those he has been leading have developed as leaders in their own right. Since joining the Traditional Turbine Co., Harry had been constantly working to help both his management colleagues and employees understand how they relate to each other. Harry worked tirelessly to persuade others to coordinate their efforts. That they actually started implementing change still came as a shock to Harry.

Case Study 7.3   The Traditional Turbine Co.—
Turning the battlefield green

Harry had grown accustomed to fighting some new battle everyday, but as the product development team became consumed with the details and complexities of delivering

→

the Toronto Light and Power and Budapest University contracts, Harry felt disconcerted. Back in the pub with Per, discussing how he felt about this desirable, but still rather strange state of affairs, Per commented, "I don't think that there is anyone left to fight."

"There is always someone else to fight," responded Harry, although in truth he knew that this time there wasn't. The last few weeks Harry felt the product development team meetings were more like social events rather than business meetings. In the sessions, they discussed new bids Per was working on with sales, allocation of personnel on future contracts, and the positive and negative aspects of the Toronto Light and Power and Budapest University contracts.

Harry and Per inevitably ended up back in the pub after these meetings. With fewer technical problems to discuss, their attention turned to how the product development team could work more effectively. In essence, without explicitly mentioning it, the conversations really pointed to how Harry could work differently.

As a consequence of the "therapy" sessions with Per, Harry found that during product development team meetings he was no longer directing current issues, but painting pictures of an imagined future. In this imagined future there were more and more contracts for axial exhaust turbines, the sales department worked more closely with engineering who in turn continued to organize around contract teams.

As they discussed that morning's product development team meeting, Per commented:

> I heard the project managers discussing their costs while I worked on another axial exhaust bid in sales. They have just revised their costs down 40% based on the hours booked so far on the Toronto Light and Power and Budapest University contracts. They honestly
>
> $\rightarrow$

believe that it's a consequence of the excellent job they have been doing!

Once Harry and Per had stopped laughing at the absurdity of the idea Harry thought for a moment and then said, "It's better that way. They have to believe they did it themselves if they are to believe in it at all. But, my friend, you and I must learn to live without applause."

The company completed and delivered the Toronto Light and Power and Budapest University contracts on time. Twelve months later the warranties for each contract expired and there were no contract claims. None could remember this ever happening before.

Case Study 7.3 illustrates that the product development team members now coordinated their efforts to a degree that meant Harry no longer had to fight to motivate them to produce. However, this development did not result solely because Harry was the formal leader of the product development team. The product development team's organization meant that leadership was now an emergent property of the way in which its members chose to work together.

Case Study 7.3 illustrates how Harry communicated with not only members of the product development team but also the project managers who in this context constituted the interface with the wider organization. This was not the first time Harry effectively found a way to communicate with others. Case Study 4.2, *Reaching a consensus*, illustrates how Harry organized the product development team around two formal meetings a week. Between meetings, Harry was constantly involved in discussion and debate with both product development team members and also the sales managers who were now involved with launching and selling the new product range. In so doing, Harry did not just communicate with others, but did so with the specific purpose of delineating the necessary roles the product development team needed to adopt to be successful.

Communicating and delineating roles is the fourth aspect of developing leaders and Case Study 4.2, *Reaching a consensus*, describes the first occasion Harry managed to do this.

Case Study 7.3, *Turning the battlefield green*, illustrates how Harry continued to communicate and delineate roles, but now in a different context. As the product development team reached the end of its life, Harry recognized that members must engage in dialogue about the future. Specifically, Harry focused on communicating and delineating the ongoing roles of all involved to clarify how the future would build on current success in an ongoing drive to get the best out of management colleagues and employees.

Case Study 7.3, *Turning the battlefield green*, also illustrates how Harry consciously recognized that in order for him to succeed, he needed the voluntary cooperation of others. This was not the first time that Harry recognized the importance of others' voluntary cooperation. Case Study 5.1, *Getting by with a little help from your friends*, illustrates how Harry consulted with his peer group, finally finding a novel way to address the concerns of product development team members. These members wanted approved design procedures for an axial exhaust before the company took an order for an axial exhaust turbine. However, writing a design procedure required the product development team to actually complete the design of an axial exhaust turbine, something that the Traditional Turbine Co. had never previously attempted without a contract against which to book the cost.

Harry consulted with his peer group, finally agreeing to undertake contract-related engineering without a contract for the first time in the Traditional Turbine Co.'s history. This shift in organizational policy enabled Harry to get the best out of the product development team members who were now able to work "as if" they had a contract without having the time-related pressures that they typically associated with a contract. The above may not seem to represent great or heroic leadership action, but it did represent a basic shift in organizational policy. The product development team members deeply appreciated that Harry was able to effect such change in direct response to their concerns. In their turn, the product development team members responded by fully committing to the design of the new product range. Appropriate leadership action on Harry's part was then directly responsible for getting the best out of others, the fifth aspect of developing leaders.

In addition to illustrating how Harry was becoming increasingly aware of the importance of getting the best out of others, Case Study 7.3, *Turning the battlefield green*, also illustrates how Harry spent an increasing amount of time standing back and reflecting on the world. During product development team meetings, Harry found he was telling stories about how all would work in the future. The process of reflection is not simply a form of storytelling. Even at this late stage in the product development team's development, the technical difficulty of this new approach still resulted in unexpected issues. The product development team was now well equipped to address such challenges. However, the product development team was less well equipped to manage issues associated with how their new way of working would fit into the Traditional Turbine Co. in the future. What would they do next? How could their new work method and strategies continue in the future? Through the product development team's development, Harry intuitively grasped the importance of the sixth aspect of developing leaders—standing back, reflecting on the world, and creating a vision of the future.

Reflection was a way of imagining the future and therefore, a method by which Harry could make sure product development team members were clear about the future and in the process bringing to the surface any final team challenges. The method was effective, at least in part, because it did not attempt to solve problems immediately. Harry never used his authority to force consent; instead he allowed solutions to evolve over time as team members imagined different futures at successive product development team meetings. Over time this iterative process resulted in a form of convergence between the hopes and aspirations of team members and the future needs of the organization into a shared vision of the future.

The wider organization complemented the process of imagining new futures within the product development team by laying out future strategy. Within the wider organization the product development team positively impacted the project managers as a result of their new way of working. Case Study 7.3, *Turning the battlefield green*, illustrates how the company would work in the future combined with concrete evidence that the product development team was working better. As a result, project managers unilaterally volunteered to revise their estimated hours down by 40%. In effect, the project managers accepted that the organization was past the point of no return; the strategy was now set. It was time to embed new working practices into the organization, move on, and focus on how the future would be different.

So, let us recap. We may define leadership development as expanding the collective capability of organizational members to engage effectively in leadership roles and processes. Leadership roles refer to those that come with and without formal authority and leadership processes are those that enable teams of people to work together in meaningful ways. Leadership development involves building the capability of teams of people to learn their way out of problems that they could not have predicted. We can conceptualize this as improving the capability of those involved to build commitment among members of a community in the form of mutual obligations, which they support by reciprocated trust and respect.

Leadership development is intrinsically linked with the specific issues we associate with a specific leadership role. Once a manager occupies a specific leadership role, it is no longer enough to consider how to be a better leader in a general sense. There are six separate identifiable aspects we associate with developing leaders that underpin any manager's ability to be successful in a specific leadership role:

1. Understanding context, responding to context, and, therefore, doing different things.
2. Timing and positioning the message.
3. Giving and receiving feedback.
4. Communicating and delineating roles.
5. Getting the best out of others.
6. Vision, standing back and reflecting on the world.

Together, the above will enable a manager to first identify what he or she needs to realize the latent leadership potential of others and second, gain support for the action associated with its implementation. In so doing, a manager is able to encourage growth by challenging all those involved to move on from followers taking direction to being leaders in his or her own area of responsibility, collectively working toward the realization of a shared vision.

Fitting behavior

Delivery of the first two axial exhaust turbines into service and their trouble-free operation was a major success, both for Harry personally and the Traditional Turbine Co. The product development team never disbanded and continued to meet twice a week to discuss new bids, the latest contracts, and how they would manage them. In effect, the Traditional Turbine Co. replaced its functionally aligned organizational structure with a contract-aligned structure. Although the organizational structure was never formally changed, the creation and use of cross-functional contract teams made a significant impact on how the Traditional Turbine Co. now conducted business.

No matter how we describe the Traditional Turbine Co.'s organizational structure, the sales and engineering departments underpinned interdepartmental cooperation. However, the most fundamental change in working practices was within the engineering department. The new contract teams could only form as a consequence of the engineering department being effectively dismantled, with its members forming the nucleus of each and every team.

Over time the new contract—team-based way of working successfully established itself and helped solve the Traditional Turbine Co.'s internal and external problems. As sales received new enquiries for turbines, the company progressively took for granted the need for the formation of a new contract team to bid for the inquiry and then manage the resulting contract. Over time people ceased to question this. The Traditional Turbine Co.'s culture effectively changed to one based around a new assumption: a dedicated contract team would manage all contracts. Each function within the organization still had its place, the "home" team from which contract team members came. Once they delivered a turbine, they would return to their "home" team. In effect, the Traditional Turbine Co. changed the way it worked to better align itself with the environment within which it was embedded.

Over 100 years ago, the Traditional Turbine Co. had become a great British engineering institution. Its founder had made it successful using a functionally aligned organizational structure. One hundred years later Harry realigned the organization around a contract-based structure, and in so doing, enabled the Traditional Turbine Co. to reengage with its environment and become great again.

As the new contract-based organization became embedded into the Traditional Turbine Co.'s culture, remolding "the way things are done around here," employees forgot there had ever been a leadership battle between Harry and Brian, the company's senior blade designer. The process by which the company designed a new blade did not actually change. What changed was the way in which agreement for the specification of that blade was reached. In effect, Brian was left to perform a necessary technical role but the company allowed him to continue to personally focus on past ways of working. Therefore, he did not play any part in either the Traditional Turbine Co.'s management or leadership. In contrast, Harry was living in the present and focused on the future with no inclination to think about the past. However, sometimes events conspire to bring the past to life. We rejoin Harry as the memory of the leadership battle and the reasons for it come crashing back into the present.

Case Study 7.4   The Traditional Turbine Co.—
A simple truth

Shortly after the Traditional Turbine Co. delivered the axial exhaust turbines to the Toronto Light and Power Company

$\rightarrow$

and Budapest University, Brian collapsed in the office. The rescue squad rushed him to the hospital where he died.

Before Harry joined the Traditional Turbine Co., the doctors had diagnosed Brian with an incurable heart condition. To maintain his dignity, he specifically told his wife he wanted no one to know. After the funeral, while conversing with Harry, Brian's wife suddenly asked, "Are you the one who arranged for him to go to the conference in Orlando?"

Harry confirmed that he had made the arrangements. Brian's wife continued, "I wanted to thank you. He was so much better after he returned. He enjoyed himself again for the first time since he knew about his heart."

It was a cold, clear winter day. Harry watched dust floating in the light streaming through a stained glass window. Somehow he felt he should have done more for Brian, but what? Per approached and gently uttered, "None of us knew, and he didn't want to talk about it. He wouldn't have thanked you if you had tried."

Harry knew he was right, but before he could articulate his thoughts, he felt an unexpected sense of relief. He now understood why Brian turned down the job of engineering director. Why take a job you would not have the time to do? Harry had always believed that the anger and the hatred directed at him were aimed at the engineering director as an authority figure. He believed that it was not personal, that it would have made no difference who landed the job.

However, the choices he made did not change that it had *felt* personal. He was sorry that Brian had died before his time. Nonetheless, it was a relief to finally have insight into Brian's behavior.

The chapel emptied. Remaining behind, Harry watched the dust caught in the light. Aware of the sound of someone
→

> walking toward him, Harry looked up to see Chris, the
> Traditional Turbine Co.'s chief executive, walking away
> from the front row of pews, lost in thought. As he drew
> level with Harry he stopped. As Harry looked up, he was
> sure Chris was about to say something, but he appeared to
> change his mind and started walking again. Harry turned
> his attention back to the dust and light.

Case Study 7.4 illustrates that a way to avoid having to
managing yourself is to blame those around you for your problems. If everything that is wrong with the world is wrong as
a consequence of others, then you avoid having to recognize
the need for personal change. If we reflect upon those we have
known and how we felt about them, we will realize that there
were times when our feelings toward others were more about
us than them.

When we consider Harry's behavior through the facing the
future stage, it is clear that he had matured into his role. Harry
was not only leading the product development team. He had
made a primary contribution to the leadership development of
key members of the Traditional Turbine Co. The working practices developed within the product development team became
embedded within the wider organization. More than anything
else, we associate the facing the future stage with ongoing roles
and responsibilities with the key objective a mutually acceptable
reconciliation between the ongoing needs of the individual and
the organization.

The Traditional Turbine Co. case study illustrates that despite
Harry's driving force at the center of a product development initiative, as he won the battle and the first contracts were placed, he
recognized that the management must allow the rest of the organization to engage. The company now requires others who had previously been uninvolved to be involved and consequently, Harry's
role as a warrior was redundant. Harry did not react badly to this
change of role, reinventing himself as a peacekeeper. In so doing,

Harry demonstrated the first leadership behavior we need at the facing the future stage:

- Accept that a low profile is now the appropriate leadership style.

Harry brought focus to managing the project managers because he took responsibility for the product development team's relationship with the project managers. Within this particular context, that responsibility took the form of finding a way for the product development team to deliver two contract turbines without losing sight of its goal—to create a single generic design that could accommodate contract to contract variations. Harry was well aware that members of the product development team were specialists and could not be in two places at once. Left to their own devices, Harry knew each project manager would focus on his or her own contract, competing to attract the best people.

Harry did not tell the project managers they could not have the best people, but did not break up the product development team either. Harry found a middle way—a way that prevented the product development team from disbanding while still forming two contract teams. Thus, Harry demonstrated the second leadership behavior we need at the facing the future stage:

- Discourage other managers from removing key team members for "important" jobs elsewhere.

Keeping the product development team intact was critical as the company needed to create a single generic turbine design that could accommodate contract-to-contract variations. That was the product development team's goal, and had always been its goal. Notwithstanding, Harry recognized that it was still possible for the product development team to fail if it morphed into two contract teams. Case Study 7.2, *One little victory*, illustrates that the product development team members slipped into old habits designing bespoke turbines. That the product development team members kept catching and correcting each other enabled the team to continue toward its goal. To deviate from the path the product development team was following, to change focus from designing a generic turbine that could be applied to many contracts would have invited failure. Harry intuitively knew that he must ensure the product development team's goal was not changed. In so doing, Harry demonstrated the third leadership behavior we need at the facing the future stage:

- Resist strongly any attempt to change the team's goal at this late stage.

Case Study 7.3, *Turning the battlefield green*, illustrates how Harry increasingly came to regard product development team meetings as social events. This was Harry's term for the process of painting pictures of the future, or looking back at the present from some imagined future. At the time Harry could not have explained this action. However, that busy people with two major contracts to deliver never missed a product development team meeting indicates the importance product development team members placed on Harry actions.

The process of imagining new realities was a process of recognizing that no one wanted to disband the product development team. All involved struggled to come to terms with what they would do next after the state of grace they had come to enjoy ended. Harry's painting pictures of the future and imagining new realities was a form of therapy for both him and other product development team members. An ability and willingness to engage others in this way denote key leadership capability, enabling all involved to move on to new challenges. In so doing, Harry demonstrated the fourth leadership behavior we need at the facing the future stage:

- Recognize that the loss we associate with disbanding the team is because of the "death" of the team social system.

Product development team meetings focused on the specification associated with bids that sales were likely to convert into new contracts. Discussion also covered what was working well and badly as the Toronto Light and Power and Budapest University contracts progressed. This discussion, combined with a debate about how the future might differ from the present facilitated dialogue as to potential future assignments. Product development team members identified potential linkages between their own hopes and aspirations, what should and what could be done differently, and the opportunities open to them. In so doing, Harry demonstrated the fifth leadership behavior we need at the facing the future stage:

- Discuss with individual team members their expectations of the team, if they were fulfilled and requirements from their "follow on" team.

The reorganization of the Traditional Turbine Co. around contract teams embedded the new working practices that the product development team developed in the wider organization. The interdepartmental cooperation between the sales and engineering departments resulted in the organization's most experienced engineers actually knowing what opportunities would become available in the near future for the first time. Consequently, individuals could align their aspiration with future opportunities. In so doing, Harry demonstrated the sixth leadership behavior we need at the facing the future stage:

- Ensure that the management system is in place to organizationally identify "follow on" goals, and assign individuals to teams delivering goals most likely to fulfill individual expectations.

So, let us recap. During the facing the future stage managers need to accept that a low-profile leadership style is appropriate, quietly discouraging other managers from attempting to either disband the team prematurely or attempting to remove key members for "important" jobs elsewhere. A key aspect of a leader's role during the facing the future stage is to recognize the sense of loss members will feel at the destruction of their team's social system.

Leadership action must focus on helping members come to terms with the reality that the state of grace they have come to enjoy is coming to an end. Discussion should focus on establishing members' hopes and aspirations, helping to ensure that they are as far as possible aligned with available opportunities. Changing management systems or organizational structure to ensure new ways of working are embedded is critical. Doing so ensures that what was responsible for facilitating high performance of one team becomes "the way we do things around here" and in so doing, helps to ensure improved performance across the wider organization.

Key learning points

- The facing the future stage comprises two elements, managing yourself and developing leaders.
- Managing yourself starts with listening to what others have to say and then reflecting on what they say before proposing any new course of action.
- Listening and reflecting on what people say helps a manager see the big picture and form a view on how best to contribute to it.
- As a manager moves from listening, reflecting, and forming a view of the bigger picture he or she must reach out to others and engage, even when it would be easier for all involved to disengage.
- We can facilitate reaching out to others and engaging by learning to control anxiety and not taking ideas and suggestions personally.
- As a manager learns to listen, reflect on what is said and engage with others, they also learn to trust others and as a consequence of their considered behavior, begin to gain the trust of those with whom they work.
- Managing yourself well ultimately improves your credibility in the eyes of others, and being seen to have credibility enables a manager to propose and initiate leadership action.
- We may define leadership development as expanding the collective capability of organizational members to engage effectively in leadership roles and processes. It involves building the capability of teams of people to learn their way out of problems that we could not have anticipated.
- Building the capability of a team to learn its way out of problems starts with understanding context, responding to context, and therefore doing things differently.

- As we start to understand the contextual reality of a situation and the challenge a team faces, we also start to understand the need for specific individuals to engage in specific action. Timing and positioning the message is critical when we attempt to influence those involved to take action.
- We closely link influencing others to take necessary action to the ability to give and to encourage feedback.
- The process of agreeing signifies what we should do and how we should facilitate this by communicating with others and delineating their roles within the organization.
- It is only through communicating with others and finding creative ways to address their concerns that a manager can get the best out of others.
- In order to develop the latent leadership potential of those they lead, a manager must develop a shared vision of how the world will be different in the future when all involved have been successful.
- During the facing the future stage leaders help those involved match their hopes and aspiration for the future with the opportunities available within the organization. If done well, this can provide an incentive for people to undertake challenges to help ordinary people develop themselves, taking on wider and more demanding roles and responsibilities that in combination with hard, focused, purposeful work enable ordinary people to achieve extraordinary results.

Want to know more?

- For further insight on being successful as a manager, refer to Olivier (2001).
- For more information on better managing yourself, see Drucker (1999).
- A wealth of information exists on the philosophies and approaches to developing leaders. For leadership as a source of competitive advantage, see McCall (1998) and Vicere and Fulmer (1998).
- In order to perform effectively in a leadership role, see McCauley et al (1998) and Day (2001).
- For leadership, teamwork and developing a cadre of leaders, refer to Hooijberg et al (1999) and Drucker (2004).

- For the training and development of leaders, see Fiedler (1996) and Wenger & Snyder (2000).
- For viewing leadership as a social process, building commitment within communities, see Salancik et al (1975) and Wenger (1998).

CHAPTER 8

Grace under pressure

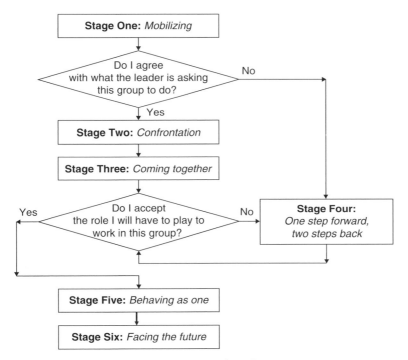

Figure 8.1   The integrated group development process

Source: Compiled by the authors

So, what has been learned? You must develop leadership capabilities if you are to become a better leader. The most relevant
capabilities change from one stage to the next of a team's development. As such, the capabilities most relevant at one stage may
not be at the next. The chapters you have read thus far presented
the elements we associate with each stage of a team's development, and in doing so, clarified the capabilities you must focus
on at each stage if you are to become a better leader.

We used the case study, the Traditional Turbine Co., to illustrate how Harry and the Traditional Turbine Co.'s other key characters exemplify leadership capabilities. Yet, if you had asked Harry at the time what stage the product development team had reached through its development or which leadership capability he utilized in his ongoing effort to make himself a better leader, he would not have been able to tell you. Long after the events described in the case study, Harry met up with some of his former colleagues and through that reunion, he reflected on his actions and described what he had learned. Harry indicated that having the necessary leadership capabilities alone was not enough. Indeed, knowing that one leadership capability was more appropriate than another in a particular context, while a prerequisite, was still not enough to guarantee that leadership action would be effective. To be consistently effective, Harry needed to develop very particular qualities—qualities that, looking back Harry concluded, had made him appear accomplished in the eyes of others when taking leadership action.

It is perhaps most difficult to appear accomplished when taking leadership action under pressure. In this situation, Harry concluded that it was necessary to have what he termed "grace under pressure." Grace under pressure indicates that when under pressure, one must retain a sense of awareness of both the situation within which one finds oneself and others who are also involved. Harry favored the term "grace under pressure," as to lead is to put yourself under pressure, and having grace when under pressure is to remain rational when others are perhaps not, and in so doing, inspire confidence in those around you.

As such, grace under pressure refers to particular qualities of an individual that underpin that individual's ability to deploy appropriate leadership capabilities. We may think of each quality as a distinct and separate "grace." In this context, we can think of a grace as a particular quality we observe in an individual that makes him or her appear accomplished and graceful. The graces that underpin an ability to deploy appropriate leadership capabilities are very different from the leadership capabilities themselves. A leadership capability refers to a form of professional development, a skill an individual has both developed and become capable at applying in a particular context.

In contrast, a grace is a form of personal development, with that development occurring as a consequence of many cycles of action followed by reflection. Over time, as an individual takes action and then reflects on the consequence of his or her action, that individual is progressively more able to behave in an accomplished manner. In the eyes of others, he or she progressively develops grace under pressure.

At the time the events we described in the case study took place, Harry could not have conveyed to you the qualities he later came to refer to as graces. Despite his undoubted professional success, personally he lived in the present and focused on the future. The past was just too raw and painful for him to analyze, let alone discuss with others. Only much later and long after he left the Traditional Turbine Co. did Harry finally understand himself what it meant to have grace under pressure and the graces that underpinned his ability to select the leadership capability appropriate to the context. We rejoin Harry as insight starts to dawn, prompted by the most unlikely of circumstances.

**Case Study 8.1   The Traditional Turbine Co.—
Ten years later**

Winter seemed to be less gray and overcast that year. It was colder and clearer than usual, the sky cloudless as Harry's driver pulled up in front of Heathrow's Terminal Five. Still early, sunlight sparkled on the frost.

"Looks like a good day for flying," the driver commented as Harry paid his fare and grabbed his bag.

Entering the terminal, Harry watched the people busily rushing to catch their flights. With four hours to spare, Harry was relieved he could take his time and retreat into the BA Executive Lounge. As he poured himself a steamy cup of mocha coffee, Harry heard a voice call out his name.

"Harry?" The voice was familiar, but he could not quite place it. "Is that you, Harry?"

$\rightarrow$

Harry looked up and to his complete surprise Chris, the chief executive of the Traditional Turbine Co. was standing before him. Harry had left the Traditional Turbine Co. years ago and had not encountered his old boss since.

Harry looked into Chris' face. There were a few more lines and a few more gray hairs, but there was also an unrecognizable twinkle in his eye. Engaging in conversation as though they had last seen each other yesterday, Harry was happy to see that Chris was so much more relaxed than he remembered him. When he paused, Harry took the opportunity to comment on this transformation. "You look as if you are enjoying life these days."

Chris continued:

> Yes, I have to admit it is a relief not to be under pressure now. I retired this time last year and, looking back, I probably should have done so years ago. Don't get me wrong, I'm very proud to have achieved what we did at the Traditional Turbine Co., but it really was time for me to go. In the end, I was the last of my generation to move on.

Harry sat back in his chair, contemplated this comment, and then realized that he had moved on from the Traditional Turbine Co. for much the same reason that Chris had retired. "Now that you mention it, looking back, I realize that I decided to leave after Per retired. We had developed the product range, new people were coming into the company, and, without Per, it just seemed like the right time to go."

There was silence for a while as the two friends reflected on the conversation. Chris then broke the silence. "I saw Per again recently."

"How is he these days?"

$\rightarrow$

"Frail, but still in good spirits."

As Chris spoke, Harry suddenly knew that he wanted to see his old friend again. Before he could articulate this thought, Chris spoke again. "We should get together, you know. It's been ten years now and that seems as good an excuse as any. Why don't I give John, Natasha, Doug, and Per a call to work something out?"

As Harry walked toward his departure gate passing shops and restaurants, the idea of a reunion seemed appropriate. He realized that he was really looking forward to seeing his old friends, talking about old times, and perhaps making some sense of them.

Case Study 8.1 illustrates that the passage of time enabled Harry to see past his preconceptions about Chris. Harry recognized that he had, at times, felt under pressure when working at the Traditional Turbine Co., and so it was hardly surprising to learn that Chris had too. At the time the events we describe in the case study took place, neither Harry nor Chris was able to speak to the other about the pressure they were under. However, the passage of time enabled them to acknowledge that Chris, John, Natasha, Doug, Per, and Harry had all been under pressure. As the change process in the Traditional Turbine Co. progressed, they each developed, learning to deal with the pressure, and by the end they had learned to do so with good grace.

When we reflect on the Traditional Turbine Co. case study, the particular qualities that the key characters developed provide an insight into the nature of what Harry later came to term the graces that underpinned his ability to take leadership action. Throughout the case study the key characters remained grounded despite the pressure they were experiencing. Taking leadership action and choosing one course of action in preference to others can only be effective if you are grounded, accepting, and understanding of the reality of a situation. As such, the first grace is *grounded under pressure*.

Second, the Traditional Turbine Co.'s key characters were able to deal with a succession of difficult situations requiring great personal resilience on their part. The case study illustrates that the Traditional Turbine Co. was, at times, a tough place to work, and made more so when attempting to drive unpopular change. To survive a leader must be resilient. As such, the second grace is *resilience under pressure*.

Third, despite finding themselves under pressure, the Traditional Turbine Co.'s key characters never stopped believing that the only way to succeed was to work together. As organizations progressively shift toward knowledge-based working, the ability to influence and be influenced by a team during the implementation of a common task is becoming increasingly important. As such, the third grace is *collaboration under pressure*.

Fourth, as the Traditional Turbine Co.'s key characters worked with others, they accepted that they must be adaptable, changing plans as new information came to light. The nature of team work is one that depends on members building on each other's suggestions and strengths as they develop solutions to the problems they face. As the team identifies solutions, they may involve all concerned working in ways very different from those initially anticipated. As such, the fourth grace is *adaptability under pressure*.

Fifth, the Traditional Turbine Co.'s key characters never burdened others with an overlarge ego. They had the maturity to remain focused on the issues at hand, irrespective of their pressures. It is critical for a leader to embrace a mature approach to all aspects of managerial work if he or she is to gain the trust of others. As such, the fifth grace is *maturity under pressure*. Thus, we have identified the five graces which managers should consider and embrace when taking leadership action:

- Grounded under pressure.
- Resilience under pressure.
- Collaboration under pressure.
- Adaptability under pressure.
- Maturity under pressure.

Grounded under pressure

Why is it so hard to be grounded under pressure and to accept reality for what it is? It is so obvious when we watch others avoiding reality that they are doing so. The obese man claims he has no idea why he is overweight while eating a doughnut. An employee refuses to use a computer and then claims to have no idea why he loses his job. It is not hard to see that these people are avoiding painful realities. The obese man is overweight because he eats too much and rarely exercises. The manager who fires the employee does so because he refused to maintain and update his skills and has consequently become progressively less relevant to a changing organization. If people acknowledged these painful realities, they would inevitably realize a compelling need for unwelcome change.

The defensive processes we all engage in, to a greater or lesser extent, are a form of self-deception. Scholars who have studied the psychology of self-deception have concluded that the dynamic of information flow within and among us points to a particularly human malady: to avoid anxiety, we close off crucial portions of awareness, creating blind spots. This applies both to self-deception and shared illusions, leading to delusion, the cloudiness of mind that leads to misperception of the object of awareness. The cure for delusion is insight—seeing things as they are—which equates to a comprehension that is undistorted by the defensive urge to avoid anxiety.

We rejoin Harry as he arrives for the reunion dinner. This meeting will remind all of past events and interestingly, with the passage of time, the Traditional Turbine Co.'s key characters will see past their cloudiness of mind. The painful realities they had been avoiding for ten years finally come into awareness.

Case Study 8.2 The Traditional Turbine Co.—
Denial and isolation

Walking into the restaurant, Harry felt a sudden sense of relief as his old friends crowded round and shook his hand,
→

asking how he was and what he was doing now. Catching up on their lives, clearly, everyone was pleased to be there.

Gathered around the dinner table, John proposed a toast which temporarily interrupted the laughing and joking, but soon enough they resumed with renewed enthusiasm. As the starter arrived, the conversation lulled. Chris seized the opportunity to speak to everybody for the first time.

"You know, despite my organizing this evening, I really wasn't sure if I wanted to come, but I'm glad I did." A gentle silence fell as they reflected on Chris' comment. Chris continued. "While organizing this reunion I found myself thinking about things we did together and actually, some things we did, but not together." Chris paused before continuing. "Do you remember the time you ordered the first axial exhaust casing without telling me?"

"You found out about that?" Harry asked, slightly apprehensively. He had always assumed that Chris had not noticed that particular transgression.

"Yes, John and Natasha told me after we won the first order. They didn't really have much choice as it was the only way to explain the rationale to deliver in nine months what should have taken 14."

"Sorry. Should have mentioned it, I suppose ... ." said Harry.

Chris responded:

> Don't apologize!
>
> It wasn't a very pleasant experience, realizing that you had no other choice than to go behind my back, but I did learn a hard lesson. You need to be realistic. It's I that should be apologizing to you. By making the assumption that you couldn't design a casing that we could use on any contract, I now realize that I became part of the problem.

$\rightarrow$

I never forgot that. I have always remembered that I must be realistic, even when reality isn't very nice. I don't blame you for what happened. Well, not now, although looking back I probably did at the time!

Listening to Chris, the others perceived that there was no resentment in his words. But in fact, up until that moment, Chris had avoided the painful reality that the group had gone behind his back. At the time, believing that they were against him had been easier than accepting the truth that under pressure he had been unable to see reality for what it was.

Case Study 8.2 illustrates that Chris was finally able to say what he had always known but had been unable to acknowledge. While the others might have accepted the reality of their situation, he had not. His anxiety at the prospect of a reunion sprang from his fear of bringing the past to life. If the past was brought to life, it would make it harder for him to avoid the reality that the success for which he had taken credit as the Traditional Turbine Co.'s chief executive was partly in spite of his inability to accept and deal with reality, not because of it.

In truth, Chris had for many years wanted to acknowledge the debt he owed John, Natasha, Doug, Per, and Harry. Case Study 7.4, *A simple truth*, illustrates how he found himself alone in an empty chapel with Harry and had tried to find words to express himself. However, the need to avoid anxiety overwhelmed him, causing his mind to blank. Before he knew it he was leaving the chapel. Cloudiness gripped his mind thus sparing him from facing a painful truth for a little longer—ten years longer as it turned out.

Cloudiness of mind is a luxury leaders cannot afford. It is vital to remain grounded, acknowledging the reality of a situation whatever the pressure. Only by seeing a situation as it really is can one take positive action to impact events as they unfold. That is why the first quality of leadership is grounded under pressure, underpinning every leadership capability at every stage of a team's development.

Resilience under pressure

Why is it so hard to be resilient under pressure? Clear evidence indicates that many people are not. Listen to many conversations in a bar or restaurant when people are not under pressure and you might conclude that these people are going to change the world. However, the next day they drag themselves to work and are very different. Their grand plans and great ideas have evaporated as they watch the clock waiting for the moment they can escape from their dreary job only to dream once again with their friends. It never enters their head that they have created their own miserable reality one piece at a time as they persistently fail to face up to and follow through on the tough decisions in life.

If we reflect on the Traditional Turbine Co. case study, more then anyone else, Doug had to face the inevitability of unwelcome and unwanted change. As Harry tore up the Traditional Turbine Co.'s historic product range, he was also tearing up Doug's life work—a product range in which he had invested over 30 years. To see your life's work torn up in this way is to find yourself under pressure. Rising to the challenge of leading the team that will rebuild it requires a level of resilience that is more than difficult to comprehend, but that is precisely what Doug did. We rejoin the reunion as it gets into full swing.

Case Study 8.3   The Traditional Turbine Co.—Don't look back in anger

Laughing and joking, the temporary seriousness evaporated as the old friends engaged in conversation. Chris realized that he had unconsciously made assumptions that he had then defended rather than challenged. The others

→

recognized a part of themselves in what he said, but did not feel the need to dwell on the subject.

During his tenure with the Traditional Turbine Co., Harry had spent much time with the product development team, so it was natural for him to also spend much of the evening talking with Doug and Per. After all, it was remarkable that ten years later their competitors were still not offering a comparable product range.

"You know," Harry said, "The devil is in the detail. Our competitors probably have sold an axial exhaust turbine, but have had in-service problems and then stopped."

"You could be right," said Doug. "The detail wasn't easy. In the end I had to make the exhaust end bearing fixed. We had never done that before. That was why we needed to rewrite every design procedure, not just those dealing with the exhaust."

The three friends were quiet for a moment before Per spoke. "That you nailed the design procedures, got them right in the end, is all the more surprising when I remember how Harry and I really had to argue our case to persuade you to commit to the project at all!"

Doug was thoughtful for a moment before speaking:

> I remember you two coming to visit me and not taking 'no' for an answer. Told me it was my job as chief draftsman to get what had been done down on paper. I remember Harry saying, 'if you don't find a way, no one will.' Now I come to think about it, I really hated you both for putting me under such pressure!
>
> But what Chris said earlier is true. You have to be grounded and accept reality for what it is. I have always been able to recover from shock. I don't like feeling as if I want to run away, and so I get my head down in the end and get on with it. I came round to the idea of a
>
> $\rightarrow$

new product range eventually, and I can say that when I finished that first layout I did privately admit to myself that you were right.

"I don't remember you ever mentioning that before!" said Harry. They all laughed before Doug answered. "Well, it's easy enough to forgive someone for being wrong. What I just can't forgive is someone for being right! I remember at the time I didn't like being wrong, but I learned a hard lesson. You have to listen and be adaptable, even if you don't like what you hear.

Case Study 8.3 illustrates that Per and Harry for the first time recognized the scale of Doug's contribution to the new product range. It was Doug, and not Per or Harry, who led the effort to turn problems into solutions with realistic detailed drawings that would serve as blueprints to actually manufacture a viable product line. Yet, Doug had opposed Harry's actions when he joined the Traditional Turbine Co. However, looking back, who could blame him for that? When he joined the Traditional Turbine Co.'s Board of Directors, Harry was inexperienced and naïve. From a purely objective perspective, Doug's initially negative attitude was entirely rational.

Yet, over time Doug changed his mind, and if we look at ourselves in the mirror, how many of us can honestly say that we changed our mind about someone who initially made a poor first impression and did so under real pressure? Despite knowing better than anyone else the complexities of delivering axial exhaust turbines without design procedures, Doug resolved to work tirelessly through countless design issues without complaining or seeking recognition.

Resilience under pressure is a difficult concept to convey to those who have never experienced pressure. There are times when it really would be easier to stop, but you don't, not because you are a hero or superhuman, but for no other reason than you choose not to. Why persist? Why bother? Why care? Because the manager chooses to! Resilience under pressure is as much an attitude of mind as it is a quality of leadership. It is recognizing that strength of character is as necessary as leadership skill. Ultimately, it's a matter of pride.

For those who presume to lead others, giving up is not an option as people perceive this poorly. It is vital to engage, focus, and find a way when events conspire against you. Through preparedness to do more, risking, and caring more than others think prudent you are able to truly become resilient under pressure. That is why the second quality of leadership is resilience under pressure, underpinning every leadership capability at every stage of a team's development.

Collaboration under pressure

Why is collaborating under pressure so hard? When there is no pressure it is easy to draw a veil over our behavior. We are polite. We show interest in others. However, when situations become difficult we quickly pull back the veil. No longer is it a priority for us to engage with those who are not aligned with our own way of thinking. As we succumb to pressure, we retreat into a safe place, focusing on what matters to us. As we disengage, we become increasingly marginalized and increasingly unable to lead.

If we reflect on the case study, Natasha had the most compelling reasons not to engage with Harry as the pressure started to mount. Natasha came from a working class background, had left school at 16, and worked her way up the hard way. In contrast, Harry was middle class, privileged, and had been shielded from the harsh reality of real-world survival. Coming from worlds apart, Harry and Natasha found a way to come to a meeting of the minds. We rejoin the reunion as the six friends laugh and joke while waiting for dessert.

Case Study 8.4   The Traditional Turbine Co.—
Bargaining with the devil

It was already dessert time! The evening had flown by as the friends lifted their glasses for another toast. Natasha and John confessed that Harry had pressured them to sell the idea of a new product range to Doug to "soften him up" before Per and Harry's full frontal assault. That Doug was genuinely surprised at the news just made it funnier.

"You didn't exactly escape without Harry putting you under pressure though, did you?" Doug retorted after Natasha finished describing how badly he reacted to their efforts. "I remember plotting with Harry how we would slip Per into your department unnoticed."

With a thoughtful expression, Natasha answered, "No, I suppose not. I woke up one day, came into the office and found Per running it for me. Nothing personal Per, but you were as welcoming as the bubonic plague."

"No offense. I've been called worse before and probably will be again."

"It really wasn't rational, but when I realized you had invaded my department, I was apoplectic with rage. You had double-crossed me!"

Pausing, Natasha stopped laughing and remembered the anger she had really felt:

> It wasn't nice, but I learned that if you are really committed to working in a team, you have to accept that it will be necessary to give something up. Since then I have quite consciously thought through the difference between what I need and what I want. When I am able to separate the two in my mind, it becomes much easier to let the things go that I want. It's not easy, but looking back at what we did, it's obvious to me now that we would never have been able to do it without collaborating.

Case Study 8.4 illustrates how Natasha learned to accept that to enjoy the upside we associate with collaborating with others, it was also necessary to accept the downside. It is necessary to give something up when working with others. In a general sense, we forfeit autonomy and control. Without collaboration you are autonomous and, for better or worse, have control over the course of action you choose to pursue. As soon as you collaborate with others, the reality that what is best for the team might or not be best for you personally comes into sharp focus.

Despite the problems inherent in working together, Case Study 8.4 illustrates that Natasha recognized that the Traditional Turbine Co.'s key characters were able to do together what none could do alone. Consequently, because of their belief in the value of good working relationships, they were ultimately able to collaborate despite individually having to forfeit something important. Natasha succeeded in her professional relationships because she worked at making them successful. A belief in the fundamental need for good working relationships meant that they were willing to put time and effort into building and maintaining them. Good working relationships, in turn, made it easier to forfeit something when collaborating, and in so doing, do what was right for the team.

For those who presume to lead others it is simply not enough to be purely task focused. Leaders must build a network of relationships which they can draw upon, particularly when under pressure. Only with the help of a good network can we address and resolve difficult and unforeseen problems. That is why the third quality of leadership is collaboration under pressure, underpinning every leadership capability at every stage of a team's development.

Adaptability under pressure

Why is it so hard to adapt under pressure? Many people fixate on a particular solution and fail to see the importance of working differently in response to new ideas. The need to adapt is crucial when we respond to unforeseen problems. We facilitate solutions to such problems when we are willing to adapt, so all team members cooperate rather than oppose the solution or do as they wish.

Those aspiring to improve their leadership must work at developing the skill of adaptability. If we reflect on the Traditional Turbine Co. case study, John had the lowest profile role but was also involved in making and implementing difficult decisions. Other key characters wanted him around and went out of their way to make sure he was. In Board meetings John answered most of Chris' questions and presented the most. John reported, without drama, company decisions at Board meetings. If Doug were the Traditional Turbine Co.'s engine, then John was the lubricating oil enabling it to function without excessive friction. We rejoin the reunion as the evening winds down over coffee.

Case Study 8.5   The Traditional Turbine Co.—Black dog

The restaurant was generally less noisy as Harry drank his coffee. On balance, he thought it had been a remarkably good evening. That Chris, Doug, and Natasha could speak openly and comfortably was a compliment to the rest of them. Unknowingly, Harry suddenly found himself wondering if John had anything he wanted to say. A low-key kind of guy, he probably wouldn't volunteer unless somebody asked. "John, is there anything you remember from our time together at the Traditional Turbine Co.? Anything you learned that really stands out in your mind?"

Pausing, John reflected on their team efforts. "I remember that you didn't seem to be able to put any kind of plan together and stick to it! You kept getting stuck, coming up with some new work-around, and then almost immediately got stuck again. I remember feeling angry at you for not being able to fulfill your promises."

$\rightarrow$

John continued,

> I started to realize that it was not that you didn't plan so much as you couldn't plan. What you where trying to do was too difficult to make any kind of detailed plan possible. There were too many unknowns. Realizing this, I also recognized that I had to adjust. Instead of complaining that things were not working out as expected, I became involved in finding a way round the problem.
>
> I didn't like it. There was supposed to be a plan with a time scale and a budget and I wanted you to deliver the new product range on time and on budget. However, I learned that it is not always so simple. The difficulty of our task meant that there would be unforeseen and unforeseeable problems. I could either roll with it and help solve them, or criticize from the sidelines. I guess I learned that it is better to be part of the solution.

As John stopped speaking, Per spoke up. "We had some unforeseen problems, but not all of them were unforeseeable. Both Harry and I learned that we had to plan better toward the end. Because we just don't have it in us to plan, we eventually involved project managers. In hindsight we should have involved them earlier."

"It's a tricky balance." said Harry. "It's not just adapting when circumstances change. It's also about having a flexible attitude towards how you work. I learned that I needed to plan more and plan earlier. As I remain completely incapable of doing so, a project manager is now a mandatory part of every product development team I have formed since leaving the Traditional Turbine Co.!"

Chris said:

> That's slightly ironic. We have been listening to an accountant, who by definition had the least opportunity
> $\rightarrow$

of any of us to be flexible in his professional role, talk about flexibly adapting! It seems that John learned that to be part of a team you must abandon rigidity and predictability. You must accept that just because something has always been or was supposed to be done one way does not mean that it should or will be done that way in the future.

The mood lifted as the waiter brought more coffee. Harry could not help but think how everybody had taken away something different from their experience. What he had always thought of as the truth was in fact, only one point of view.

Case Study 8.5 illustrates that leadership action does not have to be high profile or heroic in order to be effective. The role John chose was effective largely because it was not. However, beyond John's preferred style was a leadership quality he both naturally possessed and had worked to develop. He would think before he spoke and had the flexibility of mind he needed to offer considered responses in unexpected situations.

How many can really say that we are adaptable, particularly when we are under pressure? How many vent their irritation on those who speak up and complain that their plans are to fail and that they are forced to rethink? We live in an uncertain world, however, where the best laid plans regularly go astray. If we reflect on the Traditional Turbine Co. case study, there were many occasions when team players needed to reconsider the action and implement new decisions in light of changing information or circumstances.

For those who presume to lead others, dogmatically persisting with plans they develop on the basis of assumptions that have become obsolete is not an option. Leaders must vitally recognize the reality that the world does change in unexpected ways and therefore, they must be prepared to both replan and adapt to circumstances as they change. That is why the fourth quality of leadership is adaptability under pressure, underpinning every leadership capability at every stage of a team's development.

Maturity under pressure

Why do apparently capable, experienced, and knowledgeable adults revert to childlike emotions when under pressure? We have all seen it. When things do not go as planned or intended, there is always one who starts ranting at everyone else or who sulks because he or she has not gotten his or her own way. Yet, while we ourselves engage in such behavior, we expect our own leaders to be exempt. Leaders should be wise and insightful, always knowing the best thing to do. Rightfully and properly so, we expect such behavior from our leaders, and if occasionally our own behavior does not match up to such high ideals, we rationalize that this is perfectly acceptable given the circumstances—except it's not.

To expect one thing from our own leaders while at times behaving very differently with those we lead is not reasonable. Behaving well in front of the chief executive and in an inconsiderate way toward more junior staff is contradictory and unprofessional. It indicates that an individual is not and may never be ready for the responsibility we associate with leading others.

If we reflect on the Traditional Turbine Co. case study, clearly, had there been a prize for "most improved student," Harry would have secured first place. However, Harry was not universally held in the highest regard within the Traditional Turbine Co. All Board members did not feel comfortable approaching Harry for confidential advice. Without doubt, Per was best able to remain calm and rational when others were becoming emotional and losing their perspective. Per was everpatient with people and never came across as the all-knowing wise man. We rejoin the reunion as the conversation shifts to a more serious subject matter.

Case Study 8.6 The Traditional Turbine Co.—
The unconditional agreement of acceptance

Harry found his thoughts drifting back to John's comments and realized that sometimes he had fixated on the task at hand and what he wanted to achieve. Sometimes he was so focused that he did not realize his inability or unwillingness to adapt. Commenting to Per that adaptability was not his strong point, Per was about to agree, but then changed his mind. "No doubt adaptability is important, but it's not the only important thing. Do you remember the time you tried to persuade the product development team to take more risk? You kept telling members to guess, but they wouldn't. Finally, I had to tell you to let me tell them to guess instead."

Harry hadn't recollected the incident until Per mentioned it, "You persuaded them to do something I couldn't, so it made sense to switch roles. I can tell you I was really angry about it though! I blamed you for a while, then the product development team, and finally the project managers who were safely out of the way so couldn't object to me blaming them!"

Per thoughtfully responded, "No, it was definitely your fault that they wouldn't guess when you asked them. You didn't know enough to tell them how to guess. I'm glad to see you're over it now."

The two friends laughed before Harry spoke again. "I kept repeating that line from the song by the Rolling Stones, *You Can't Always Get What You Want*, but if you try sometimes you'll get what you need."

"Better not give up your day job. I don't think you are going to make it as a rock star!"

"I guess the point I'm trying to make is that I learned the hard way that there is no point in sulking, getting angry, or becoming emotional.

$\rightarrow$

Listening to them, Chris commented on something he always wanted to know. "But you always got on so well, cracking jokes, and finding humor in the most difficult of situations."

Per thoughtfully responded, "It's the way Harry and I deal with pressure, and make it easier for other people to deal with pressure. Some people hold their head in their hands and cry; others laugh. You have to do one or the other, although at times I concede that our jokes were so bad they could make you cry."

Harry sat back in his chair and reflected on this comment. Per was right. Humor played a large part in discussing the undiscussable when under pressure. It was hard to accept that you can't always get what you want in life, but the sooner you learn to accept that and to do so with good grace, the better. If he couldn't do so with good grace, then doing so with good humor was better than not doing so at all.

Case Study 8.6 illustrates that even though Chris had worked with Per and Harry for years, only now he had insight into a reality that others had always known. For Per and Harry the humor was a coping mechanism that allowed them to discuss difficult issues in a less stressful way. Their humor was a mechanism to give and ask for feedback and make others feel able to engage. It was a way for them to lift the spirits of others who might otherwise just give up.

For those who presume to lead others it is essential to find a way to be human and for others to perceive you as someone with humanity. Per and Harry found that humor worked for them, but what worked for them would not necessarily work for others. We must each find a way to engage those we lead at a human level, not as leader and follower. Only by being human and having humanity and the maturity to do so under pressure can we get the best out of others. That is why the fifth quality of leadership is maturity under pressure, underpinning every leadership capability at every stage of a team's development.

The audacity of hope

Why do people give up under pressure? The evidence that they do is all around us. It is more usual for organizational initiatives to fail than to succeed, but why? We conceive many excellent initiatives that would benefit our organization if we implemented them. More often than not, these great ideas just float in the air but never crystallize into action. A reason for this is that when under pressure some people seek to escape. They either slump in front of the television watching reality shows or drink excessively to temporarily forget their daily problems and challenges. It is easier to opt out than to take action. Fear of change often plays a role in capable peoples' reluctance to initiate, thus preventing action which translates into results.

In the Traditional Turbine Co. case study, if anyone had cause to want to escape the problems of his world it was Harry. There were moments when Harry wanted to give up, but he remained steadfast. We rejoin the reunion as Harry sips his brandy, reflecting on the evening's conversations.

Case Study 8.7   The Traditional Turbine Co—
An antidote for despair

Harry wondered how others succumbed to despair when after no more than a moment he could find a way to struggle on. "There must be a reason," he thought. After all, it was only natural to abandon hope in the most difficult of times. And quite suddenly, without expectation, Harry was talking about something that had never previously occurred to him:

> I know now the one common factor. Hope. It gives a sense of mission in life, and when I think about everything
> $\rightarrow$

that happened during my time at the Traditional Turbine Co., I don't think I ever lost hope for more than a moment before pulling myself together.

I held onto hope in the form of determined optimism and that helped to maintain my spirits. It enabled me to endure more tests when everything became such a strain. My optimism was both a form of rationalization for my suffering and simultaneously a form of temporary denial. I now see why I was able to lead others. My optimism encouraged people to embrace their own hope and my continued enthusiasm filtered downward, especially in difficult times. They showed confidence in me because I allowed for such hope, realistic or not.

In retrospect, I realize that I never conveyed a sense of hopelessness to those around me, even while acknowledging the seriousness of a situation. As a direct consequence, others took their own strength from me, finding the strength to make a comeback in one way or another.

Harry stopped talking, as an epiphany hit him for the first time. A great weight had been lifted from him. He felt a sense of closure and knew it was time to move on.

Case Study 8.7 illustrates that Harry had finally recognized a truth that had, up until that moment, eluded him. Hope sustains us. The ability to deal with difficult situations is a consequence of holding onto hope. Hope enables us to have grace under pressure. Hope is a state of mind that enables us to be grounded, resilient, collaborative, adaptable, and mature under pressure. It is hope that underpins our ability to have grace under pressure and the state of mind Harry recognized and embraced during his tenure at The Traditional Turbine Co. Hope sustains us in particularly difficult times and is the mental state that is the essence of an individual's relationship with a team.

It's only a model

The ideas and concepts around which we wrote this book can help you to get the best out of the teams within which you work, but it is not a substitute for the inner drive mandated of those who presume to step into a leadership role. We, the authors, firmly believe that anyone who wants to be a better leader can be. Not everyone, however, wants to be a leader. You must want to make a difference and have an idea about how to do it, otherwise you are a follower. Good leaders are enthusiastic; they motivate people. They have humanity and humility and, at times, must be tough and demanding but always fair. Leaders must deliver the goods, so they must be clear and direct about the tasks at hand. You must sacrifice your reputation as an all round "nice" guy without resorting to aggression. You must remain positive and always communicate, expressing ideas simply and directly. This book, therefore, will help you become a better leader, but only if you really desire this goal. A love of office and the privileges of rank are not enough.

Throughout this book we have used the Traditional Turbine Co. case study to illustrate what a team's developmental stages means in practice. At another level it clarifies the significance of grace under pressure because the Traditional Turbine Co. case study is a story about people who find themselves under pressure. To say that the Traditional Turbine Co. is a story is not, however, in any way a criticism. A story can transform dry and abstract concepts into compelling pictures in the reader's mind.

When contemplating the use of stories, scholars have concluded that we construct them about ourselves—where we come from and where we are going. Five key elements are present in all great stories:

- A protagonist the listener cares about. The story must be about a person or team to whose struggle we can relate.
- A catalyst compelling the protagonist to take action. Somehow the world has changed so that something important is at stake. Typically, the first act of a play is devoted to establishing this fact. It's up to the protagonist to put things right again.

- Trials and tribulations. The story's second act commences as obstacles produce frustration, conflict, and drama, and often lead the protagonist to change in an essential way. The trials reveal, test, and shape the protagonist's character. Time is spent wandering in the wilderness, far from home.
- A turning point. This represents a point of no return, which closes the second act. The protagonist can no longer see or do things the same way as before.
- A resolution. This is the third act, in which the protagonist either succeeds magnificently or fails tragically.

This is the classic beginning-middle-end story structure defined by Aristotle more than 2,300 years ago which countless others have used since. It reflects how the human mind wants to organize reality. That is why the Traditional Turbine Co. case study uses this classical structure to tell the story of Harry, our protagonist.

So, let us recap. All groups pass through stages as they develop into high-performing teams. The leadership capabilities appropriate at one stage are not necessarily appropriate at the next. Grace under pressure underpins the ability to apply leadership capabilities appropriately. In this context, grace refers to the five qualities of leadership that collectively enable individuals to form teams that comprise environments within which their members are able to do together what no individual could do alone. Above all, a state of mind sustains the ability to have grace under pressure and that state of mind is hope—the essence of an individual's relationship with the teams of which they are a part. Hope sustains us in particularly difficult times and enables us to go on and in so doing, find pathways through hindrance we would not otherwise have found.

Chapter 1

Aristotle (1986), *Nichomachean Ethics*, Translated by Irwin, J., Hacket Publishing Company, Indianapolis, IN.

Avolio, B.J., Jung, D.I., Murry, W., & Sivasubramaniam, N. (1996), "Building Highly Developed Teams: Focusing on Shared Leadership Processes, Efficacy, Trust and Performance," in Beyerlein, M.M., Johnson, D.A., & Beyerlein, S.T. (Eds.), *Advances in Interdisciplinary Studies of Work Teams*, Vol. 3, pp. 173–209, JAI Press, Stamford, CT.

Bernard, L.L. (1926), *An Introduction to Social Psychology*, Holt, New York.

Chidambaram, L. & Bostrom, R.P. (1996), "Group Development (I): A Review and Synthesis of Development Models," *Group Decision and Negotiation*, Vol. 6, pp. 159–187.

Fiedler, F.E. (1967), *A Theory of Leadership Effectiveness*, McGraw-Hill, New York.

House, R.J. and Mitchell, R.R. (1974, Fall), "Path-Goal Theory of Leadership," *Journal of Contemporary Business*, Vol. 3, No. 4, pp. 81–98.

Kakabadse, A.P. (2000), "From Individual to Team Cadre: Tracking Leadership for the Third Millennium," *Journal of Strategic Change*, Vol. 9, pp. 5–16.

Kakabadse, A.P. & Korac-Kakabadse, N. (1998), "History of Leadership," in Kakabadse, A.P., Nortier, F., & Abramovici, N.B. (Eds.), *Success in Sight: Visioning*, pp. 35–72, International Thomson Business Press, London.

Manz, C.C. & Sims, H.P. (1993), *Business Without Bosses*, John Wiley & Sons, New York.

Martin, R. (2007), "How Successful Leaders Think," *Harvard Business Review*, R0706C, June, Vol. 85, No. 6, pp. 60–67.

Nietzsche, F. (1969), *The Will to Power*, Vintage, New York.

Pearce, C.L. & Sims, H.P. (2000), "Shared Leadership: Towards a Multi-Level Theory of Leadership," in Johnson, D.A. & Beyerlein, E. (Eds.), *Advances in Inter-Disciplinary Studies of Work Teams, Vol. 7 Team Development*, pp. 115–139, Elsevier Science, New York.

Sheard, A.G. (2007), "An Examination of Leadership Development: A Role Based Perspective," PhD Thesis, University of Northampton.

Sheard, A.G. & Kakabadse, A.P. (2002), "From Loose Groups to Effective Teams: The Nine Key Factors of the Team Landscape," *Journal of Management Development*, Vol. 21, No. 2, pp. 133–151.

Sheard, A.G. & Kakabadse, A.P. (2004), "A Process Perspective on Leadership and Team Development," *Journal of Management Development,* Vol. 23, No. 1, pp. 1–106, Monograph Edition.

Sheard, A.G. & Kakabadse, A.P. (2007), "A Role Based Perspective on Leadership Decision Taking," *Journal of Management Development,* Vol. 26, No. 6, pp. 520–622, Monograph Edition.

Stogdill, R.M. (1974), *Handbook of Leadership: A Survey of Theory & Research,* Free Press, New York.

Tuckman, B.W. (1965), "Development Sequences in Small Groups," *Psychology Bulletin,* Vol. 63, No. 6, pp. 384–399.

Tuckman, B.W. (2001), "Development Sequences in Small Groups," *Group Facilitation: A Research and Applications Journal,* Vol. 3, Spring, pp. 66–81.

Tuckman, B.W. & Jensen, M.A. (1977), "Stages of Small-Group Development Revisited," *Journal of Group & Organization Studies,* Vol. 2, pp. 419–427.

Chapter 2

Drucker, P.F. (2004), "What Makes an Effective Executive," *Harvard Business Review* No. R0406C, June, Vol. 82, No. 6, pp. 58–63.

Farson, R. & Keyes, R. (2002), "The Failure-Tolerant Leader," *Harvard Business Review* No. R0208D August, pp. 64–71.

Goldenberg, J., Horowitz, R., Levav, A., & Mazursky, D. (2003), "Finding Your Innovation Sweet Spot," *Harvard Business Review* No. R0303J, March, pp. 120–129.

Korac-Kakabasde, N. & Kakabadse, A.P. (1998), "Vision, Visionary Leadership and the Visioning Process: an Overview," in Kakabadse, A.P., Nortier, F., & Abramovici, N.B. (Eds.), *Success in Sight: Visioning,* International Thomson Business Press, London.

Olivier, R. (2001), *Inspirational Leadership,* The Industrial Society, London.

Reiss, G. (1992), *Project Management Demystified,* E & FN Spon, London.

Sethi, R., Smith, D.C., & Park, C.W. (2002), "How to Kill a Team's Creativity," *Harvard Business Review* No. F0208B, August, pp. 16–17.

Surowiecki, J. (2004), *The Wisdom of Crowds,* Little Brown, London.

Tuckman, W. (1965), "Development Sequences in Small Groups," *Psychology Bulletin,* Vol. 63, No. 6, pp. 384–399.

Chapter 3

Analoui, F. & Kakabadse, A.P. (1991), *Sabotage: How to Recognise & Manage Employee Defiance,* Mercury, London.

DeVries, M.K. (2001), *The Leadership Mystique,* Prentice Hall, London.

Diamond, M.A. (1993), *The Unconscious Life of Organisations: Interpreting Organisational Identity*, Quorum Books, London.

Jehn, K. (1995), "A Multi-method Examination of the Benefits and Detriments of Inter-group Conflict," *Administrative Science Quarterly*, Vol. 40, No. 2, pp. 245–282.

Olivier, R. (2001), *Inspirational Leadership*, The Industrial Society, London.

Thomas, K.W. (1976), "Conflict and Conflict Management" in Dunnette, M.A. (Ed.), *Handbook of Industrial and Organisational Psychology*, pp. 889–935, Rand McNally, Chicago, IL.

Weiss, J. & Hughes, J. (2005), "What Collaboration? Accept—and Actively Manage—Conflict," *Harvard Business Review* No. R0503F, March, Vol. 83, No. 3, pp. 93–101.

Chapter 4

Caldwell, B.S. & Taha, L.H. (1993), "Starving at the Banquet: Social Isolation in Electronic Communication Media," *Interpersonal Computing and Technology: An Electronic Journal for the 21st Century*, Vol. 1, No. 1, pp. 11–28.

Diamond, M.A. (1993), *The Unconscious Life of Organisations: Interpreting Organisational Identity*, Quorum Books, London.

Duck, S. (1994), *Meaningful Relationships*, Sage Publications, London.

Hinde, R.A. (1997), *Relationships A Dialectical Perspective*, Psychological Press, Hove, East Sussex.

Knowles, R.N. (2002), *The Leadership Dance: Pathways to Extraordinary Organisational Effectiveness*, The Center for Self-Organizing Leadership, Niagara Falls, NY.

Jaina, J. (2001), *Relationships and Self Efficacy Beliefs*, PhD Thesis, Cranfield University, Bedford, England.

Jaina, J. & Tyson, S. (2004), "Psychological Similarity in Work-Based Relationships and the Development of Self-Efficacy Beliefs," *Human Relations*, Vol. 57, No. 3, pp. 275–296.

Stang, D.J. (1973), "Effect of Interaction Rate on Ratings of Leadership and Liking," *Journal of Personality and Social Psychology*, Vol. 27, pp. 405–408.

Chapter 5

Adair, J. (1986), *Effective Teambuilding*, Gower, Aldershot.

Bohm, D. (1990), *On dialogue*, David Bohm Seminars, Ojai, CA.

Cheng, M., Dainty, A.R., & More, D.R. (2003), "The Differing Faces of Managerial Competency in Britain and America," *Journal of Management Development*, Vol. 22, No. 6, pp. 527–537.

Gladson Nwokah, N. & Ahiauzu, A.I. (2008), "Managerial Competencies and Marketing Effectiveness in Corporate Organisations in Nigeria," *Journal of Management Development*, Vol. 27, No. 8, pp. 858–878.

Jones, M.O., Moore, M.D., & Snyder, R.C. (1988) (Eds.), *Inside Organisations*, Sage, Newbury Park, CA.

Kakabadse, A.P. (1987a), "The Syntax Corporation Part One," in Kakabadse, A.P. & Tyson, S. (Eds.), *Cases In European Human Resource Management*, pp. 65–69, Heinemann, London.

Kakabadse, A.P. (1987b), "The Syntax Corporation Part Two, Three, Four & Five," in Kakabadse, A.P. & Tyson, S. (Eds.), *Cases In European Human Resource Management—Teachers Guide (Second Edition)*, pp. 54–83, Routledge, London.

Kilmann, R.H. & Saxton, M.J. (1983), *The Kilmann—Saxton Culture Gap Survey*, Jossey-Bass, San Francisco, CA.

Lowe, K.B. (2003), "Demands, Constraints, Choices and Discretion: An Introduction to the Work of Rosemary Stewart," *The Leadership Quarterly*, Vol. 14, pp. 193–238.

McClelland, D.C. (1971), *Assessing Human Motivation*, General Learning Press, New York.

Schein, E.H. (1992), *Organisational Culture and Leadership*, Jossey-Bass, San Francisco, CA.

Stewart, R. (1982), "A Model for Understanding Managerial Jobs and Behaviour," *Academy of Management Review*, Vol. 7, No. 1, pp. 7–13.

Stuart, R. & Lindsay, P. (1997), "Beyond the Frame of Management Competencies: Towards a Contextually Embedded Framework of Managerial Competence in Organisations," *Journal of European Industrial Training*, Vol. 21, No. 1, pp. 26–33.

Trice, H.M. & Beyer, J.M. (1985), "Using Six Organisational Rites to Change Culture," in R.H. Kilmann, M.J. Saxton, & R. Serpa & Associates, *Gaining Control of the Corporate Culture*, Jossey-Bass, pp. 370–399, San Francisco, CA.

Chapter 6

Herzberg, F. (1987), "One More Time: How do You Motivate Employees?", *Harvard Business Review*, September–October, Vol. 65, No. 5, pp. 109–120.

Kakabadse, N.K. & Kakabadse, A.P. (2005), "Discretionary Leadership: From Control / Co-ordination to Value Co-Creation" in Cooper, C.L. (Ed.), *Leadership & Management in the 21st Century*, pp. 57–106, Oxford University Press, Oxford.

Kakabadse, A.P., Kakabadse N., & Lee-Davies, L. (2008), *Leading for Success: The Seven Sides to Great Leaders*, Palgrave McMillan, London.

Katzenbach, J.R. & Smith, D.K. (1993), *The Wisdom of Teams*, McGraw Hill, Maidenhead.

Miller, E.J. & Rice, A.K. (1967), *Systems of Organization: The Control of Task and Sentient Boundaries*, Tavistock Publications, London.

Robbins, P.R. (1984), *Essentials of Organisational Behaviour*, Prentice Hall International, Upper Saddle River, NJ.

Roberts, V.Z. (1994a), "The Organisation of Work, Contributions From Open Systems Theory," in Obholzer, A. & Roberts, V.Z. (Eds.), *The*

Unconscious at Work, Individual and Organisational Stress in the Human Services, Routledge, London, pp. 187–196.

Roberts, V.Z. (1994b), "Conflict and Collaboration, Managing Inter-Group Relations," in Obholzer, A. & Roberts, V.Z. (Eds.), *The Unconscious at Work, Individual and Organisational Stress in the Human Services*, Routledge, London, pp. 187–196.

Senge, P.M. (1997), *The Fifth Discipline*, Century Business, London.

Chapter 7

Day, D.V. (2001), "Leadership Development: A Review in Context," *Leadership Quarterly*, Vol. 11, No. 4, pp. 581–613.

Drucker, P.F. (1999), *Management Challenges for the 21st Century*, Butterworth-Heinemann, Oxford.

Drucker, P.F. (2004), "What Makes an Effective Executive?", *Harvard Business Review*, June, Vol. 82, No. 6, pp. 58–63.

Fiedler, F.E. (1996), "Research on Leadership Selection and Training: One View of the Future," *Administrative Science Quarterly*, Vol. 41, pp. 241–250.

Hooijberg, R., Bullis, R.C., & Hunt, J.G. (1999), "Behavioural Complexity and the Development of Military Leadership for the Twenty-First Century," in Hunt, J.G., Dodge, G.E., & Wong, L. (Eds.), *Out-of-the-Box Leadership: Transforming the Twenty-First-Century Army and other Top-Performing Organisations*, pp. 111–130, JAI, Stamford, CT.

McCall, M.W. (1998), *High Flyers: Developing the Next Generation of Leaders*, Harvard Business School, Boston, MA.

McCauley, C.D., Moxley, R.S., & Van Velsor, E. (Eds.) (1998), *The Center for Creative Leadership Handbook of Leadership Development*, pp. 403–432, Jossey-Bass, San Francisco, CA.

Olivier, R. (2001), *Inspirational Leadership*, The Industrial Society, London.

Salancik, G.R., Calder, B.J., Rowland, K.M., Leblebici, H., & Conway, M. (1975), "Leadership as an Outcome of Social Structures and Process: A Multi-Dimensional Analysis," in Hunt, J.G. & Larson, L.L. (Eds.), *Leadership Frontiers*, pp. 81–101, Kent State University, Kent, OH.

Vicere, A.A. & Fulmer, R.M. (1998), *Leadership By Design*, Harvard Business School, Boston, MA.

Wenger, E. (1998), *Communities of Practice: Learning, Meaning, and Identity*, Cambridge University, Cambridge, England.

Wenger, E. & Snyder, W.M. (2000), "Communities of Practice: The Organisational Frontier," *Harvard Business Review*, January–February, Vol. 78, No. 1, pp. 139–145.

accreditation, of experience, 130
activity planning, 36
adaptability under pressure, 222,
    231–5
Aristotle, 4

behaving as one stage of group's
    development, 144
  boundary management, 156, 161
  collaborative team, 158, 161
  effective team management, 166
  embracing dialogue, act of, 173
  engaging others, 148–9, 165–75
  ethnocentrism, 157
  fitting behavior, 175–80
  highest-performing teams, 146
  inter-team transactions, 156–9
  key learning points, 180–1
  leadership behavior, 177–9
  multiple dialogue, 173
  open system, 148, 153–4
  polylogue, 173–4
  practical indicators, 151–3
  team development, 149–51
  team members; decision-making
    power, 166; delegation and
    empowerment, 169
  teams working with other teams,
    147–8, 153–65
  Traditional Turbine Co.,
    case study, 155–6, 159–60,
    161–3, 167–8, 170–2, 175–6
  transition into, 149–50, 151
behavioral variables, 129
born-to-lead school of
    leadership, 3–4
boundary management, 156,
    161, 165

capability, 128, 130–2
choices, 130–1
close monitoring, 28
cognition, 32
collaboration under pressure, 222,
    229–31
collaborative team, 158, 161
coming together stage of group's
    development, 108–9
  fitting behavior, 97–102
  group development, 80–2
  key learning points, 102–3
  leadership behavior, 100–2
  management and leadership,
    78–9
  practical indicators, 82–4
  Traditional Turbine Co.,
    case study, 85–6, 93–5, 97–9
  transition into, 83
  work-based relationships, 80,
    84–92
  working in groups, 80, 92–7
competencies, 128–30
conceptual framework
  group development, 5–10
  group-based leadership,
    importance, 2
  leadership in 21st century, 3–5
  leadership with group
    development, 1
  unusual traits of leader, 1
conflict, 145
  avoidance, 63, 70
  management, 50, 60–70, 73
  relationship conflict, 50, 51–2
  task conflict, 50, 51
  understanding conflict, 50,
    53–60, 73

confrontation stage of group's
   development, 6, 48, 74, 108–9
   associated conflict, 112
   conflict management, 50,
      60–70, 73
   conflicting priorities, 49
   fitting behavior, 70–6
   group development, 50–2
   key learning points, 76–7
   leadership action in selling
      process, 72–3
   leadership behavior, 74–5
   practical indicators, 52–3
   Traditional Turbine Co.,
      case study, 55–6, 61–72
   transition into, 51
   understanding conflict, 50,
      53–60, 73
constraints, 130, 131
cooperation, 31
coordination, 32
creative thinking under time
      pressures, 28–9
creativity and innovation, 13, 18–30
   close monitoring, 28
   cohesion and open
      conversation, 27
   failure-tolerant leader, 28
   time pressure and, 28–9
   Traditional Turbine Co.,
      case study, 19–26
culture
   building blocks of, 114–15
   change, 128–9
   dynamics of, 113
   group, 105, 115, 116, 129
   leadership and, 113–14

data gathering and fact finding, 21–2
decision making, 13, 30–6
   challenges of managers, 31–2
   distributing leadership
      responsibilities, 31
   by team members, 166
demands, 130, 131

effective managers, 12–13
effective team management, 166
embracing dialogue, act of, 173
ethnocentrism, 157

facing the future stage of group's
      development
   fitting behavior, 207–14
   key learning points, 214–15
   leadership behavior, 211–13
   leadership development, 185–6,
      198–207
   managing yourself, 184–5, 186,
      190–8
   practical indicators, 188–9
   self-insight, 183–4
   team development, 186–8
   The Traditional Turbine Co.,
      case study, 191–3, 194–6, 201–3,
      208–10
   transition into, 187
failure-tolerant leader, 28
floor time management, 91
forming the group, 13, 16–18

gated review process, 37, 39–41
goal-based planning, 36–7
grace under pressure, 217
   adaptability under pressure, 222,
      231–5
   audacity of hope, 238, 239
   collaboration under pressure,
      222, 229–31
   definition, 218, 219
   grounded under pressure, 221,
      223–6
   maturity under pressure, 222,
      235–8
   resilience under pressure, 222,
      226–9
   stories, key elements of, 240–1
grounded under pressure, 221,
      223–6
group development, 5–10, 107–10
   breakdown points, 7–8

group development – *continued*
  coming together, 6–7, 80–2, 108–9
  confrontation, 6, 50–2, 108–9
  group, definition, 144–5
  integrated group development
    process, 8–10
  linear development sequence, 7
  mobilizing, 6, 14–15
  one step forward, two step back,
    107–10
  trigger transition, factors, 108

hope, audacity of, 238, 239

"ignorance paradox", 4
informal organizations, 79–80
integrated group development
    process, *see individual stages*
intercultural clash, 121–3
interdependency between
    members, 31
inter-team transactions, 156–9

leadership, 43–5, 78–9
  behaviors, 44–5, 74–5, 100–2,
    139–41, 177–9, 211–13
  born-to-lead school of, 3–4
  capability, 218
  culture and, 113–14
  functional approach, 5
  functions and characteristic
    activities, 79
  group development and, 1
  management and, 43, 78
  self-development school of, 4–5
  as social process, 199–200
  in 21st century, 3–5
leadership development, 185–6, 199
  communication and delineating
    roles, 185, 204–5
  context understanding, 185, 199
  definition, 198, 206
  feedback, giving and receiving,
    185, 200–1, 203
  getting best out of others, 185, 205

  messages, timing and positioning
    of, 185, 200
  vision of future, 185–6, 205–6
linear group development
    sequence, 7

management, 78–9
  boundary, 156, 161, 165
  conflict, 66, 73
  of failure, 28
  functions and characteristic
    activities, 79
  group's creativity and, 27
  leadership and, 43, 78
manager
  challenges of, 31–2
  conflict management, 50,
    60–70, 73
  floor time management, 91
  leadership behavior, 74–6
  self-insight, 183–4
  understanding conflict, 50,
    53–60, 73
  working relationship, 87–8
managing yourself
  anxiety control and personal
    criticisms, 185, 196–7
  credibility, 185, 197–8
  developing trust in others, 185, 197
  engaging with others, 185, 193–4
  listening and reflecting, 184–5,
    190–1
  seeing the bigger picture and
    contributions to it, 184–5, 191
maturity under pressure,
    222, 235–8
mobilizing stage of group's
    development, 6, 12, 73–4
  activity planning, 36
  close monitoring, 28
  cohesion and open
    conversation, 27
  creative thinking under time
    pressures, 28–9
  creativity and innovation, 13, 18

mobilizing stage of group's
development – *continued*
customers' needs, 25–6
data gathering and fact finding,
21–2
decision making, 13, 30–6
failure-tolerant leader, 28
fitting behavior, 41–5
forming the group, 13, 16–18
gated review process, 40
goal-based planning, 36–7
group development, 14–15
informal communication
practices, 22
innovative implementation of
creative ideas, 29–30
interdependency between
members, 31
key learning points, 46–7
leadership behavior, 44–5
newness, 14
poor performance in formal
meetings, 35
practical indicators, 15–16
task activity, 14–15
Traditional Turbine Co.,
case study, 19–20, 21, 23–5,
33–4, 38, 41–2
transition into, 15
wary of jumping to conclusions,
20–1
ways of working, 13–14, 36–41
multiple dialogue, 173

one step forward, two steps back
stage of group's development,
8, 104
competence and capability, 105,
107, 128–36
fitting behavior, 137–42
group culture, 105
group development, 107–10
intercultural clash, 121–3
key learning points, 142–3
leader developed new group
culture, 127

leadership behavior, 139–42
management role, responsibilities
associated with, 138–9
practical indicators, 110–12
roles and responsibilities, 139
shared assumption, 105,
105–6, 129
Traditional Turbine Co.,
case study, 117–20, 123–4,
125–6, 132–3, 135–6, 138
transition into, 111
truth, stranger than fiction,
124–5
the way things are done around
here, 106, 112–28
open system, 148, 153–4

polylogue, 173–4
psychological similarity, 89

relationship and social interaction,
88–9
relationship conflict, 50, 51–2
resilience under pressure, 222,
226–9

self-development school of
leadership, 4–5
self-insight, 183–4
social interaction and relationship,
88–9
Socrates, 4

task conflict, 50, 51
team development
behaving as one stage, 149–51
facing the future stage, 186–8
team, definition, 145
tensions, existence of, 145
Traditional Turbine Co., case study
behaving as one stage, 155–6,
159–60, 161–3, 167–8, 170–2,
175–6
coming together stage, 85–6,
93–5, 97–9
confrontation stage, 55–6, 61–72

Traditional Turbine Co., case study
behaving as one stage – *continued*
facing the future stage, 191–3,
194–6, 201–3, 208–10
grace under pressure, 219–21, 223–5,
226–8, 230, 232–4, 236–7, 238–9
mobilizing stage, 19–20, 21, 23–5,
33–4, 38, 41–2
one step forward, two steps back
stage, 117–20, 123–4, 125–6,
132–3, 135–6, 138

ways of working, 13–14
activity planning, 36
gated review process, 37, 39–41

goal-based planning, 36–7
Traditional Turbine Co.,
case study, 38
wisdom, 4
work behavior, 129
work-based relationships, 80
judgment about behavior, 90
moderation of behavior, 84
psychological similarity, 89
social interaction and
relationship, 88–9
talking, 90–1
Traditional Turbine Co.,
case study, 84–7
working in groups, 80, 92–7